THE IZON (IJAW) PEOPLE OF LONDON:
FROM IMMIGRANTS TO CITIZENS 1808 - 2024

To Preye

THE IZON (IJAW) PEOPLE OF LONDON:
FROM IMMIGRANTS TO CITIZENS 1808 - 2024

BY

Niger Delta Peace Initiative and Development (NDPiD) HERITAGE PROJECT 2023 - 2024

FUNDED BY

The National Lottery Heritage Fund

THE HERITAGE PROJECT
NIGER DELTA PEACE INITIATIVE AND DEVELOPMENT
https://ndpid.org/

The Izon (Ijaw) People of London

CONTENTS

ABOUT NDPID

The Niger Delta Peace Initiative and Development (NDPiD) is dedicated to supporting the Niger Delta derived communities, such as the Izon (Ijaw) People resident in the United Kingdom. NDPiD has been pivotal in initiating various community-building activities that enhance the quality of life while fostering unity and cultural pride. NDPID actively engages in advocacy and community development. The organization supports various causes, including educational programs for youth, cultural preservation initiatives, and social integration efforts. NDPID addresses social justice and equality issues, ensuring the Izon people's voices are heard in broader societal discussions. Through workshops, seminars, and cultural events, NDPID promotes understanding and cooperation between the Izon community and other cultural groups in London. During the Covid-19 pandemic, NDPID played a critical role in supporting communities with free training on "Managing the Covid-19 Crisis in London," supported by the National Lottery Community Fund.

While NDPID's efforts in Nigeria are noteworthy, this book project is about enhancing our community involvement in London. The community-building activities and advocacy efforts in the UK are of primary interest to our funders and stakeholders. The successful funding of this project by the National Lottery Heritage Fund has been critical in bringing this project to fruition.

The President and the Executive Team at NDPID express their heartfelt appreciation to the Heritage Fund, Chapter Researchers and Writers, Editors, and all persons who contributed to the book *The Izon (Ijaw) People of London.* Their support and dedication have been invaluable in highlighting the resilience, culture, and achievements of the Izon community in the United Kingdom.

Annah Buseri
President NDPiD

THE PROJECT TEAM

Mr Jeffery Osuya, NDPiD Projects Committee Chairman & IT Technical Support
Mr Benaebi Oguoko, Project Manager
Dr Akpobibibo Onduku, Project Advisor
Ms Keziah Joseph, Project Admin Officer
Mr Martins Biu, Project Accounts Officer
Ms Annah Buseri, Audio Transcriber
Mr Robin Walker, Publication Designer
Ms Ibiba Don Pedro, Proofreader & Editor

Contributing Writers & Researchers

Dr Kemefasu Ifie

Dr Kemefasu Ifie is an Associate Professor in Marketing Loughborough Business School, United Kingdom. He holds a BSc; OAU Nigeria, MSc; Northumbria University UK and a PhD from Loughborough University, UK.

Tarelayefa Igedibor Beth-Ingo

Tarelayefa Beth-Ingo is a Petroleum Reservoir Geologist & PhD Research Scholar. Currently, he is a Visiting Lecturer in Environmental Engineering & Sustainability, Faculty of Science & Engineering, School of Architecture & the Built Environment, the University of Wolverhampton Springfield Campus, United Kingdom.

Benaebi Benatari Oguoko

Benaebi Oguoko is an Environmental Consultant and Researcher on African Global Studies. He holds a BSc (Hon) Environmental Science from London Metropolitan University (formerly University of North London) UK.

Dr John Areye Mekemi Kiapene

Dr John Kiapene is head of the Maths & ICT Department at Oldbury Wells School United Kingdom. He holds a PhD, MSc, BSc (Ed), NCE. He is an Educational Consultant and Researcher who is particularly interested in ICT Integration and Mathematics Education.

FOREWORD

London, a cosmopolitan city, had an immigrant population that comprised about 40% of its residents in the 2021/2022 estimates. Within this group, some are of African descent, and a smaller portion identifies as Izon (Ijaw, Ijo). If you are an academic or a general reader interested in understanding how this small Ijaw community settled in London, this book is essential. It's crucial reading for scholars, the public, and the Ijaw people, making it a must-read.

While the Windrush Generation of Black Caribbean immigrants to the UK is widely discussed, many are unaware that direct African immigration, particularly from West Africa, began centuries earlier. There is a common misconception that Africans are recent arrivals in the UK. However, this book reveals that Africans have been migrating to Britain for at least 400 years, with Ijaw individuals from West Africa being part of these early groups.

The Izon (Ijaw) People of London traces the history of the Ijaw presence in London from 1808 to 2024, but it delves deeper into the Ijaw people's initial encounters with European visitors on the West African coast. The narrative includes the involvement of the Ijaws in the Atlantic slave trade, both as victims and facilitators and tracks the rise of the British Empire. It explores how Ijaw individuals arrived in Britain under various circumstances, such as traders, exiled royals, sailors, soldiers, scholars, and students from newly independent Nigeria, continuing up to the present day.

The book provides readers with a rich historical background on the Ijaw people, explaining the origins of their relationship with the British. It reveals that the Ijaws resisted formal colonization and their incorporation into the British-created colony of Nigeria. Despite this, they made the most of their situation, with enterprising young men traveling to Britain, where they formed the earliest Ijaw communities in London and other cities. Once settled, they became industrious residents, playing a role in the city's economic growth.

For readers interested in the impact of immigrant populations on their host nation, this book provides insights into how they have integrated with the White British population and the challenges they have encountered. It also offers a study on identity, covering aspects from ethnicity to citizenship and the legal status of immigrants. The book explores what it means to be a citizen when one or one's parents have emigrated, addressing the concept of being a perpetual outsider while holding onto ethnic identities. The research shows that ethnic and cultural associations, rather than hindering assimilation, assist immigrants in navigating their new environment, ultimately aiding their integration into the host society. The book supports its conclusions through oral history interviews, academic research, and the archives of key Ijaw associations in London.

The book also highlights the achievements of several prominent Ijaw individuals who have made London their home, showcasing the contributions the Ijaw community has made and continues to make to London's economic development. It explores how London became their home, whether through being born there, moving there at a young age, or relocating later in life to seek better opportunities.

For young Ijaw people born and brought up in London and the UK, this book is important as it gives them a deeper understanding of their identity, the motivations behind their parents' migration, and how to handle the challenges of having an immigrant heritage while being a citizen.

This book uncovers a largely overlooked chapter of Black Britain, shedding light on the African communities in the UK that frequently remain invisible to those studying Black History. It is a significant contribution to the broader understanding of minority ethnic nationalities as citizens of the United Kingdom.

Rowland Ekperi
Patron NDPiD

CHAPTER 1: GENERAL INTRODUCTION

The Ijaw People have had significant presence in London for some time. Historically, the Ijaws have a documented presence in London for over 215 years, but this is not common knowledge or in the public domain. There is no doubt that many of the earliest Africans that came to live in London and indeed, in the United Kingdom were from the coastal West African regions. While individual ethnic nationality names are not mentioned and also many of the original indigenous people's names might have been changed, we can still discern that a number of them came from the Ijaw Ethnic Nationality. In this project entitled *The Ijaw (Izon) People of London: From Immigrants to Citizens 1808 - 2024,* we have captured the earliest known and even forgotten Ijaw personalities who came to live in London and some, who eventually became citizens of the United Kingdom.

The objective of this project, is to create a documented historical heritage record of the presence of Ijaw (Izon) people in London based on oral interviews of elderly Ijaw people, younger persons as well as, written accounts that narrate the individual and collective experiences of Ijaw (Izon) people as immigrants arriving in London for various reasons. The project involves telling the stories of how the early immigrants lived, worked, formed self-help community associations, improved themselves educationally and became citizens, while in some cases raising children born in London as British citizens of immigrants.

The objective is to present this in writing, visual/audio documentation to the Ijaw community in London and the wider London community, through the libraries of the London boroughs that they have historically lived and worked. The project aims to record the Ijaw cultural heritage in London and the contributions of Ijaw people to London life. We hope to trace the very first known Ijaw immigrant known by name, right back to 1804 based on research findings. We wish to tell the story of the Ijaw community associations and how they provided vital welfare services to their members, outside of local authority services. We aim to tell the story of the younger professionals, artists and ordinary Ijaw people, who now make up the Ijaw community in London and how they have enriched the cultural vibrancy of London. Our timeline covers the period from 1804, though we have a more enriching account of Ijaws from the 1940s.

Finally, we want to document the Ijaw cultural heritage that has survived in London and with attention to how much of it retains aspects of the original, that is practiced in the Ijaw homeland and how much has been socially influenced or modified by Ijaws in London over the decades.

PART ONE

THE HISTORICAL & CULTURAL BACKGROUND OF THE IZON (IJAW) PEOPLE

CHAPTER 2: METHODOLOGY AND PHILOSOPHICAL UNDERPINNING OF THE PROJECT

In order to gather some of the vital information necessary for writing the book with this title, the project created and adopted a methodology for gathering essential information based on qualitative research methodology, which could be defined as a technique for collecting, analysing and reporting "people's subjective experiences or interpretations of the world" (Roberts et al., 2019, p. 4). Furthermore, the project used exploratory techniques to interpret the rich, in-depth data of the Ijaw communities, using both inductive and deductive approaches (Roberts et al., 2019).

One outstanding strength of qualitative research is that, it provides rich, deep exploration and description of the phenomenon being studied (Dzakiria, 2012), that is from the people's personal experiences, from an insider point of view (Johnson and Onwuegbuzie, 2004) to establish the factual narratives of the historic perspective of the Ijaws in London.

Although, qualitative research has been criticised (Patton, 1999), firstly for its lack of generalisation beyond the population of study because of the constructivist (underlying philosophy of qualitative research) view of the world as complex and subject to multiple interpretations (Dzakiria, 2012), it is the only suitable approach for this kind of research and interestingly, this study is limited to only the Ijaws in London. Another well-known criticism of qualitative studies is the lack of scientific rigour in data analysis (Cope, 2014), followed by a lack of uniformity in its analysis (Patton, 1999). To ameliorate these weaknesses, the researchers shall address and minimise the associated subjectivity by employing the principle of neutrality in the data collection and analysis, to establish credibility and trustworthiness (Sandelowski, 1986).

After a careful study of the methodological dilemma, the paradigmatic conflicts, the aims and objectives, and finally, the research questions enumerated in the introductory section, this study adopts the interpretative as the philosophical underpinning. Interpretative paradigm opined that social reality resides in the participants. Unlike the study of natural sciences and inanimate objects, the knowledge of truth (reality) dwells in the subjective perspectives of the participants. The choice of interpretative paradigm was because objectivity will not produce the anticipated oral history of the migration of the Ijaws in London. Secondly, the methodological approach (ethnography) explained in the next section, can only coexist with this paradigm.

Ethnography

The project uses ethnographic discourse that emphasises the importance of studying a social context in this case, the activities of the Ijaw (Izon) community in London, through the collection of first-hand natural data directly from the participants (Hammersley, 2006). The decision to settle for ethnography was informed by three pillars, in line with Aldiabat and Le Navenec (2011) justification for ethnographic studies. Firstly, the researchers want to understand and interpret alternative realities, in addition to the participants' viewpoint through photographs and document analysis and recorded live events of the Ijaws in London. Secondly, NDPiD wants to record and preserve deeper understanding of the culture and value system of the Ijaws in London on behalf of the Ijaw Community, which can only be obtained through empirical study. While finally, capturing the migration and socio-economic contributions of the Ijaws, individually and collectively to London is a complex and multifaceted topic that mostly suits the principles of ethnography.

Consistent to the resolution principles of the tension between the "participants and analytic perspective" - that is the analysis perfectly reflects the perspectives of the researched and the outcome of the study accurately describes the activities of the participants engaged in and their course of actions (Hammersley, 2006); NDPiD has carefully selected a project manager who lives among the participants, who takes part in Ijaw activities in the London metropolis and the researchers were carefully chosen and thus, have superb knowledge of the culture and tradition of the Ijaws. This can be disadvantageous due to interference and over familiarity, which could affect the quality of data. To avoid the negative effect of this, the researchers tenaciously uphold the principle of neutrality and asked participants to authenticate the interview data after transcription.

This heritage project was carried out within a year (against the several years' recommendations of ethnographic studies) in response to the time stipulations of the Heritage Fund. The project therefore, was designed to document the surface of historical events through participants' construct in a particular setting, as opposed to seeking to understand the deeper social factors that shaped the whole of society, since the time frame could not permit holistic context discovery. Despite the short time period of the study, this work is expected to capture the historical artefacts, the local and wider history of the Ijaws systematically in the historical background section.

Population and Sample of the Study

The population for this Oral History Heritage Project, is the Ijaws currently living in the London Boroughs, and a few who once lived in London. There are approximately over 500 Ijaw families living in London and its Metropolis and this could translate to up to 2500 or more Ijaw persons. This figure is an approximate based on noted community events, where up to 500 Ijaw persons are known to have attended, with each one being a part of a nuclear family. However, due to the impracticality of interviewing all members of the population, a convenient sample of 20 persons deliberately selected to achieve spread across age groups, professionals, gender, originating clans and regions were selected for the ethnographic study. Though, non-randomization has its setbacks, in the prevailing circumstances a non-probabilistic sampling is the best approach to achieve the objectives and research outcomes of the project, as outlined in the introduction.

Research Instruments

In consonance with the multifaceted sources of data collection in ethnography, the main instrument of data collection in this study is face-to-face interviews. However, we shall complement interview data with photographic evidence, recordings from archives, family testimonies, genealogies and observation of events (festivals and other traditional events) happening during the duration of this project.

An open interview structure was used to give participants the opportunity to freely elaborate and tell their experiences and stories. The interview was made up of 5 sections. Firstly, the demographic data and other interview information in accordance with National British Library archives. Secondly, there is a section that traces the history, value system, cultures and events of the Ijaws in London. Thirdly, a section to capture the migration stories of the Ijaws including the benefits and challenges. Fourthly, the professional engagements and contributions of Ijaw migrants to the London economy, social and cultural life.

Ethical Issues and Management

Following the universally accepted standard of sound academic practices, ethical issues shall be taken seriously throughout this study. We shall deviate from the 'Deontological approach' (the universality of ethical decisions) and the 'Teleological viewpoint' (the belief that ethical decisions are relative to a particular culture and time). We shall align with the utilitarianist viewpoint (the belief that ethical decisions are made, based on the consequences and benefits for the participants and the larger society) (Akaah, 1997) in line with the constructivist views of the study. Ethical questions of the study cover justice, benevolence and non-maleficence, integrity, confidentiality, anonymity and autonomy. We shall ensure that the entire research process, its benefits and participants' rights and protections shall be clearly explained to the participants and organisations involved in the study. During data collation, analysis and reporting, we shall ensure that all participants' names used are in recognition of their contributions or pseudonymised following participant's permission and preferences. Consistent with the General Data Protection Regulations (GDPR) 2018 and Personal Data Protection Acts, no personal data of participants and any information that could identify them will neither be released to a third party, nor used for a reason or stored other than for the needs of this study.

During the interview, we ensured that participants signed a consent form. All participants were briefed on the subject matter and the procedure for the interview before the actual interview Participants were reassured that the purpose of the study is purely for documentation of heritage purposes, and no part of the information gathered and data generated, would be divulged to a third party under any circumstances other than the National Lottery Heritage Fund, who provided the grant that funded the project and Tower Hamlets Local History and Library Archives, who would archive the oral history recordings.

Concerning the actual interview, the participant agreement form, participants' information sheet, interview recording agreement, interview sensitive review form, interview content summary and procedure for the interview, shall be sent in advance to participants prior to the fieldwork. The essence of this, was to ensure that participants adequately understand their involvement, full adherence to ethical issues; ensuring participants have a broad idea of the themes of the interview.

Actual Interview

The interviewers must have the following
1. Interview data sheet
2. Interview content summary
3. Interview participant agreement
4. Interview recording agreement to be signed by interviewer and interviewee at the end of each interview
5. Interview sensitivity review form
6. Interview guide
7. A Photographer
8. Audio recording machine

9. A volunteer or an assistant
10. Any other important fact here

Conducting the Interviews

We anticipated conducting 20 face-to-face interviews. These interviews were carried out during the period of August 2023 to March 2024. We ended up with 17 direct interviews. The structure of the interview was open-ended.

The Interviewees

Archhishop Doye Agama
Rev. Francis B. Akpanari
Ms Larraine Okorodudu
Ms Edith Akenkide
Mrs Edna Knight
Mr Ombrai Oguoko
Dr Boma Douglas
Mr Rowland Ekperi
Ms Sokari Ekineh
Mr John Opuogulaya
Mr Joshua Garry
Mr Enei Edonya
Mr Lawrence O. Dorgu
Mr Datoru Ben Paul Worika
Mr John Ogetti Kpiaye
Mr Macdonald J. Mopho
Mr Patience Agbabi

Various themes that came out of the interviews combined with other informal oral histories, are developed in subsequent chapters of this book.

BIBLIOGRAPHY

Aldiabat, K. and C. L. Le NavenecL. 2011. *Clarification of the blurred boundaries between grounded theory and ethnography: differences and similarities.* Turkish Online journal of Qualitative Inquiry 2: 1-13.

Martyn Hammersley (2006) *Ethnography: problems and prospects,* Ethnography and Education, 1:1, 3-14.

CHAPTER 3: HISTORICAL AND CULTURAL BACKGROUND
OF THE IZON (IJAW) PEOPLE

The history of Ijaw on its own, is enough for a voluminous book. Since the focus of this documentation varies slightly, we decided to give a concise history to offer our readers a historical perspective. The term Ijaw is the Anglicisation of Ijo or Ejo. Other commonly used variations include Izon (Ijon), Ezon (Ejon), Uzo, and Uzon (Ujon). All these names refer to the Ijaw people. These names were used throughout the Niger Delta and its environs and they are used interchangeably. This heritage project shall use the spelling "Ijaw".

The Ijaw people are found predominantly in present day Nigeria and their natural homeland, is the Niger Delta and surrounding coastal areas. Historical researchers indicate that the Ijaw people are one of the oldest ethnic nationalities in Nigeria. They have existed as a distinct ethnic group, with a unique language for over 5,000 years, while evidence for Niger Delta habitation goes back to at least 800 BCE.[1]

Who are the Ijaw people? Accordingly;

- They have a shared genetics, language, culture, history and environment
- The Ijaws (Ijo, Izon) are an Ethnic Nationality of Africa that inhabit the Niger Delta and immediate environment of Nigeria
- Founded by the ancient people known as the Oru (Orubo) of various extended families, led by the ancestor Father Ijo (Izon)
- Genetically, they can trace back to these founding extended families and communities
- They speak Ijaw (Izon) language and its dialects and also variant languages, due to social and ethnic mixing with neighbouring non Ijaw speakers.
- They share in common, a riverine culture, community culture and spiritual way of life
- Have a common history of development within the Niger Delta and its immediate hinterlands
- Archaeological and geological evidence for settlement of the Niger Delta, goes back at least 2500 years.

According to their own traditions captured in scholarship, the Ijaws are descendants of autochthonous or ancient, aboriginal people - an ancient tribe of Africa identified as the "Oru" or "Kumoni". These Oru people originated from the ancient aquatic civilisations of Middle Africa, that spread to create the ancient Egyptian and ancient Sudanese civilisations.[2] The ancient Oru people migrated to the Lake Chad aquatic civilisation, most probably during the period (c 5000-2000 BCE) and further migrated from there, to the Lower River Niger and Niger Delta region, through the ancient waterways that link up the Nile Valley to West Africa, chiefly by means of watercrafts such as reed boats and wooden carved canoes. Knowledge about this remote period remains limited. However, in traditional mythology the early ancestors are described as descended from the sky or emerging from the waters, symbolising their divine origin and that most probably, they were spiritual initiates. They were deeply devoted to spiritual culture and deeply connected with water as the symbol of spiritual culture, evident in the legends of mermaids and water people.

According to historical research, following a route that brought ancient people to the Niger/Benue region, a fertile basin that supported human societies, the ancient Oru established in the present Ife region and then the present Benin City region of Nigeria. Upon their arrival in the Benin region, they established permanent settlements and embarked on expeditions into the Niger Delta. During these journeys, they encountered other remote Oru communities, whom they acknowledged as kindred people. They recognised their shared heritage as Oru people such as language, culture and aquatic environment adaptation and formed communities as a united people. Accordingly, from what we can discern from the ancestral mythology traditions, various Oru families led by Father Ijo (Izon) settled the central Niger Delta in antiquity and gave birth to the Ijaw ethnic nationality. Up until the 19th century, the Ijaws were also known by their ancient names of Kumoni and Oru. European visitors identified the name ORU, as a distinct reference to the Ijaw people.[3] These ancient ancestors interacted with neighbouring non Ijaw speakers and through time, variant dialects and divergent languages came to be spoken amongst the Ijaw related clans. However, the most important relationship is the shared genetic relationship that has evolved through generations of exchanges of the human genome.

Over time, Ijo (Ijaw) or Izon emerged as the collective name for the entire ethnic group. It evolved from the personal name Ijo, which belonged to one of the ancestors, while it also means TRUTH. As mentioned earlier, the ancestor Father Ijo represents the pivotal moment that the Ijaw people emerged as a distinct and separate people from their ancestral Oru forebears that also merged, or were assimilated to other ancient peoples.

Territory and Population

The Ijaws are the most populous indigenous inhabitants in the Niger Delta region of Nigeria. The estimated population of the Ijaw People is over 10 per cent of the national population of Nigeria, or over 20 million. It is the fourth largest ethnic group in Nigeria, and cannot by any means be considered an ethnic minority. The people have naturally lived in the riverine areas mainly because their ancient aquatic culture and main occupation of exploiting marine environments such as fishing, riverbank farming and salt making, and their origin has much to do with water.

After Nigeria gained independence, through a series of regional and state creation exercises, the Ijaw ethnic nationality homeland has been balkanised into the current states of Akwa Ibom, Rivers, Bayelsa, Delta, Edo and Ondo States. Presently, the Ijaw (Izon) ethnic nationality comprises of the following clans, kingdoms and related kinship communities, that are indigenous to the aforementioned states of Nigeria:

1.   ABUA-ODUAL (RIVERS STATE)
2.   AKASSA (BAYELSA STATE)
3.   ANDONI (EASTERN OBOLO, AKWA-IBOM & RIVERS STATES)
4.   APOI (WEST, ONDO STATE)
5.   APOI (CENTRAL, BAYELSA STATE)
6.   GBARAUN (BAYELSA STATE)
7.   AROGBO (ONDO STATE)
8.   BASSAN (BAYELSA STATE)
9.   BILLE (RIVERS STATE)
10.   BOMA (BOMO, BAYELSA STATE)
11.   BUSENI (BAYELSA STATE)
12.   EGBEMA (EDO & DELTA STATE)
13.   EKPETIAMA (BAYELSA STATE)
14.   ENGENNI (RIVERS STATE)
15.   EPIE-ATISSA (BAYELSA STATE)
16.   FURUPA (BAYELSA STATE)
17.   FURUPAGHA (EDO/ DELTA STATE)
18.   GBARAIN (GBARAN) (BAYELSA STATE)
19.   GBARAUN (BAYELSA STATE)
20.   GBARANMATU (DELTA STATE)
21.   IBANI (BONNY) (RIVERS STATE)
22.   IBENO (AKWA-IBOM STATE)
23.   IDUWINI (BAYELSA & DELTA STATES)
24.   ISABA (DELTA STATE)
25.   KABO (BAYELSA & DELTA STATES)
26.   KALABARI (RIVERS STATE)
27.   KE (RIVERS STATE)
28.   KOLOKUMA (BAYELSA STATE)
29.   KULA (RIVERS STATE)

Figure 1. Map of Africa indicating the Ijaw people.

    30.   KUMBO (BAYELSA & DELTA STATES)
    31.   MEIN (BAYELSA & DELTA STATES)
    32.   NKORO (KALA OKIRIKA, RIVERS STATE)
    33.   OBOTEBE (DELTA STATE)
    34.   OGBE-IJO (DELTA STATE)
    35.   OGBEIN (OGBOIN, BAYELSA STATE)
    36.   OGBIA (OGBEYAN, BAYELSA STATE)
    37.   OGULAGHA (OGULA, DELTA STATE)
    38.   OKORDIA (BAYELSA STATE)
    39.   OLODIAMA (CENTRAL) (BAYELSA STATE)
    40.   OLODIAMA (WEST, EDO STATE)
    41.   OPEREMO (OPOROMO, BAYELSA & DELTA STATES)

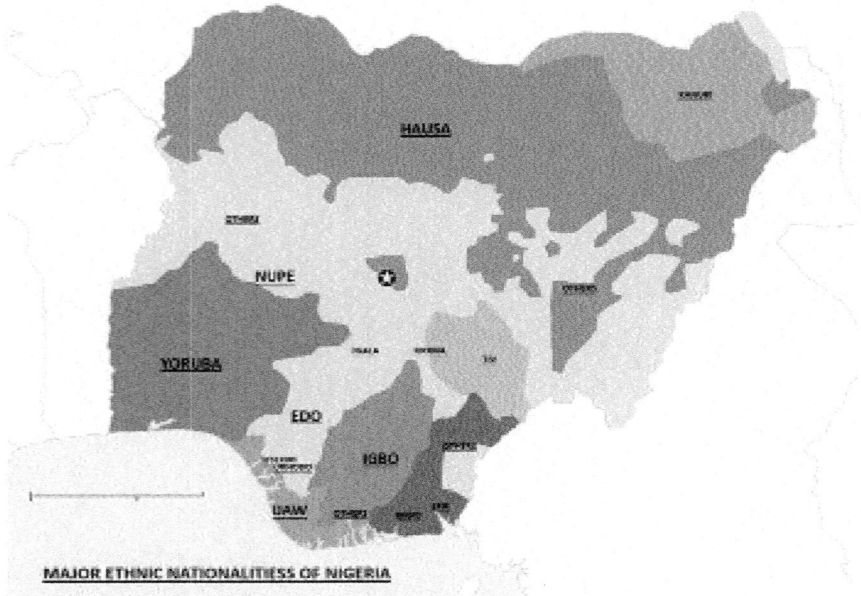

Figure 2. Map of some of the major ethnic nationalities of Nigeria.

42.   OPOBO (RIVERS STATE)
43.   OPOROMA (BAYELSA STATE)
44.   OPUKUMA (BAYELSA STATE)
45.   OYIAKIRI (EBENI, BAYELSA STATE)
46.   SEIMBIRI (DELTA STATE)
47.   TARAKIRI (CENTRAL, BAYELSA STATE)
48.   TARAKIRI (WEST, BAYELSA & DELTA STATES)
49.   TUNGBO (BAYELSA STATE)
50.   TUOMO (DELTA STATE)
51.   UKOMU (EDO ESTATE)
52.   WAKIRIKE (OKIRIKA, RIVERS STATE)
53.   ZARAMA (BAYELSA STATE)

Traditional Culture - Marriage

Like most traditional indigenous African people, the Ijaws lived as extended families, and practiced both monogamy and polygamy. Marrying at least two wives was and still is normal and legal. Most families, especially in the past, stayed under the same roof, with each wife entitled to their own living quarters, usually within the same massive or closely linked buildings. The Ijaw wives, unlike other ethnicities in Nigeria, are not ranked but, are treated equally and have equal access to their husband. Interestingly, these large families and other extended family members, such as uncles, nephews, etc., ate from the same table. This reinforced kinship and kindred kindness.

Among the Ijaw people a prospective groom, also pays a bride-price to the bride's family as a part of the rites of marriage. There are at least two forms of bride-price. Bride price-only marriage, is where the groom pays only the bride price to the wife's family, typically in cash. In this type of marriage, the children trace their line of inheritance through their mother to her family. This means that when they grow up, the children have more choices as to where they can live, with their fathers' or mothers' people. The second type of marriage is a complete bride price payment, where the groom's family pays a bigger bride-price, meaning the children belong to the father's family.

The Ijaws have also gravitated towards monogamy, attributable to westernisation, Christianity and recently feminism. Some persons who have had first-hand experience of polygamy, hold the view that it has its benefits and disadvantages, but regretted that the new wind of monogamy in Ijaw land means that, people are giving up the benefits of healthy competition, less reliance on parents' wealth and getting used to life's realities - crisis management within the extended family network.

Traditional Culture - Occupations and Economic Activity

The Ijaws were traditionally, mainly fisher folk and farmers, who lived around riverine areas. Their habitation of these seafood rich aquatic environments, ensured that they produced more than their needs. Besides sharing with others (extended family members and distant relatives) and smoking some for rainy days, they exchanged the rest of the products of their fishing activities, for items they needed, using trade by barter in the olden days. Even in the present, some communities still make a living from fishing.

Additionally, the Ijaws were and still are peasant or subsistence farmers, now called 'smallholder farmers', who till the soil for agricultural produce such as yams, sugarcane, potatoes and corn, to mention a few. Prominent farming activities that expose them to the rest of the world, especially the international community, are palm-wine tapping and palm oil production. The Ijaw people thrive on a livelihood centred on fishing, complemented by farming crops like paddy-rice, plantain, yam, cocoyam, banana, and various vegetables. Additionally, they engaged in trading activities. Notably, they cultivate tropical fruits such as guava, mangoes, and pineapples. Moreover, the Ijaw people process smoke-dried fish, timber, palm oil, and palm kernels for export purposes. This robust economic system sustains their communities and contributes to their overall prosperity.

The Ijaws are also known for palm oil processing. Ijaw women pounded, macerated and boiled palm groves and used the extracted oil for cooking and making delicacies. Palm oil played an essential role in the Industrial Revolution because both crude palm oil and palm kernel oil (oil extracted from the palm kernel) were used as raw materials for the production of many items such as shampoo, detergents, cosmetics, toothpaste, lipstick, deodorants, animal feeds, biofuel. Palm oil is native to the Ijaw people in Niger Delta, and this exposed them to trade with the British in the 19th-century, post-slave trade (Leis, 1964).

Palm wine tapping is another traditional occupation that announced the Ijaws to Nigeria and the rest of the world. The palm wine, which is fermented to produce alcoholic gin, is made from the raphia palm tree, found in swampy areas such as the Niger Delta (Leis, 1964). The sumptuous palm wine and fermented gin which have numerous health benefits, are consumed widely and also used as raw material in producing anything with alcoholic content. The Ijaws produced palm wine and the fermented gin in quantities beyond their immediate needs. Therefore, the excess traditionally was exchanged for other needs.

As a maritime people, the Ijaws have long been engaged in the merchant shipping sector during the early and mid-20th century, before Nigeria's independence. However, with the emergence of oil and gas exploration in their territory, some have transitioned into employment within this lucrative industry. Additionally, many Ijaws have found occupation in the civil service of the Nigerian states of Bayelsa and Rivers, where their presence is dominant. Regrettably, larger population of the Ijaw people are unemployed because of the exploration of crude oil in the region, which has rendered their rich ecosystem useless for fishing, farming, lumbering, palm production and distillation.

During the 1970s and 1980s, the government of these states initiated extensive overseas scholarship programs, resulting in a notable influx of Ijaw professionals in Europe and North America. This phenomenon, is often referred to as the Ijaw Diaspora.

The Ijaw people were among the earliest Nigerian communities who had contact with Europeans. They later played a significant role as intermediaries in the transatlantic trade in captives, facilitating transactions between European visitors and the inland populations. This was particularly true before the discovery of quinine, a time when West Africa was notorious for its high malaria prevalence, earning it the grim moniker of the "White Man's Graveyard."

Within the Ijaw community, specific kin-based trading lineages emerged and evolved into substantial corporations known as Houses. Each House had a democratically elected leader and maintained a fleet of war canoes to safeguard trade and fend off rivals. Additionally, fishing and farming have long been integral occupations for the Ijaw people.

Given their maritime heritage, many Ijaws found employment in the merchant shipping sector during the early and mid-20th century, well before Nigeria's independence. The Ijaw people's historical significance, economic activities and contributions to various sectors, underscore their rich cultural heritage and resilience. Presently the Ijaws like other Nigerian Indigenous people, are employed by government agencies from the Federal down to the local government level. They are also employed or engaged in self employment in the oil and gas sector and private sector of Nigeria.

Traditional Culture - Food

The Ijaw ethnic nationality, stands proudly as one of the traditional communities that boast remarkable food security. The Ijaw people have cultivated diverse cuisines within their vibrant culture, ranging from ceremonial dishes to everyday delicacies and traditional snacks. Among the countless culinary treasures of the Ijaw people, we find the tempting delights of 'Kekefiyai,' 'Polofiyai,' 'Kiri-igina,' and 'Opuru-fulou.' Additionally, the Ijaw people take great pride in their mastery of preparing fried and roasted fish and plantains, the delectable Okodo and many other mouth-watering creations.

These unique delicacies do not only define the Ijaw ethnic nationality but, also serve as a unifying force, showcasing the rich cultural heritage of the people. The Ijaw people have skilfully crafted various rare local dishes in Nigeria. These culinary wonders are created from the finest ingredients, including fish, clams, oysters, periwinkles, yams, and plantains (terms used may be different in some Ijaw dialects).

♦ Among the most renowned dishes, we find the illustrious 'Polofiyai.' This sumptuous soup, prepared with yams and palm oil, boasts an unparalleled richness.

♦ Another culinary masterpiece is the esteemed 'Kekefiyai,' a pottage that combines the flavours of chopped unripe (green) plantains, fish, other seafood, or even game meat (bush-meat), all harmoniously blended with the lusciousness of palm oil.

♦ For those seeking a truly indulgent experience, the Ijaw people offer an exquisite combination of fried or roasted fish and plantain. Picture succulent fish expertly fried in palm oil, served alongside perfectly cooked plantains, creating a symphony of flavours that will leave the taste buds dancing with delight.

♦ Kalabari Sea-Harvest Fulo: Indulge in the exquisite flavours of this rich mixed seafood soup or stew, perfectly complemented by the delightful accompaniments of foofoo, rice, or yams. A true culinary masterpiece that will transport the taste buds to new heights of satisfaction.

• Owafiya (Beans Pottage): Immerse yourself in the heart-warming goodness of this delectable pottage, crafted with the finest beans, palm oil, and a choice of fish or bush-meat. This dish is served alongside processed cassava or starch and celebrates flavours and textures.

• Geisha Soup: Prepare to be captivated by this soup's simplicity and yet undeniable allure, made from the exquisite geisha fish. With just a touch of pepper, salt, and water, this culinary gem is brought to life through a brief but intense boiling process. It is a true testament to the power of minimalism in creating extraordinary taste experiences.

• Opuru-Fulou (Prawn Soup): Embark on a journey of flavours with this tantalising soup, also known as prawn soup. Immerse yourself in the rich combination of prawn, Ogbono (Irvingia gabonensis seeds), dried fish, table salt, crayfish, onions, fresh pepper, and red palm oil. A symphony of ingredients that will leave you craving for more. And let us not forget the Wakirike people's beloved Onunu, a delightful blend of pounded yams and boiled overripe plantains, pounded together with a dash of palm oil, a true delicacy that will transport you to culinary bliss.

• Kiri-Igina: Prepare to be amazed by this unique creation that defies traditional cooking methods. Crafted without fire, this dish showcases the harmonious blend of Ogbono (Irvingia gabonensis seeds), dried fish, table salt, and crayfish. A testament to the ingenuity of culinary artistry.

• Ignabeni: A delectable soup made with a choice of yam or plantain, expertly seasoned with tea bush leaves, a hint of pepper, succulent goat meat, and flavourful fish.

Traditional Culture - Beliefs about Birth, Death and Life After

In traditional Ijaw culture, a man is believed to be incomplete until he marries, has a biological child and can build a roof over his head for his family. The birth of a child is a significant event in Ijaw land, worthy of celebration (Beredugo et al., 2018).

When a woman loses a child severally, customarily it is believed that the same child can return to be born by the woman. The deceased bodies of such children are marked before burial so that, they can be recognised if they return. In one such burial, according to those who carried out the act, a nail was used to pierce through the side close to the eye of the deceased child. Amazingly, the boy, now about fifty-two years old, was born with conspicuous marks. The birth of this child, marked the end of infant mortality for the woman in question.

Figure 3. Ijaw Kalabari Ancestral Screen.

The Ijaws clearly understand and appreciate that at the appointed time, a person will leave this world to the world beyond. In the Kabowei clan, when the oldest man (or traditional ruler) dies, there are no immediate announcements. The family gets water from a big fish's bubbles to bathe the deceased before a formal announcement is made with canon shots. But, the death of an ordinary person is immediately announced with weeping and wailing of family members (Ariye, 2013). Lastly, those without children are buried quietly.

Traditionally, the remains of an ordinary person are buried the next day. Family and relatives will gather to play traditional drums throughout the night, in case the dead wakes up. If nothing happens, the deceased is buried the next day. except prominent leaders like the oldest man or the traditional rulers are embalmed for a couple of days for distant relatives to gather before their burial. The current practice of keeping the remains in the mortuary for months and, on rare occasions, years with some people going as far as building a house and spending frivolously for the burial of a deceased, were alien to the Ijaws.

In the traditional beliefs of the Ijaws, it is firmly held that one is constantly under the watchful gaze of one's ancestral spirit. As a sign of gratitude and to ensure future wellbeing, it is customary to pay homage to the deceased and offer prayers to them. Before each meal, a small portion of food is reverently cast to the ground, accompanied by reciting the names of ancestors. Additionally, a dedicated food and drink offering is set out exclusively for them every eight days.

Furthermore, a significant ritual occurs every seven years, where a goat's blood is ceremoniously sprinkled in front of symbolic images or pillars representing the revered ancestors. It is strictly forbidden by tribal law to speak ill of these spirits. Should anyone utter disrespectful words about the deceased and refuses to apologise, the offended family retaliates by speaking unfavourably about the wrongdoer's deceased relatives. However, when sincere apologies are extended, a collective atonement ceremony is performed by all parties involved.

The Ijaws' ancestral beliefs and practices are deeply ingrained in their cultural fabric, serving as a testament to their reverence for the past and their commitment to maintaining harmonious relationships with their forebears. One can also seek solace and guidance from the spirits at sacred shrines during times of dire need. Every individual is believed to possess two souls - the eternal ego and the life force that departs with the physical body. While both souls depart upon the final breath, the life force can also flee in moments of intense fear. Should this soul fail to return, the body succumbs to death. On the other hand, the eternal soul takes on the form of a ghost, shadow, or reflection upon leaving the body, hence the cautionary belief against stepping on shadows. Mirrors are often employed to divert the attention of evil spirits towards the reflected image of the soul, rather than the actual soul itself.

Like numerous faiths around the globe, the Ijaw people also acknowledge the presence of a Ghost King, Nduen-Ama, and a ghost messenger named Ffe, who manifests as a skeletal figure and administers punishment by striking the base of the skull with a formidable staff. A ferryman known as Asasaba also guides virtuous souls across the river of existence, facilitating their reincarnation into trees, animals, or other living entities. Although various ethnic groups hold distinct beliefs regarding the forms of reincarnation for good and evil souls, they all share a common belief in karma. For instance, in one clan, a righteous soul may be reborn as a cow, elephant, or leopard, while in another clan, virtuous individuals may find themselves reincarnated as trees. Conversely, in a third clan, only malevolent individuals are believed to transform into plants after death. The Ijaw people hold their ancestors in the highest regard, revering and cherishing their memory. Speaking ill of these revered ancestors is strictly forbidden and considered taboo. Moreover, the Ijaw people are renowned for their practice of ritual enculturation, a form of traditional citizenship rites. This fascinating tradition involves individuals from unrelated groups, undergoing sacred rites to become part of the Ijaw community.

Traditional Culture - Religion and Spirituality

The Ijaws today are predominantly Christians, with Catholicism and Anglicanism being the most prevalent varieties of Christianity among them. A significant proportion, still adhere to the original traditional spirituality and belief systems of the Ijaw people. Traditionally, the Ijaw practised their spirituality before the arrival of Christianity. This spiritual culture included the acknowledgment and veneration of the Supreme Creator, and its' manifestations as the forces of nature, also referred to as water spirits in some literature, and what has become now known as the deities or divine manifestations. The Supreme Creator is called by various names such as Tamarau, Tamuno, Ayibarau, Ayiba, Aziba, Woyengi, Woyin, Woyinma to name a few.[4]

The Ijaws traditionally believed that water spirits are like humans with personal strengths and weaknesses and that human beings dwell among the water spirits before birth (most probably water symbolises the spirit realm[5]). The role of prayer in the traditional Ijaw belief system, is to maintain living in the good graces of the water spirits among whom humans dwelt before being born into this world. They believed that when the people offend the water spirits, they suffer heavy flooding and are destroyed with high waves and that

Figure 4. Water Spirit Masquerade Head, wood, early 20th century.

this fate could only be fended off, by the sacrifice of goats and chickens in rituals carried out by the mediator priests.

Each year, the Ijaw hold celebrations lasting several days in honour of the spirits. Central to the festivities lies the pivotal role of masquerades. These captivating spectacles feature men adorned in intricate attire and exquisitely carved masks. As they sway and twirl to the rhythmic beats of drums, they embody the very essence of the water spirits, their dancing reflecting their connection's sheer quality and intensity. The magnificence of these masquerades, is believed to signify the spirits' possession as they dance on their behalf (Fabiyi & Oloukoi, 2013).

Traditional Cultural - Art, Music, Festivals and Games

The Ijaw people boast of a rich artistic heritage, with their traditional river masks crafted from intricately carved wood standing out as the most renowned. These masks, known as 'Owuamapu,' are powerful representations of water spirits. They skillfully combine geometric shapes with animalistic and abstract qualities, creating captivating depictions of human heads.

The Ijaws have long embraced their cultural traditions in music, relying on drums, percussion planks, and other idiophones to create enchanting melodies. These instruments continue to grace cultural festivals, accompanying mesmerising dances such as the Fisherman's Dance, the 'Egbelegbele Sei,' and the Wind and Trees Dance. Alongside these traditional instruments, contemporary horns and other musical devices have found their place in the Ijaw's repertoire.

Over the years, the Ijaw people have also witnessed the emergence of new musical genres. Notably, a unique strain of gospel music has taken root, resembling reggae or ska. This genre, infused with the soulful sounds of trumpets and other horns, deviates from the traditional American gospel style. The Ijaw's famous music scene remains faithful to its roots, emphasising the use of horns, percussion and steady, slow beats.

In addition to their mastery of masks and music, the Ijaw people have gained fame for their exceptional memorial screens. These screens, meticulously carved from wooden planks, are poignant tributes to the departed. Traditionally, they were created to honour members of trading families who had passed away. These remarkable works of art were cherished within the trading houses, adorned with food and drink offerings.

The Ijaw people's artistic prowess is genuinely awe-inspiring, with their river masks, musical rhythms and memorial screens, serving as testaments to their rich cultural heritage. The Ijaws have carved a place for themselves in the annals through their masterful craftsmanship and unwavering dedication to tradition.

Figure 5. Ijaw Ancestral Plaque.

Ijaw people exhibit distinct characteristics, values, customs, and culture that shape their identity and contribute to their resilience and success. Their close-knit communities, strong values of loyalty and respect, vibrant customs, and rich artistic expressions, all play a pivotal role in defining them.

The Ijaws known for their strong sense of community, have distinct characteristics that set them apart. Resilience is one prominent trait observed among them as they have thrived, despite historically facing marginalisation and environmental challenges. This resilience can be attributed to their deep connection with nature and adaptability to maritime lifestyles. Additionally, Ijaw people are known for their ingenuity, excelling in various fields such as literature, arts, music, and architecture.

Values among the Ijaws highlight the importance of community, honour, and respect. Individual success is celebrated, but communal prosperity takes precedence. The Ijaws uphold the principles of 'iroko' and 'ikan', emphasising loyalty, honesty, and truthfulness. These values guide interpersonal and societal relationships, fostering a shared sense of responsibility and unity. Furthermore, respect for elders is ingrained and the wisdom and counsel of the elderly are valued and sought after in decision-making processes throughout Ijaw land.

Customs and traditions play a vital role in the Ijaw culture, shaping various aspects of daily life. One notable tradition is the 'Iselekere' ceremony, a coming-of-age ritual for young girls. The ceremony celebrates womanhood and marks their transition into adulthood. Another significant custom is the 'Owu' festival, where the Ijaw people honour their ancestral spirits through cultural displays, music, dance, and masquerade performances. These customs reinforce cultural preservation and promote social cohesion within the community.

The Ijaw culture is rich in artistic expressions, reflecting their connection with nature and spirituality. The performing arts, particularly music and dance, are central to their culture. Traditional musical instruments such as the 'oboko' (a xylophone) and 'obu' (a flute) are used during ceremonies and festivals. Dance forms like the 'Owigiri' and 'Ijimere' showcase elegant movements that depict various aspects of their marine lifestyle and spiritual beliefs.

Wrestling is a traditional sport that has its roots in the Ijaw ethnic group of Nigeria's Niger Delta region. Known as 'Igbe,' this form of wrestling has been practised for centuries and has gained popularity as a sport and cultural tradition. It is essential to discuss the significance of Ijaw wrestling within the larger contexts of Nigeria's cultural heritage, its social impact, and its role in preserving the values and identity of the Ijaw people.

From an intellectual perspective, studying Ijaw wrestling allows us to explore the historical context of this traditional sport. It provides insights into

the sociocultural evolution of the Ijaw society and their way of life. To fully
comprehend the sport, one needs to delve into the rituals, techniques and rules
associated with it and the cultural symbolism attached to wrestling events. This
enables us to appreciate the significance of Ijaw wrestling as a manifestation
of the cultural beliefs, values, and communal bonds of the Ijaws. The strongest
wrestler in traditional Ijaw community, the one who no one can defeat, is
crowned as the revered 'Olotu' of the village. The sport profoundly impacts the
social fabric of Ijaw communities. Ijaw wrestling events are critical social
gatherings, where people from different villages come together to celebrate,
bond, and build relationships. It fosters unity, promotes physical fitness and
strengthens the sense of communal pride. Every male child was trained to
wrestle in the traditional Ijaw villages as a sign that they can protect their
families. Sometimes, especially in the traditional era, people give their children
in marriage to great wrestlers with the hope that they would protect them from
other stronger families.

REFERENCES

1. Derefaka A A (2003) *Archaeology and Culture History in the Central Niger Delta*, pp.
19-20.
2. Neiketien P B (1941) *A Short History of Tarakiri Clan*, p. 27.
http://uzornwaelehiablog.blogspot.com/2016/08/ijo-political-evolution-in-niger-delta.html
Talbot P A (1926) *The Peoples of Southern Nigeria vol 2*, pp. 1-2.
Brookes G E (1986) *A Provisional Historical Schema for Western Africa Based on Seven
Climate Periods (ca. 9000 BC to the 19th Century)*, African Studies Notebooks Flight. 26,
Cahier 101/102, Milieux, histoire, historiographie (1986), pp. 43-62.
Banigo Y (2006) *JO ULTIMATE AUTOCHTHONY: STILL AN UNANSWERED
QUESTION?* Journal of the Historical Society of Nigeria Vol. 16 (2005/2006), pp. 30-35
(6 pages) Published by: Historical Society of Nigeria.
Further evidence of this can be found in language studies, for example comparing Lafofa
a Nile Valley (Sudanese) language with Ijo or Ijoid. University of Jos Lafofa a distant
Ijoid related language "Conclusion 1. Lafofa could be Ijoid's closest relative:- a) meets the
Ijoid diagnostic of SOV word order and sex gender, b) 30% lexical similarity to Ijo,
Defaka (Ijo-Defaka 40% similarity) c) extensive resemblances in gender and animacy
morphemes, d) evidence that Talodi material is added to an Ijoid-like substrate, 2. Lafofa
has an article like Mande. Question: Is Lafofa closer overall to Ijoid than Mande?"
3. Alagoa E J (1964) *The Small Brave City State*, p. 7. Crowder S (1970 2nd Edition)
*Journal of an Expedition Up the Niger and Tshadda [Benue] Rivers undertaken by
Macgregor Laird in 1854* - Missionary Research and Travels no.15, p. 10. Mockler A F
(1897) *From up the Niger, Narratives of Major Claude MacDonalds Mission to the Niger
and Benue Rivers West Africa.* p. 13. Ancient traditions talk about the Oru aborigines who
are referred to as the water people or deities who founded spiritual initiation societies.
4. These names literally mean The Creator, referred to in the feminine gender, and Our
Mother. The Supreme Being is largely perceived as a Female, an All Encompassing
Divine Mother.

5. There is increasing understanding that Water is a grand symbol for what we call the Spiritual Realm or Metaphysical Realm. This Water Symbol cuts across religions.

BIBLIOGRAPHY

Abejide, S. T. (2022) *The Structure of Ijaw Political Economy in the Colonial Administration, C. 1900-1960s: An Assessment,* KIU Journal of Social Sciences Vol. 8(1): 101-108.

Alagoa, E. J. and Tamuno, T. N. *Land and People of Nigeria Rivers State.* (1989 Riverside Communications).

Alagoa, E. J, Anozie F. N, and Nzewunwa, N. *The Early History of the Niger Delta.* (1988 Helnut-Buske verlag Hamburge).

Alagoa, E. J. *The Small Brave City State.* (1964 University of Ibadan Press). *A History of the Niger Delta - an historical interpretation of Ijo oral traditions.* (1972 University of Ibadan Press).

Alagoa, E. J., Tekena N T, Clark, J. P. T. *The Izon Of The Niger Delta* (2009 Onyoma Research Publications).

Ariye, E. (2013). *The Ijo (Ijaw) People of Delta State: Their Early History and Aspects of Social and Cultural Practices.* Historical Research Letter, 8, pp.25-30.

Asiegbu, J. U. J. *Nigeria and its British Invaders - 1851-1920.* (1984 Nok Publishers Nigeria).

Azorbo, T. G. and Ufford-Azorbo (2013). *FEMALE VIRGINITY AND MARITAL HONOUR AS VIRTUOUS ACTS AMONG THE IJAW PEOPLE IN AKPOS ADESI'S EBIDEIN-ERE*

Beredugo, L. I., Emmanuel, L. Oniso, J. I. and Aluye-Benibo, D. (2018). *BIRTH PREPAREDNESS AND COMPLICATION READINESS IN AMASSOMA COMMUNITY OF SOUTHERN IJAW LOCAL GOVERNMENT AREA, BAYELSA STATE, NIGERIA.* 3rd Edition Lautech Journal of Nursing. Accessed on 17/08/2023 available online from https://lautechjournalofnursing.com/wp-content/uploads/2019/01/Lautech_3rd_Edition_Nov-Dec_20181.pdf#page=176

Burns, A. *History of Nigeria.* (1978 George Allen and Unwin Ltd).

Fabiyi, O. O. and Yesuf, G. U. 2013. *"Dynamics and Characterization of Coastal Flooding in Nigeria: Implication for Local Community Management Strategies."* Ife Research Publications in Geography 12 (1&2): 45-61.

Ferryman-Mockler, A. F. *Up The Niger-Narratives of Major Claude MacDonald's Mission to the Niger and Benue Rivers West Africa.* (1892 George Philip and Sons London).

Leis, P. E. and Hollos, M. *Becoming Nigerian in Ijo Society.* (1989 Rutgers University Press).

Leis, P. E. (1964). *Palm Oil, Illicit Gin, and the Moral Order of the Ijaw.* American Anthropologist, Aug., 1964, New Series, Vol. 66, No. 4, Part 1 (Aug., 1964), pp. 828-838.

Nieketien, P. B. *A Short History of Tarakiri Clan* (1941).

Oduma Magazine vol 2 August 1974.

Okereke, I. E. (2019). *Science Process Skills Practised in Palm Wine Tapping.* Journal of CUDIMAC (J-CUDIMAC) Vol 6, accessed online on 08/08/2023 from http://cudimac.unn.edu.ng/journals-2/

Olaniyan, R. *Nigerian History and Culture.* (1985 Longmans).

Owonaro, S. K. *The History of Ijo (Ijaw) and her Neighbouring Tribes in Nigeria.* (1949) Niger Printing Press Lagos).

Talbot, P. A. *The Peoples of Southern Nigeria vols 1-4.* (1926 Oxford University Press), *The Tribes of the Niger Delta-Their Religion and Customs.* (1932 The Sheldon Press London), *A Sudanese Kingdom.* (1931).

The African Diaspora-Africans and Their Descendants in the Wider World to 1800. (1987 Ginn Press).

PART TWO

IZON (IJAW) AND BRITISH RELATIONS DURING THE ERA OF THE ATLANTIC SLAVE TRADE AND BRITISH EMPIRE

CHAPTER 4: ORIGINS OF TRADE, FIRENDSHIP AND PROTECTION TREATIES BETWEEN THE IZON (IJAW) AND BRITAIN

From historical records, the Portuguese were the first Europeans to contact the Ijaws of the Niger Delta from 1450 onwards or even before, while the English or British arrived about 100 years later. In 1440-44, the Portuguese sea captain named Diniz Dias landed in Upper Guinea (North West Africa). About the same time, a group of Berbers and other Africans were 'acquired' or captured from the North/West coast and taken to Portugal as exhibits. For the first half century (1450-1500), Europe itself was the main market for African captives. Large numbers of captives were brought to Spain and Portugal, where they performed the same duties that they were to perform in the Americas.

The enslavement of Africans by Europeans is traditionally held to have started in 1441. Antam Goncalves, a young Portuguese mariner, sailed to Rio De Oro on the coast of Southern Morocco. "O how fair a thing it would be" said Goncalves to his crew, "if we, who have come to this land for a cargo of such petty merchandise, were to meet with the good luck to bring the first captives before the face of our Prince." Later joined on the coast by Nuno Tristao, "a youthful knight very valiant and ardent," they kidnapped twelve Africans and gave them as a present to Prince Henry of Portugal. One of the captives, of noble birth, revealed particulars of the land from which he came to the Portuguese. With this intelligence, the prince sent an embassy to Pope Martin V to state his plans for more conquests and enslavement. Welcoming the new crusade, the Pope offered to grant "to all of those who shall be engaged in the said war, complete forgiveness of all their sins" … In 1443-4 Nuno Tristao sailed once more down the West African coast. His crew seized 29 men and women from canoes they were paddling near the shore. In Lisbon, the cargo of captives silenced critics who saw the expeditions as a waste of resources. A Portuguese account suggests: "their covetousness now began to wax greater. And as they saw the houses of others full to overflowing of male and female slaves, and their property increasing, they thought about the whole matter and began to talk among themselves". The Portuguese agreed to fund six ships under Gil Eanes and Lancarote. Their campaign led to the initial capture of 165 men, women and children "besides those that perished and were killed." Eventually they sailed home with 235 captives.[6]

The Izon (Ijaw) and the Encounter with the Europeans

Being a coastal marine people, settling along inland rivers, coastal creeks and estuaries, the Ijaws were one of the earliest West African people to have encountered the European, and hence Portuguese, and English captive dealers that enslaved the captives. One of the earliest and main areas from which these captives were acquired was the area that became known as the Slave Coast, which consisted of the river's estuaries, Mahin, Benin, Escravos, Forcados, and Ramos, plus some of the eastern delta estuaries, such as the Koluama River, Nun River etc. They collectively became known as the "Slave Rivers" due to the number of captives taken or acquired from this region. This so-called Slave Coast corresponds to the Ijaw country, and most of the earliest victims of the Atlantic slavery system were the Ijaw and other coastal peoples. Ijaw traditional historians remember this era very well;

> There are three distinct periods often spoken of in the Tarakiri clan, with regard to the coming into contact with European influences. First, the period of "Omoni-beke" meaning, 'the period of the slave trade' This was the period of intensive piracy and inter-tribal wars. Slave raiding during this period was an incident of daily happening. To travel a short distance from one village to another, one had to equip himself with all necessary fighting material or had to wait for an opportunity to go in the company of many people. Sometimes, people would band up themselves and would go to raid a village at night. Men, women and children would be captured and sold away to slave dealers. There was no law and the strongest man was at liberty to exercise his will no matter whether he was right or not.[7]

The ships of the Portuguese gave the search for gold the highest priority. They were well aware that West African gold reached Europe by way of the Sahara. To move in on the trade monopolised by the Arabs, Portuguese ships made their way down the coast of West Africa. In some cases, they contacted places that had gold, in others, there was no gold. If there was no gold, they could at least raid for captives. The raid on peaceful coastal communities then began.

In 1480, the Ijaw coastal town of Kula in the eastern delta was visited by some Portuguese sea merchants. The Portuguese received a hostile reception and turned back never to trade there again;

> 1480 The Portuguese are stated to have first landed at Kula, where they met with such a hostile reception that their visit to that neighbourhood was not repeated.[8]

In 1485, the Portuguese issued themselves a royal privilege; claiming for themselves the sole right to trade and acquire captives from the five slave

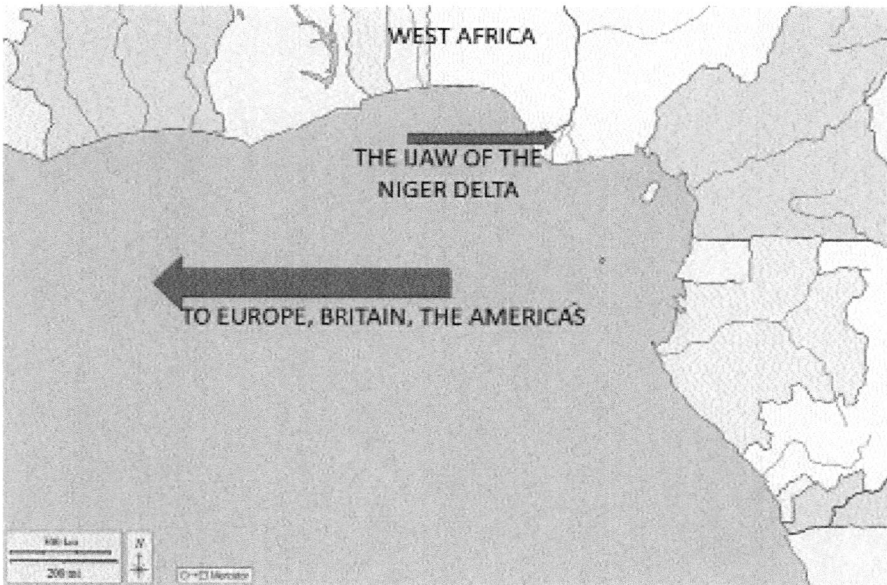

Figure 6. West Africa meets Europe, 16th century AD.

rivers, which were Mahin, Benin, Escravos, Forcados and Ramos. Arriving in the Niger Delta, they observed the Ijaws (Ijo, Izon), of whom they made various comments of;

> Beyond these there are other Negroes called Jos [Ijo], who possess a large territory; they are a warlike people.[9]

The 1588 English Contact with the Izon (Ijaw) of the Niger Delta

In about 1588, the English Sea Captain Welsh made contact with the Ijaws of the Benin Coast and was taken to Benin. He procured 22 barrels of palm oil and other goods. This is the first recorded contact of the Ijaws with the English or British.[10] Later on, palm oil was developed and used as an industrial lubricant, in tin-plate production, street-lighting, and as the fatty semi-solid for candle making and soap production in Europe and the Americas.

With regards to the earliest Trans-Atlantic slave trade in captives from slave raiding, which involved various Ijaw communities, many Ijaw victims would have found themselves in the Americas[11] and England. The Testimony of Olaudah Equiano in the 1780's (*The Interesting Narrative of the Life of Olaudah Equiano* 1789) and others, tell us that Africans were living in England as captives and free persons. Furthermore, that the free Africans organised

Figure 7. Olaudah Equiano.

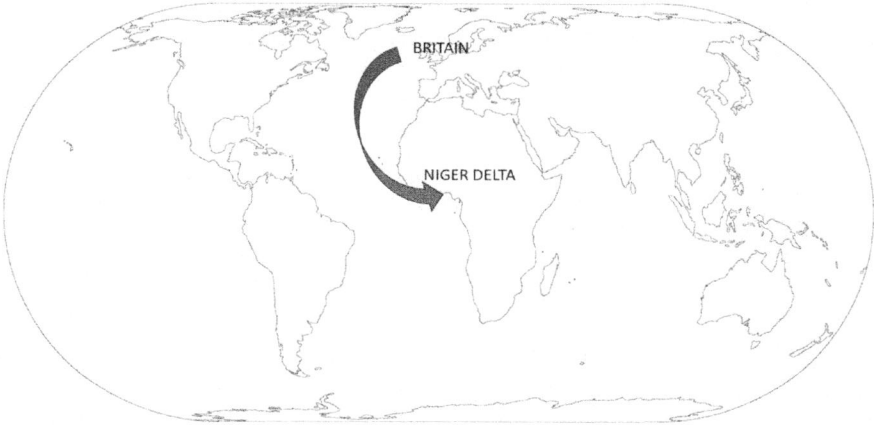

Figure 8. Britain meets the Ijaw Niger Delta, 19th century AD.

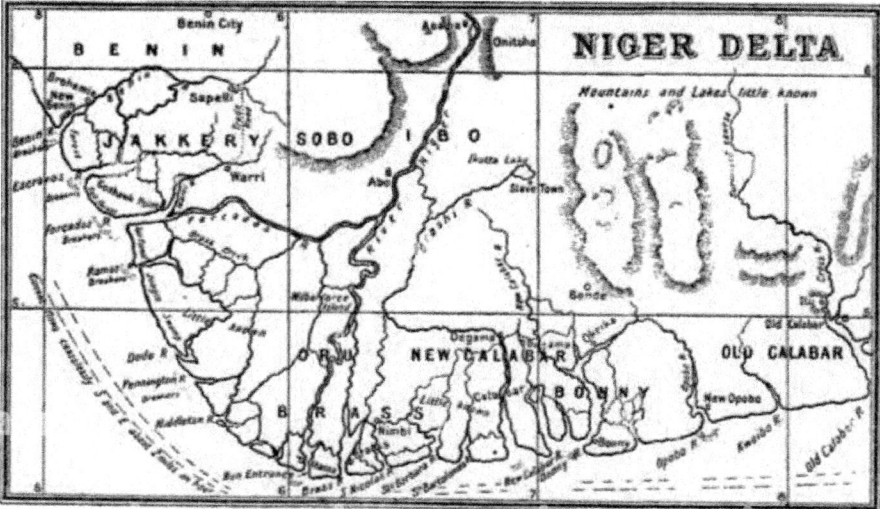

Figure 9. Niger Delta map of 1898 by H. Bindloss.

themselves under the name of 'The Sons of Africa' in order to fight for the abolition of the Trans-Atlantic slave trade. Ijaw individuals would have been amongst them, since Equiano himself had come from the Lower Niger region of present-day Nigeria, and the Niger Delta was a hotbed of captive raiding activity. This would then constitute the first informal migration of unknown Ijaw persons to Britain.

The British Presence along the Niger Delta Coast - 1833 Onwards

The British presence in the Ijaw country, begins with the enforcement of the abolition of the slavery act. Between 1807 - 1833/4, Britain abolished slavery with the Abolition Act (1833). To enforce this act, they stationed a navy squadron off the coast of West Africa in present-day Gulf of Guinea, at Fernando Po Island. To stop the slave trade in captives, the British contacted Ijaw kings and communities along the Niger Delta coast, notably Ibani (Bonny) Nembe (Brass), Kalabari, Iduwini and Ogulagha.

Britain, which had now taken an economic interest in the Niger Delta or Oil Rivers, due to the abundance of the oil palm, stepped up negotiations with coastal rulers about the undesirability of trading in captive human beings, and the possibility of switching over to the trade in agricultural produce, mainly palm oil. In the Niger Delta, their mode of negotiations was by the signing of treaties of protection backed up with threats of using armed force. This was the beginning of British colonialism and imperialism in the Niger Delta and the establishment of direct links between the Ijaw Niger Delta and Britain (United Kingdom). The capturing of the Lander brothers, Richard Lemon Lander (8 February 1804 - 6 February 1834), and John Lander, British explorers of western Africa, who were the first Europeans to follow the course of the river Niger and discover that it led to the Atlantic, by the Ibos of Asaba in 1830 and taken as prisoners and their subsequent release secured by traders from the Ijaw City States of Nembe and Ibani (Bonny) is an indication of gradual historic ties between the Ijaw people and Britain.

Treaties Signed Between Izon and the British

A treaty is a binding formal agreement, contract, or other written instrument that establishes obligations between two or more subjects of international law.[12] Britain gradually gained control of the Niger Delta (Oil Rivers) using both diplomatic (treaties) and military (gunboats) diplomacy. Treaties thus defined the character of the British penetration in such a way that by 1900, political control was formally established over the Niger Delta (Oil Rivers). An effective suppression of the slave trade (which needed to start from the

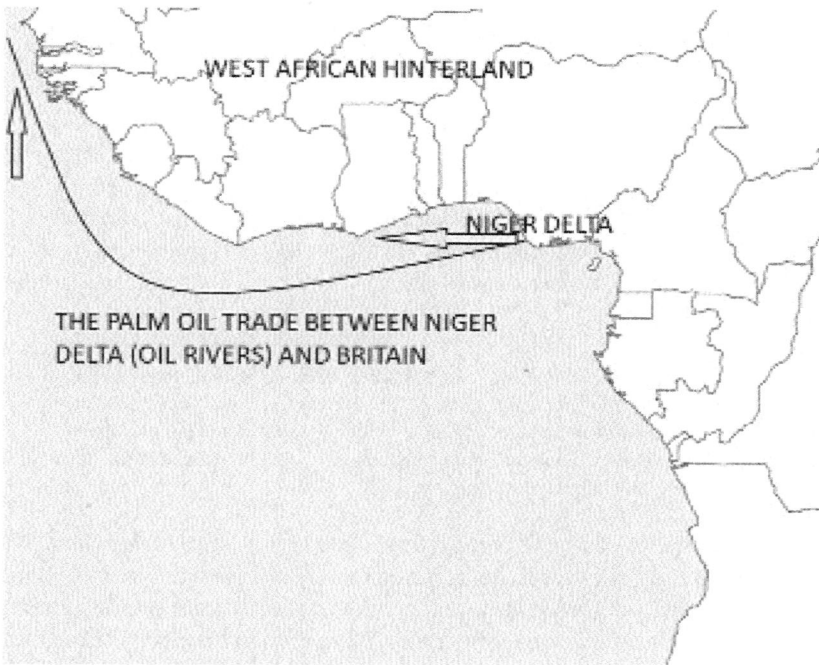

Figure 10. Palm Oil Trade, 19th century.

hinterland) could only be achieved with the use of treaties. The slave-trade treaties thus provided the legal and diplomatic basis, to put a stop to a trade that was no longer profitable to the commercial and industrial demand of Britain.

Several treaties were signed between the Ijaws of the Niger Delta and Britain in the 19th and 20th centuries, related to the abolition of the slave trade and the establishment of the palm oil trade. Colonel (later General) Sir Edward Nicolls, one of the enthusiastic and dynamic Governors of Fernando Po, 1829-34, had taken a distinct liking to the Niger Delta and indulged in activities few of which the Colonial Office sanctioned. Foremost among these was his passion for treaty-making. He claimed that the most effective means of exterminating the Delta slave trade was not the suppression movement led by the Navy but, the negotiation of alliances with the Delta states, which through treaty obligations, would side with Britain against the slave dealer. Such city-states as did support the British Navy against the dealers in people, signed the treaties because it paid them to do so. Therefore, between 1834 and 1885 (and further ones in 1888) the various Ijaw Autonomous clans and kingdoms, signed Friendship and Protection Treaties with the British Crown (her Majesty Queen Victoria) placing themselves under consular protection for the purposes of trade with British mercantile interests exclusively.[13] These treaties essentially gave Britain a large degree of control over the signer's territory, allowing the British to conduct foreign relations on the part of the ruler and to interfere in local politics in the interest of peace and free trade. This is best exemplified by Ibani (Grand Bonny); In 1839, King Dappa Perekule (corrupted to Pepple by Europeans) of Ibani-Ijo (Bonny) accompanied by the regent Alali (or Annie Pepple of the European records), his high priest, and Alali's secretary, were invited on board the British naval ship HMS Scout by Commander Robert Craige, for discussions on how to stop the slave trade and switch over to the trade in palm oil;

> Captain Craige assured the King that England ever dispensed justice, and would encourage the lawful commerce of the Bonny in every way; that she would send out ships in abundance for their palm-oil and other products; and if the Bonny men directed their attention properly to these, he was certain they could easily get rich without exporting slaves.[14]

This was then, the beginning of the large-scale trade of palm oil between the Ijaw Niger Delta and British merchants based mostly in Liverpool and London. Therefore, the trade continued as usual, with malice, suspicion and double dealing still a prominent feature of the trade, not in human beings this time, but agricultural produce (palm oil). For instance, a European extract from 1863 details this:

> On the 26th of January we entered Bonny, the wealthiest of these rivers of corruption. Here the [European] traders dare not live ashore but inhabit the huge hulks of ancient merchantmen ... West Africa is essentially a land of oils; this is its real wealth; and the export of ivory and gold are small in comparison. The commissions are large, to tempt these factors to brave a climate whose dangers they [i.e., Europeans] assist with their intemperance, and still more with their insanity ... These black traders are now almost too much for the white ones in these matters of low cunning which enter so largely into commerce of a petty nature. The days have gone by when charcoal powder and coralline could be passed upon the simple natives with impunity. A little can still be done with false weights and measures, but the good old days are gone forever, and the natives have learned to turn the dirty tables upon those who could once cheat them as they chose ... Among the whites there is no real unity; nobody trusts his neighbour. This gives the blacks a great advantage ... Rivals as they are, they can at least combine with that honesty which is always the best policy. If a Negro, for instance, cheats a white, the latter puts up with it. His brother members of the Association would freely promise to refuse to deal with the Negro, but he knows very well that a canoe loaded with palm oil could not be resisted by any of them. On the other hand, if a white man flagrantly offends, the native traders unite and 'shut the trade' to him. A case of this kind happened not long ago in Benin. They found that a certain trader used a smaller cowries-

Figure 11. Anchorage off Bonny.

tub than the others; they also found that while the other salt-tubs had one stave across it, to make the salt fall light and take up more space, his had two. A council was held: the trade was shut; not a canoe came near him; and he was forced to leave the river.[15]

The growth of palm oil export trade in West Africa, and particularly in the Ijaw area, which begun due to the availability of palm trees that grow naturally in the Niger Delta and immediate hinterland environment, the homeland of the Ijaws, was an important factor in rising relationship between Britain and the Ijaw people. The Niger Delta area, particularly Ibani (Bonny) and Elem-Kalabari, became significant points of entry, partly due to the abundance of palm tree in its hinterland, and because of the easy transportation route provided by the Niger River for oil export across the Atlantic Ocean. It has been noted that the preparedness of the Delta's hinterland region for the palm oil trade dates back to centuries of old internal development. This contact was facilitated by the hinterland oil producers' prior knowledge of extracting oil from oil palm fruit; the existence of a desire for commerce; established trading links between the coastal people and the inland areas, which all facilitated the rapid growth of the palm oil export business in the early 19th century. The growth in the palm oil export trade, could therefore be said to have responded to the immediate and indirect effect of the overseas trade in human captives, and not to the decline of such exports, but to palm oil production growth that already existed in the Niger Delta.

Figure 12. Another scene of anchorage off Bonny.

Figure 13. Palm oil workers, 1890s.

Therefore, the 19th century contact of the Ijaws with Britain was further established through palm oil trade, due to increasing demand for soap and industrial processes which required palm oil, in Britain that became the driving force behind the growth of palm oil export and the British involvement in the trade. During the period of Industrial Revolution, palm oil as a commodity also served as lubricants for the British industries as well as, the increasing need for personal hygiene by the Europeans, largely necessitated the growth of palm oil export demands.

By the mid-19th century, the British merchants had exported large numbers of palm oil products from the Niger Delta into London and Liverpool, with the Ijaw traders maintaining constant supply of palm oil to the merchants. The main contact centres for the palm oil export trade in the Niger Delta and the whole of West Africa between 1840 and 1855, were Elem-Kalabari and Ibani City States and the central Delta. It therefore becomes clear that, palm oil was the centre of the relationship between the British traders and the coastal trading Ijaw people. During this period of trading in palm oil, Ibani (Bonny) was the richest part of the Ijaw Delta City States in the palm oil trade and had by 1855, exported palm oil worth between 15,000 and 20,000 tons to Europe. Other rival Ijaw City States to Ibani such as New Kalabari, Brass and later Opobo, had also established trade relations with the British and had exported about 4, 000 and 2,280 tons of palm oil to Liverpool respectively. This contact promoted further trade relations between the British and the Niger Delta (Oil Rivers) signified by the export of products such as palm kernel and groundnuts that became export trade articles in the second half of the 19th century.

The British Courts of Equity and the Defence of Commercial Treaties

The Court of Equity was established in Ibani (Bonny) in 1850 after the appointment of the first consul, John Becrooft, in 1849 (Ikime, 1977, p. 31). This treaty was established by the British primarily to regulate trade between the British and the indigenous merchants. The court was composed mainly of European supercargoes, with a few leading traders of Bonny extraction. The jurisdiction of the court also covered the whole of the coastal area of modern Nigeria and extended to Benin Republic, and the Cameroons. The main function of the court, was originally to settle disputes arising from trade between European supercargoes and delta traders with John Becrooft as the chairman of the court. This created an important inroad into the Niger Delta.

By 1885, the British had signed a series of treaties with the "Chiefs and People of the Oil Rivers" or Niger Delta, who were mostly the Ijaws. These treaties were supposed to be treaties of "Friendship and Protection", which were to result in the Ijaw people of the Niger Delta being incorporated into the

Figure 14. Ibani Chiefs with British Naval Office,1896.

emerging British Empire. By June 5,1885, the Oil Rivers consisting of Benin coast, Brass (Nembe), Ibani, Calabar, Elem-Kalabari, Opobo including the rivers and creeks of the Ijaw geographical Niger Delta, were declared by the British Government through an 'order in council', as the Oil Rivers Protectorate (Niger Delta Protectorate), and placed under consular jurisdiction. Later on, in November of the same year of 1885 at the conference of European powers (Berlin conference); the European gathering acknowledged British Protectorate jurisdiction over the Niger Delta. This is achieved by Britain through the presentation to the gathering the Treaty of "Friendship and Protection". After this, more Ijaw clans and kingdoms signed treaties with the British. In 1893, by an Order in Council, the Oil Rivers Protectorate was renamed the "Niger Coast Protectorate."

By 1898-1900, what was then known as native courts were established in the Niger Delta. On 27th December 1899, by Order in Council, the name of the Niger Coast Protectorate (Oil Rivers Protectorate) was changed to Southern Nigeria Protectorate. The Niger Delta becomes the structural foundation for the British colony of Nigeria. This is the period when the Ijaw Niger Delta lost its identity as a separate sovereign political entity, through the formation of this structural foundation, along with Calabar, Benin and Lagos regions, for the creation of Southern Nigeria.

REFERENCES

6. Walker R (2006) *When We Ruled,* p. 544.
7. Nieketein P B (1941) *A Short History of Tarakiri Clan,* pp. 21-24.
8. Talbot P A (1926) *The Peoples of Southern Nigeria vol 1,* p. 238.
9. Hodgkin T (1960, 1975) *Nigerian Perspectives,* p. 123.
10. Robins J E (2021) *Oil Palm A Global History,* https://academic.oup.com/north-carolina-scholarship-online/book/42533/chapter-abstract/356844529?redirectedFrom=fulltext accessed between 01/08/23 and 31/11/23
11. One-third of the basic words in Berbice Dutch Creole, including words for 'eat', 'know', and 'speak' are of Niger-Congo origin in West Africa, from a single language-cluster, the Eastern Ijaw languages. The language borrowed its lexicon largely from Dutch (57%) and Eastern Ijo (38%), with only 1% of its lexicon stemming from Arawak varieties. It is considered a unique Creole language because it consists of only one African language influence, with 0% of its structure or lexicon stemming from parts of Africa outside of Eastern Ijo. Wikipedia accessed in October 2023, and https://ohbeautifulguyana.files.wordpress.com/2014/03/echoes-of-berbice-dutch-creole.pdf As evidence that Ijaw people were taken to the Americas or got to the Amercas during the Atlantice slavery period.
12. https://www.britannica.com/topic/treaty accessed between 01/08/23 and 31/11/23
13. In 1844, Some prominent Ijaw Clans and Kingdoms met and established for the purposes of unified trade and foreign policy, what was then called The Ijo League.
14. Hodgkin T (1960, 1975) *Nigerian Perspectives,* p. 303.
15. Hodgkin T (1960, 1975) *Nigerian Perspectives,* p. 347.

BIBLIOGRAPHY

Ade Ajayi, J. C. *Christian Missions in Nigeria 1841-1871: The Making Of Educated Elite,* 1965, London: Longman Group.

Akinrinade, S. & Falola, T. *Europe and Africa: Prelude to the Partition.* In A. Sesay (Ed), *Africa and Europe: From Partition to Independence or Dependence?* 2011, New York: Routledge.

Anene, J. C. *Southern Nigeria in Transition 1884-1906, Theory and Practice in a Colonial Protectorate.* 1965 Cambridge: Longman Group.

Asiegbu, J. U. J. *Nigeria and its British Invaders, 1851-1920: A Thematic Documentary History.* (1984, New York: Nok Publishers)

Brett, E. A. *Colonialism and Underdevelopment in East Africa: The Politics of Economic Change (1919-1939),* 1973, New York: NOK Publishers Ltd

Crowder, M. *West Africa Under Colonial Rule.* London: Hutchinson & Co. Dike, K. O. (1956). *Trade and Politics in the Niger Delta.* (1966, Oxford: Clarendon Press)

Falola, T. & Heaton, M. *A History of Nigeria. New York,* (2008, Cambridge University Press)

Hertslet, E. *The Map of Africa by Treaty, Vol. I* (British Colonies, Protectorates and Possessions in Africa). London: (1967 Frank Cass and Co. Ltd)

Hopkins, A. G. *An Economic History of West Africa.* London: (1975 Longman Publishers)

Ikime, O. *The Fall of Nigeria: The British Conquest.* London & Ibadan: (1977, Heinemann Education Books)

Orugbani, *A. Nigeria Since the 19th Century.* Port Harcourt: (2005 Paragraphic Press

Tamuno, T. N. *Some Aspects of Nigerian Reaction to the Imposition of British Rule,* Journal of the Historical Society of Nigeria, 3 (2) (1965)

Uzoigwe, G. N. *European Partition and Conquest of Africa: An Overview.* In A. Adu Boahen, (Ed.) *General History of Africa VII* (1985 Berkeley: MIT Press)

Walker, R. *When We Ruled* (2006, Every Generation Media)

PART THREE

BACKGROUND TO THE SETTLEMENT OF IZON (IJAW) PEOPLE IN LONDON

CHAPTER 5: IZON (IJAW) PEOPLE, KINGS AND PRINCES KNOWN TO HAVE LIVED IN LONDON AND DISTRICTS FROM 1808

The early Ijaw presence in London should be seen within the context of the transatlantic slave trade, its abolition, the Palm Oil trade and the rising power of the British Empire and eventual inclusion of Ijaw people into this empire. According to Abiodun Adeniyi, PhD;

> S. Shyllon (1977) argues, for instance, that the coming of blacks to Britain began from the "generally accepted date of their arrival in 1555". This was when: Five Africans were brought into Britain. Over the next century, more and more Africans were imported. By the middle of the 17th century, at least, a thriving black community had been established, and Britain had ceased to be a white-man's country (1997:3). From that year, the experience of blacks in Britain began to assume different dimensions. Though they came as slaves, an initial covert activism in 1756 began a process of flight and resistance. Olaudah Equiano, Ottomah Cugoano, and Ignatius Sancho were amongst prominent activists. Slavery began declining in 1772, and with the 18th century rise of industrial capitalism, which the trade aided (Skinner, 1982:13), its economic importance reduced. The effective outlawing of slavery took place in 1807. From the beginning of the 20th century, therefore, black influence began to rise in Britain. Black population now comprises children of slaves and of black soldiers and seamen who settled in Britain after fighting in the Napoleonic wars. There were also Africans including students, business and sports people, apart from Caribbean professionals employed in sectors of the British economy. By the end of the Second World War for instance, 20,000 blacks in Britain were living in "dockside areas of London, Liverpool, and Cardiff.[15]

With the rise of British mercantile interests in the Oil Rivers or Niger Delta, the coastal rulers who had started trading in palm oil became merchant princes. These merchant princes came into conflict with the British mercantile establishment as well as dissatisfied members of their own kingdoms. Because of this, some were exiled and found their way to London. There is documentary evidence of notable Ijaw (Ijo, Izon) persons visiting and living in London and its suburbs during the 1800s, for example Henry Sigoin Amachree is listed to have lived in Newington Surrey about 1808.[17] We also have one Mr Isaac Benebo said to have been born in foreign parts in about 1813, and by the age of 28 years, was resident at St. Botolph Bishopgate, Botolph Without Bishopgate, Middlesex England, according to the 1841 census of Middlesex.[18]

We can also mention Ijaw persons who came to Britain to gain more 'Western Education' during this period,[19] these include the following persons;

Herbert Jumbo from Ibani, who was a student of Liverpool College, England and graduated from the University of London in 1856 as an external candidate;

John Jumbo from Ibani, who graduated from Durham University, England in 1878;

Robert Abrakassa Igbeta from Nembe, who graduated from the Isle of Man, England in 1888;

Josiah Akidiye Batubo from Buguma, Kalabari, who graduated from Colwyn Bay, Wales in 1909.

Ibani (Bonny) Royal Family in London

We have the example of a branch of the Royal Family of Ibani (Grand Bonny) Kingdom of Ijaw with the early exile of Amanyanabo (i.e. 'King') Dappa Perekule (known as King William Dappa Pepple in the documents) and young family, to London. Amanyanabo Dappa Perekule was forced to go into exile by combined British mercantile and Ibani interests;

> The Bonny state was deeply riven by the long-established tension between canoe houses that in this period was given an added dimension, by the growth of the palm oil trade. This factional struggle particularly affected the position of the Amanyanabo of Bonny during the reigns of William Dappa Pepple and his son George. Factional struggles led figures in Bonny to look for outside help, as in William Dappa's use of British assistance to gain power in 1836-1837, and in his rivals' overthrow of him in 1854. The consequence of this factional tension, was the decline of the powers of the Amanyanabo and eventually, the split of Bonny into two in 1869. The attempts to manipulate outside assistance in these struggles, merely provided an opportunity for the British to increase their influence, a process that culminated in the takeover of Bonny in 1884-1885.[20]

Amayanabo Dappa Perekule stayed in England for five years (1856 -1861) with his wife and several children. Three of King Dappa Perekule's children, namely Oruigbi Dappa-ye Perekule (also known as George Pepple), Onu Perekule (also known as Henry Pepple), and Charles Perekule (Pepple) stayed in London for up to eight years receiving an English education:[21]

> Dappa Pepple was first taken to Clarence in Fernando Po in 1854. He took with him one of his wives and a servant or two. He made at least two attempts to escape and return to Bonny. King Dappa was then sent to Ascension Island from where he continued to petition the British government for his release or for an opportunity to plead his case before the British Monarch. He was removed to Sierra Leone and finally to London in 1856. In London, King

**Figure 15. Amayanabo ('King')
Dappa Perekule, also known as
King William Dappa Pepple.**

Dappa Pepple's case was taken up by some prominent Quakers including Mr
Ayrton, a member of Parliament, and Mr Gurney, a lawyer. He was also
received by the Mayor of London, and was later baptised into the Church of
England by the Bishop of London with the name of William. He attended
service at St Paul's Cathedral and sent his son George Pepple to English
Schools ... George Pepple, also known in Bonny as Dappa-ye Oruigbigi was
proclaimed king after the death of his father, and crowned on 10th October
1866 ... George Pepple had been educated in England for eight years during his
father's exile in London, a privilege shared by his brothers, Henry and Charles
Pepple. The quality of this education was acknowledged high by even the
British traders, who became prejudiced against the new king.[22]

King Dappa Perekule (Pepple) lived at 13 Philip Terrace in Tottenham, this
house now in Philip Lane still exists. King Dappa Perekule as King Pepple,
with his family and entourage, are listed in the enumeration of the 1861 census.
They were later to move to Green Place in Tottenham. In 1861, he was recalled
to Grand Bonny and left London on 14 June arriving on 25 October. Due to
poor health, he died in 1866. He was succeeded by his son Prince Oruigbi
(Oruigbiji) Dappa Perekule (also known as George Pepple), who was in exile
in Tottenham with the family, and had 8 years of education converting to

Christianity.[23] Prince Oruigbi was educated in what is known as presently as South East London at the Boys' school at Hall Place, Bexley (currently called Hall Place and Gardens, Bourne Road, Bexley, Kent DA5 1PQ Greater London. While here Prince Oruigbi studied English, Greek, Mathematics, Scripture and History, the conventional syllabus of Victorian England at the time. A 2019 tour guide notice of the school, mentions in its advertisement:

> Community Archivist, Oliver Wooller tells the story of Hall Place as a boy's school. Hailed as the Eton of Kent, for seventy years Hall Place Academy flourished under a series of remarkable headmasters ... Then there was George Pepple, a Nigerian Prince, who returned to his homeland to become King of Bonny.[24]

On 16 March 1870, Prince Oruigbi (Now King George) sailed for England, where he called for more forceful action by the British to support him in some internal kingdom crises, a plea that was accepted. In 1879 King Oruigbi Perekule (George Pepple) fell ill, and when he recovered took his doctor's advice to take a holiday in England. In London the king was received well, and his activities were reported in the press, and he was introduced to the Prince of Wales, most probably by his Quaker friends:

> The titular king of Bonny, George Pepple, had gone to England for his health; and during his stay on our shores had been everywhere received with respect and enthusiasm. He made friends with the Lord Mayor of London, was even introduced to the Prince of Wales, and gave several addresses upon the subject of his country's welfare, and the pleasure he felt at being so well received. The most important feature of his visit, however, was the interest evinced by all with whom he came in contact in the mission work at Bonny, and he was not slow to show his earnest appreciation of its value and success.[25]

He was also presented with a steam launch at the end of his visit. Due to internal crises, there was alarm among the chiefs, about his growing power combined with the growing power of the British. Because of this closeness on 14 December 1883, King Oruigbi was deposed.

In February 1886, a protectorate treaty was concluded between Ibani - Grand Bonny and Britain. A ruling council was established, and King Oruigbi Perekule was restored to his throne in October 1888. This series of actions reflected increasing closer ties with Britain and a more subservient relationship between the Ijaw mercantile princes and the emerging British Empire. The protection treaty signed by Grand Bonny along with the other treaties signed by Ijaw Clans and Kingdoms,[26] drew the Ijaw Ethnic Nation more and more into the sphere of British mercantile and colonial interests. UK Parliamentary records show that King Dappa Perekule, father of King Oruigbi Perekule received compensation during his time in London.[27]

Figure 16. King Oruigbi Perekule, also known as King George Pepple.

When King Dappa Perekule was exiled and stayed in Britain (1856 to 1861), Ijaw ethnic nationality was not a colony of Britain. The clans and kingdoms of Ijaw were autonomous sovereign entities, some of which like Ibani (Grand) Bonny had signed protectorate treaties, purely to stop the slave trade and have exclusive trading rights with Britain or British mercantile interests. This is reflected in these quotes from a parliamentary session that dealt with compensation to King Dappa Perekule (King Pepple):[28]

> MR. GREGORY remarked, that he should be sorry to make invidious allusions to oppressed potentates, but he thought, before the Committee voted a grant of £1,200 to King Pepple, they should know something of the good he had done. He had heard something of this ex-King, and he believed that since his fallen fortunes the monarch incurred but a moderate expenditure, his chief luxuries being rum and tobacco.

> MR. AYRTON said, he had seen King Pepple the other night, and if every item in the Vote was as justifiable as the amount paid to that individual, he would pass it over without objection. That unfortunate person had been the King of Bonny, and made a treaty with the British Government, whereby he agreed to suppress the slave trade in his country for a very small sum. That treaty was, he believed, in strict accordance with the policy which the Government had for many years pursued, and the item in the Vote was for the payment of the balance of the subsidy due under that treaty. He could conceive no better way of putting down the slave trade than by entering into treaties with the chieftains on the coast; but those treaties once made should be scrupulously observed. It seemed unfortunate, however, that the end of all treaties between native chiefs and this country was the dethronement of those chiefs and the annexation of

their territory, and that had been the case with this unfortunate ex-King. He
trusted, however, that the noble Lord the Secretary for Foreign Affairs would
inquire into the circumstances and that justice would be done to him. As to the
ludicrous picture which had been drawn by the hon. Member for Galway, he
could only say that when he saw the ex-King he was as well dressed as the hon.
Member himself.

With regard to the item for the ex-King Pepple, part of it referred to the sum
which was furnished to him under the treaty which had been entered into with
him for the suppression of the slave trade.

The Oil Rivers Protectorate, by which the Ijaw Niger Delta and Calabar coast
was known at the time, was incorporated into a new colonial creation by the
British, through a series of 'Order in Councils' made by high British political
officials.

But there was a deeper price to be paid as well. The factional conflict that led
to the decline in the office of Amanyanabo was also to culminate in the British
take-over of the Delta, with treaties of protection signed with Bonny in July and
August 1884 and the declaration of the Niger Districts Protectorate in June
1885.[29]

The fact that the royal family and entourage could visit Britain and stay in
London for some time, would suggest that other Ijaw merchant princes, at the
time would also have visited London or other parts of the Britain. For example,
Prince Waribo, the son of King Jaja of Opobo, was reported to have visited as
well. There are references to an overseas educated class[30] in 19th century Grand
Bonny (Ibani) and the other City States of Elem Kalabari, Okirika and Nembe
of Ijaw people. Many of these educated citizens would have schooled in
England or Sierra Leone.

Jaja of Opobo 1821-1891

Jaja of Opobo, real name Jubo Jubogha, was the first king 'Amanyanabo' of
Opobo. He was also the founder of Opobo city-state in the present-day Rivers
State in Southeastern Nigeria. Jaja was born in 1821 at Umuduruoha,
Amaigbo, in present-day Imo State, Southeastern Nigeria, and named Mbanaso
Okwaraozurumbaa at birth. He was said to have been sold to a branch of the
Ibani royal family and renamed Jubo Jubogha by his first master. After that, he
was given to Chief Alali, the head of the Opubo Manila Group of Houses. It
was in this new master's house he was given the name "Jaja" (as the British
could not pronounce his name," Jubo Jubogha". After several years in
captivity, he earned his way out of slavery. During his captivity, Jaja gained an

apprenticeship in trading and culturalized into Ijaw-Ibani culture via undergoing traditional Ibani citizenship rites. After his master's death, he understood all the nitty-gritty of the business; Jaja took charge of the trades his master left behind and became wealthy and powerful.

Internal conflict at Ibani led Jaja to leave with his supporters to establish a new town close to Andoni in 1869 named Opubo-ama (shortened to Opobo). This new location was so strategically positioned that it attracted first-hand national and international merchants, effectively making it a monopolistic oil palm trade area. But within one year, his trade venture at Opobo brought tremendous wealth, so much that his former British trading partners lost £100,000 (in 1870), which made Bonny plead with him to return, which he declined. His activities came to the attention of Queen Victoria of Great Britain, who, impressed by his influence, recognised him as King of Opobo in 1873. And Jaja reciprocated by sending a contingent of his soldiers to assist the British in their war against the Ashanti Kingdom in the then Gold Coast, now Ghana. As a form of expression of gratitude, Queen Victoria awarded him a sword of honour, which seemed to signal a sweet relationship between Opobo City State and Britain.

At the Berlin conference of 1884, when Opobo was designated as a part of the Oil Rivers Protectorate, King Jaja became uncomfortable with the terms and felt tricked, so he continued taxation of British traders and blocked attempts at inland trade, even after he had signed a treaty with Britain in 1887 to allow free trade in his territory, by blocking John Holt of Liverpool to penetrate his market in Qua Ibo River. Still, the Liverpool supporters of the African Association pressed for decisive action against him over "falling profit rates". This was a made-up story to put pressure on Jaja. Jaja thus became infamous for resisting the British's foreign political and economic influence. For fear of Jaja's growing influence, Henry Hamilton Johnson, the then British vice-consul, invited King Jaja for negotiations in 1887 aboard a "Warship" called HMS Goshawk, under the guise of resolving the issue, with the assurance of his safety. On this basis, King Jaja honoured Johnson's invitation, accompanied by his wife Patience, his Special Advisor Emma Jaja Johnson, who was an African American who had recently emigrated back to West Africa and gained employment in Jaja's Court, a cook, a steward, three servants, and a carpenter. But upon arrival, Jaja was confronted with two difficult choices. Either he grants the Europeans access to Opobo or returns home and faces war with the British Navy. He would have to go into exile if he would not settle for that. King Jaja refused to back down. A deportation order was served on him, and was deported first to Accra, in the Gold Coast (now Ghana), where he was subsequently tried and purportedly found guilty of actions inimical Britain's trade interests and sent on exile. He was said to have been moved to London first, where he met with Queen Victoria and remained her guest at Buckingham Palace. Shortly after his arrival, he was deported to St. Vincent Island and Barbados in the British West Indies, but no one knew what transpired between him and the Queen.

After years of fighting, he eventually regained freedom against his wrongful abduction, and the British Parliament permitted him to be repatriated to his Kingdom State of Opobo in 1891 but sadly died in Tenerife, enroute to Opobo. He was purportedly poisoned with a cup of tea in June. His body was shipped to Tenerife in the Canary Islands, where he was buried. He was aged 70 years old. King Jaja's death enraged his kinsmen, who requested that his body be returned to Opobo. After several protests and pleas, King Jaja's body was exhumed and sent back to the Opobo kingdom, where it was received with much sorrow by his people, and he was properly laid to rest with a full honourable royal burial. Today, his remains are in a sacred (grave) shrine behind the palace of the Amanyanabo (King) of Opobo.

But most people tend to know Jaja more of being a young man, sold to slavery after which he became a king. That is not all King Jaja was. He significantly committed himself to the protection of the sovereignty of the African man and his territory. When Britain became the world's workshop with the introduction of machines and automation, they were looking for oil to lubricate their machines when they moved from the agrarian stage to technology. That lubrication which became known as oil was found in Africa, West Africa in particular. Jaja dominated the palm oil trade, becoming number one in terms of the sales / income. This enabled Britain in those days to drive the industrial revolution that was sweeping through the whole of Great Britain and later to other parts of the Western world. Jaja needs to be remembered for these two major contributions - defending the sovereignty of his African People (although contradicted by his supporting Britain to defeat the Asanti Kingdom) the African people and the support he gave to accelerate the industrial revolution of the world).

Prince Waribo Jaja

Prince Waribo (Warabo in British archives), whose name means 'guardian of the house', was King Jaja of Opobo's second son who was sent off to school in Britain at the former Manor House School in Cheshire, England, in 1881 at the age of 13 years old, but he was never to return. However, details about his personal experience at the school or any background information about his general health need to be more detailed; still, the young prince tragically passed away just a year later after a game of cricket. A Cheshire Archives account had it that Prince Waribo was an "apt pupil" who soon became a

Figures 17 a & b. Two photographs of Prince Waribo Jaja.

popular member of his school and the local community. It seems he apparently, and very sadly, suffered an acute inflammation of the lungs (from pneumonia or some respiratory distress syndrome) and died a week later. According to an account in the Frodsham History Archives,

> ... a Firm of Scottish traders, Couper, Johnson, and Co. of Glasgow, traded with King Jaja [born 1821 - died 1891], the paramount ruler of Opobo kingdom in Nigeria. King Jaja entrusted his second son, the 12-year-old Prince Warabo, to the care of Walter Johnstone and brought him to Frodsham, England, to be educated. After careful consideration, the young prince was placed in Manor House School, Main Street, by the principal, the Rev. R.P. Borwick. But sadly, after playing cricket on Friday, 14th. April 1882, he was seized with an acute inflammation of the lungs and died at 8.25 am on Friday 21st, April 1882. This school location now stands as the location of the 'YuenBen' Chinese restaurant. The news of his death threw shockwaves within the neighbourhood, as he was said to have been very popular with the Frodsham people. Most of the shops had to close, and pupils of Mr. R.D. Turner's school, which occupied part of Crosbie House at the time, lined the road near the church to mourn the young prince.[31]

The grave of Prince Waribo, son of King Jaja of Opobo, is still visible in the churchyard at St Laurence Parish Church, Frodsham, Cheshire. It is well known in Frodsham that amongst all the graves in St Laurence churchyard, along with the Smiths, the Joneses, and the Browns, lays an African Prince,

Prince Waribo (Warabo). His siblings are listed as Prince Saturday, Prince Albert, Prince Eugene, Princess Nai, and Prince Obiesigha (Frederick Sunday). When Waribo died, his younger brother, Prince Frederick Sunday was sent to Scotland to be educated.

Prince Obiesigha Frederick Sunday Jaja (1873-1915)

Prince Obiesigha Frederick Sunday Jaja was one of the sons of King Jaja of Opobo and was the younger brother of Prince Waribo. He was educated in London and was, in 1888, temporarily exiled with his father in the British West Indies. King Jaja died in 1891 and was succeeded by his son, Prince Frederick Sunday, in 1893. Unfortunately, when the Europeans removed King Jaja of Opobo in 1887, they did not allow his crown prince's son to succeed him immediately. They were afraid he would revolt against them. There was much commotion. Eventually he became King of Opobo. There were lots of conspiracies to undermine him.

These are just some of the Ijaw personalities captured in historical archives, who are known to have lived or visited London and England during the formative years of the growing relationship between the Ijaw People and Britain with its emerging empire.

REFERENCES

16. Adeniyi A (2016) *Evolution of Nigerian Diaspora in Britain: Issues, Perspectives, and a Continuing Debate*, p. 2.
17. Ancestry Search Ancestry.co.uk. Henry Sigoin Amachree in the Surrey, England, Land Tax Records, 1780-1832. accessed between 01/08/23 and 31/11/23.
18. Ancestry Search Ancestry.co.uk. Isaac Benebo 1841 England Census, accesses between 10/01/24 and 15/01/24. There are numerous names in the UK land, tax and census records that sound Ijaw such as Benabo, Beneby where the individuals may well have been Ijaw or of Ijaw descent.
19. Fiofori T, Daminabo A O and Ayotamuno Y (2009) *Ijo Footprints - Ijo Contributors to Nigeria and the World*, p. 53. Ijaw History Project
20. Lynn M (1995) *Factionalism, imperialism and the making and breaking of Bonny kingship c. 1830-1885*, pp. 169-192.
21. Fombo A & Alagoa EJ (1972, 2001) *A Chronicle of Grand Bonny*, pp. 24-28. Cliff Pereira & Simon McKeon. *BLACK AND ASIAN PEOPLE IN VICTORIAN BEXLEY. GEORGE PEPPLE*. Bexley Council. Archived from the original on 13 June 2011. Retrieved 15 October 2010 from https://en.wikipedia.org/wiki/George_Oruigbiji_Pepple, accessed between 01/08/23 and 31/11/23.
22. Fombo A & Alagoa EJ (1972, 2001) *A Chronicle of Grand Bonny*, pp. 24-28.
23. https://archiveshub.jisc.ac.uk/search/archives/44e838ff-fe08-34d3-9a29-0fd82697a7d9 accessed between 01/08/23 and 31/11/23.
24. https://www.hallplace.org.uk/event/a-school-for-young-gentlemen/ *Bexley, The Slavery Connection*, Teachers' Resource Notes (2007-09) Bexley Heritage Trust. accessed between 01/08/23 and 31/11/23.

25. http://anglicanhistory.org/africa/crowther/page1892/11.html. From Project Canterbury *Samuel Crowther, The Slave Boy Who Became Bishop of the Niger,* By Jesse Page, London: S. W. Partridge & Co., c. 1892. Chapter XI. Bonny a Bethel, accessed between 01/08/23 and 31/11/23.
26. https://hansard.parliament.uk/Commons/1857-07-03/debates/8e11ca44-7b05-496b-9244-717f959ad4f6/CommonsChamber Commons Chamber Volume 146: Debated on Friday July 1857, accessed between 01/08/23 and 31/11/23.
27. https://hansard.parliament.uk/Commons/1857-07-03/debates/8e11ca44-7b05-496b-9244-717f959ad4f6/CommonsChamber Commons Chamber Volume 146: Debated on Friday July 1857, accessed between 01/08/23 and 31/11/23.
28. https://hansard.parliament.uk/Commons/1857-07-03/debates/8e11ca44-7b05-496b-9244-717f959ad4f6/CommonsChamber Commons Chamber Volume 146: Debated on Friday July 1857, accessed between 01/08/23 and 31/11/23.
29. Lynn M (1995) *Factionalism, imperialism and the making and breaking of Bonny kingship c. 1830-1885,* pp. 169-192.
30. Fombo A & Alagoa EJ (1972, 2001) *A Chronicle of Grand Bonny,* pp. 24-28.
31. https://frodsham.nub.news/news/local-news/rewind-the-story-of-frodsham39s-prince-waribo-of-opobo-nigeria , accessed between 01/08/23 and 31/11/23.

BIBLIOGRAPHY

Alagoa, E. J. and Fombo, A. *A Chronicle of Grand Bonny.* (1972 University of Ibadan Press).

Alagoa, E. J. and Tamuno, T. N. *Land and People of Nigeria Rivers State.* (1989 Riverside Communications).

Alagoa, E. J. Anozie, F. N, and Nzewunwa, N. *The Early History of the Niger Delta.* (1988 Helnut-Buske verlag Hamburge).

Alagoa, E. J. *The Small Brave City State.* (1964 University of Ibadan Press). *A History of the Niger Delta - an historical interpretation of Ijo oral traditions.* (1972 University of Ibadan Press).

Arthur, R. S. 1994 *Discovering Frodsham's Old Schools - an illustrated History:*

Arthur, R. S. 2012 *Brief Lives*

Asiegbu, J. U J. *Nigeria and its British Invaders - 1851-1920.* (1984 Nok Publishers Nigeria).

Burns, A. *History of Nigeria.* (1978 George Allen and Unwin Ltd).

Cookey, S. J. S. *King Jaja of the Niger Delta: His Life and Times 1821-1891* (1974 Nok Publishers).

Crowder, M. and Ajayi, J. F. A. *History of West Africa vol 1.* (1985 Longman Group Ltd).

Fiofori, T. Daminabo A. O. and Ayotamuno, Y. (Editors). *Ijo Footprints - Ijo Contributors to Nigeria and the World* (2009 Ijaw History Project, Onyoma Research Publications).

Ferryman-Mockler, A. F. *Up The Niger-Narratives of Major Claude MacDonald's Mission to the Niger and Benue Rivers West Africa.* (1892 George Philip and Sons London).

King Jaja of Opobo (Special Memorial) From Contemporary records and pictures.

Leis, P. E. and Hollos, M. *Becoming Nigerian in Ijo Society.* (1989 Rutgers University Press).

Nieketien, P. B. *A Short History of Tarakiri Clan* (1941).

Oduma Magazine vol 2 August 1974.

Olaniyan, R. *Nigerian History and Culture.* (1985 Longmans).

Owonaro, S. K. *The History of Ijo and her Neighbouring tribes in Nigeria.* (1949 Niger printing Press Lagos).

Talbot, P A. *The Peoples of Southern Nigeria vols 1-4.* (1926 Oxford University Press), *The Tribes of the Niger Delta-Their Religion and Customs.* (1932 The Sheldon Press London)., *A Sudanese Kingdom.* (1931).

The African Diaspora-Africans and Their Descendants in the Wider World to 1800. (1987 Ginn Press).

CHAPTER 6: THE GROWTH OF THE IZON (IJAW) COMMUNITY IN LONDON FROM 1900

The Colonies of Southern Nigeria and Northern Nigeria which were known as the Southern Protectorate and Northern Protectorate, were amalgamated in 1914 and immediately London became the centre of focus for young and ambitious Nigerians who wanted to explore the world. London was an attractive city for immigrants and migrants, who did not consider themselves as such, because they were coming to settle, live and educate themselves in the capital of the British Empire at the time. Most, if not all, had the status of British Citizens or Subjects because by 1 January 1948, the British Nationality Act was passed in London. This granted people of the British Commonwealth at the time, the right to apply for British Citizenship (or British Subject). They did not ask Britain to colonise their homelands, and Britain encouraged the able and willing to come to London to work and seek further education as a part of its war promises to the colonies.

Until then, it might have been the case that Izon (Ijaw) people were migrating back and forth from the United Kingdom from as far back as the seventeenth century AD, while records of more permanent settlement go back to the early nineteenth century AD, when the Izon homeland was incorporated into the newly created British Colony of Nigeria. By the twentieth century, Izon People living in Liverpool formed the Ijaw People's Union in 1945 (later known as Ijaw Cultural Union). Following that in 1948 Ijaw People living in London formed the Ijaw People's Association (IPA) of Great Britain and Ireland. Testimonies of the descendants of these early Izon 'immigrants' community reveal that they kept in contact with their homeland and tried as much as possible to maintain their ancestral Izon (Ijaw) culture, while at the same time integrating into the wider British society.

Family wise, the English educational authorities discouraged the speaking of Ijo language in the home, as they felt it would impede the educational development of the children (see https://www.edgehill.ac.uk/the-conversation-dr-ian-cushing/).

The Ijaws of London strived to maintain and celebrate their Ijaw culture, within the context of living in the UK and later being of dual nationality, Nigerian, British or Both. They did this by holding regular Izon cultural events, teaching the Ijo language, performing both Izon traditional marriage and English church or court marriages, and maintaining some cultural customs such as traditional marriage, death ceremonies such as wake-keeping and male circumcision.

Young Ijaw men who became merchant seamen employed by the Elder Dempster Line, colonial armed forces personnel and restless seekers of further education, naturally found themselves travelling to Britain and settling in the waterside dock areas of London, Liverpool, Bristol and Cardiff. For many of the early arrivals Liverpool appears from the records to have been the first city of temporary residence, before moving to a more permanent settlement in London. Within London, some of these Izon seamen would have while on shore lived at the 'Strangers Home for Asiatics, Africans, South Sea Islanders and Others,' situated at West India Dock Road (from 1857); the story of early London East End Docks settlement is told in this article extract from 'This House is Africa':

> Through the colonial trade, the presence of black sailors from Africa and the West Indies, alongside lascars from Bengal, was well-established in East London by the twentieth century. The British Empire was dependent on continuous traffic between its colonies and the mother country, and the East End held strategic importance in these exchanges. Yet one scholar concluded that although 'the produce of the empire channelled through the East End', the 'wealth it generated came to rest elsewhere.' The First and Second World Wars accelerated the number of black sailors from the colonies landing in the UK, as more men from the West Indies and West Africa joined the merchant navy and commercial operations to support the war effort, often taking up the most dangerous and physically demanding positions on ships. The interwar and post-war years saw a severe contraction in the shipping industry, during which time many seamen from the British colonies took up longer-term residence in Stepney despite encountering difficulty there.[32]

> For twenty years after 1919, racial unrest triggered by high unemployment rates, housing shortages, structural inequality, and the UK's altered global position frequently spilled over into collective violence in dockside areas. One Ijo seaman summarized his experience of prejudice as a black sailor thus, 'When white man finish you get job. White man never finishes.' The Second World War brought with it a renewed call from the British government for assistance from sailors from the colonies and promises of welfare support to right the wrongs of the interwar period.[33]

Often, they arrived in the UK as soldiers, navy and merchant marines, serving in the British colonial forces of World War I and II. At this time the Izon community in London was not formally organised. One sad example of evidence of Izons in the service of the British empire at the time, is the case of Isaac Peppell (Perekule) Prembroke (cir 1917), who died when the ship he was serving on, the Apapa, was sunk in an attack off Anglesey on 28 November

Figures 18 a & b. Old
vintage images of Erizia,
left, and Cheif Goin, *right.*

1917. A total of 77 passengers and crew went down with the Apapa when she
sank. Isaac Peppell was buried at Bangor Glanadda Cemetery Wales.[34] We
know that he was an Izon young man as he is recorded to have come from
Bonny (Ibani) which is an Eastern Izon clan. Isaac Peppell (Pepple) is not the
only Izon seaman that we have identified to have serviced in the merchant
navy. The National Maritime Museum - Royal Museum Greenwich archives[35]
further identifies two seamen listed to be of Ijo (i.e. Izon) origin who served on
the Merchant Navy Ship Nembe. This 1915 record lists two young men Sam
Agro and Sam Jumbo in the following manner:

> Sam Agro; rank/rating, Seaman; age, 22; place of birth, Ijo; previous ship,
> Boulama. Sam Jumbo; rank/rating, Seaman; age, 24; place of birth, Ijo;
> previous ship, Boulama[36]

We have others who are difficult to identify, who would have been of Izon
origin as well. So, definitively there is documentary evidence that young Izon
men served in the colonial forces and came to the United Kingdom during that
period. Some settled in Liverpool and others London at the time as the records
show.[37] The names of some early arrivals include Mr K. A. Amachree born
1910, recorded as having lived at 243 Eversholt Street, London NW1, his
profession was listed as Engineer.[38] A Reverend Philip B. Waribo, who hailed
from Bonny, records have him leaving England for Bonny then in Southern
Protectorate of Nigeria on 4th November 1908.[39] Another example we have is in

MR. ERNEST S. IKOLI

Figures 19 a& b. Old vintage image of Ernest S. Ikoli *left*. Ernest S. Ikoli in his later years of life *right*.

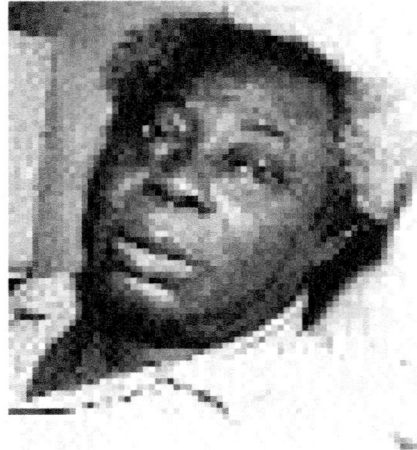

reference to Inspector S. O. Erizia, who was one of the early Izons during the colonial period to proceed to England for further education. From the records (Owonaro 1949) Inspector S. O. Erizia served as a soldier in World War 1 in England, and as a Peace Officer in World War 2 in Nigeria. Inspector Erizia hailed from Kaiama, Kolokuma Izon (Ijaw), and has descendants who currently live in London, though they came and settled at a later date.

We also know of Chief Kpakari Goin (Koin) of Amassoma Ogboin Izon (Owonaro 1949). He was also another of the early Izons to receive some technical training in England as at that early period of the 1920s.

Many more Izon pioneers arrived as merchant seamen and economic migrants in the 1930's and 40's and some others who served in the 1st and 2nd World Wars. These became the pioneer organisers of the Izon (Ijaw) Communities of London, Liverpool, Birmingham and Manchester. Because of their contribution to the war effort and their understanding of their rights as British Colonial Citizens, they came to settle in London. As part of the larger Black community in the East End of London, their views can be seen in this extract from 'This House is Africa:

> Attempting to escalate the situation, in July 1949, Ramsay orchestrated a letter, dictated by a group of Colonial House men, to be sent to the King. The letter explained, 'We come to this country because we hear you need labour, because we are British citizens, and because we help you to win this war and want to

Figure 20. Dr Adam Dagogo Fiberesima.

Figure 21. The album, *Opera Opu-Jaja*, has excerpts from a 3 act Ijaw language opera on the life of King Jaja of Opobo written by Dr Fiberesima.

see London.' Requesting an audience with George VI, the seamen hoped he would hold the Colonial Office accountable for its failures. No such public gesture was forthcoming.[40]

During the 1930's and 1940s British industry was rapidly developing, due to the impetus of the world wars and it after effects. The railways, coal industry, housing estates, were all being built. So, some of the young Izon merchant seamen living in the seamen's hostels at the time found work to support the war effort:

> The provision of seamen's hostels had become a government issue during the Second World War, with responsibility for the 'special wartime measure' for seamen from the colonies given over to the Colonial Office, action taken after the Colonial Development and Welfare Act of 1940 was passed. Colonial labour to support the war effort had been actively sought, with recruitment calls made in British colonies in the West Indies and West Africa.[41]

The young Izon men found ready employment in heavy machinery industry. The various occupations of the individuals who came to the UK at this time ranged from railway workers (engineers, wagon examiners, and labourers), factory workers, postal and clerical staff. Many sought to improve their education by going to evening schools and colleges. Others came specifically for higher education and to return after that to Nigeria.

Figure 22. The Rt Rev. E. T. Dimieari.

One of such persons was the great Nigerian nationalist, Ernest Ikoli, who was a founding member of the Nigeria Youth Movement and was also a Nigeria Independence advocate and journalist, who fought hard for Nigeria's independence.[42] We have surviving records of him being in London around 1948, staying at 23 St Mary's Gardens, Highbury, London N1.[43]

Others who educated themselves in London and other parts of the United Kingdom include the following:

Dr Adam Dagogo Fiberesima from Wakirike (Okirika) Izon, the great musical composer was a feature of the London music scene in the late 1940s and early 1950s. He came to the United Kingdom to study Electrical Engineering. During his studies in the UK, he would write short stories for the British Broadcasting Corporation and play the piano in the programme "Calling West Africa". He enrolled at the Trinity College of Music (London) where he studied music. While studying in London in the late 1940s and early 50s, he played piano in Ambrose Campbell's West African Rhythm Brothers, a prominent band in London at the time that introduced African-style dance music to the United Kingdom.[44]

We also have M. T. D. Braide from Bakana Kalabari, who obtained a Bachelor of Surgery from the Glasgow University, Scotland in 1950, and a

Figure 23. Mr Aliyi Sunjuye Ekineh, as a young Barrister at Law in the late 1940s.

doctorate in Medicine from same in 1956; M. C. A. Peterside from Opobo, who qualified as a medical practitioner from the University of London in 1948; S. Dan Jumbo from Ibani, who graduated from Cambridge University in 1951; Isaac J. Fiberesima from Okrika, who qualified from Dublin University in 1953; Ernest Dublin-Green from Ibani, who qualified as a Dentist from the University of Glasgow in 1949. He returned to become Nigeria's first Dentist; Lambert O. Bell-Gam from Opobo who qualified as a Lawyer from the University of London in 1947; Godfrey Kio Jaja Amachree from Buguma Kalabari, graduated from University of London in 1948; R. T. E. Dappa Wilcox from Ibani, graduated from the University of London in 1948; Ambrose E. Allagoa graduated from the University of London in 1949; Nabo Bekinbo Graham-Douglas from Abonnema Kalabari graduated in Law from the University of London in 1955, Masters in 1958 and Doctorate in 1963, all from the same university; Bishop Ebenezer Tamunoteghe Dimieari, the Right Reverend, was consecrated Assistant Bishop of the Niger at St Paul's Cathedral, London on June 29, 1949. He returned to Nigeria to do his work.

There were other undocumented Izon persons who studied in London and the UK and subsequently returned to Nigeria. Those that remained in the UK joined with the early Izon (Ijaw) seamen who settled in London East End Docks from the 1930s onwards. From the family and official archives such as Electoral Register[45] some of the young Izon men who arrived and lived in London from 1930s up to 1950 include the following:

A record of a Mr Suwari that died in London in 1936.[46] Mr E. A. Uranta, (Barrister at Law), who lived in London, Cornwell Crescent, Ladbroke Grove W11, in 1949; Mr Godfrey Kio Jaja (GKJ) Amachree, records show that he lived at Finchley Central, London N3, and was listed as an Administrative Officer in 1949.[47] He went on to become a Solicitor-General of the Federation of Nigeria and is so noted in the United Nations Digital Library entry dated 1961-12-28.

Early Izon (Ijaw) Residents of East London

Going back to what has now come to be described as an early Black Community in East London is Stepney, called 'London's Harlem'. This area of London, now a part of the London Borough of Tower Hamlets, had from available records, been home to Black African and Caribbean immigrants since 1780.[48] By 1944, a report claimed that at least 170 African and Caribbean settlers lived in Stepney, with about 130 being directly from Africa, and mostly West Africa:

> Despite their relatively low numbers, the perception at the time was that the majority of Cable Street's residents during the immediate post-war years were black and, as such, the area became known in the national press as 'London's Harlem'. It was also labelled 'The Coloured Quarter' by sociologist Michael Banton in his 1955 study of the area. Although some were highly qualified, many African and Caribbean men were only able to secure unskilled or semi-skilled work, with many being employed as labourers, porters and stokers.[49]

With regards to this early Izon (Ijo, Ijaw) people of London, it is rare to find an academic study or book that covers the topic. Nevertheless, the Izon presence in London in the late 1940s and early 1950s, was notable enough for one prominent academic researcher and Emeritus Professor Michael Banton[50] to write about the Izon (he uses the spelling IJO) as a part of his field studies of Black Immigrants in an English City in the emerging Race and Ethnic Relations studies that sought to explain the behaviour of immigrant communities in the United Kingdom after the 2nd world war, when Britain still retained many of its colonies. Professor Banton focuses on the Ijo in his book, Banton, M. (1955), *The Coloured Quarter: Negro Immigrants in an English City,* on several pages (18-38, 201, 218, 219 and more). Furthermore, an important research paper referenced in the aforementioned book, that discusses the Izon men of East London in the early 1950s is *The Social Groupings of Some West African Workers in Britain,* under the Department of Social Anthropology, University of Edinburgh, September 1953 Man © 1953 Royal Anthropological Institute of Great Britain and Ireland Pages 130 - 133, also by Professor Michael Banton.

In summary this paper along with the book, explores the social interaction between some of the identified West African ethnic nationality populations of East London Stepney (Tower Hamlets). In the early 1950s, the East End of London close to the docks was the cultural centre for Black people and other immigrant populations from India, Pakistan and Malta. The community was quite fluid, and people moved in out of residence; however, it was seen as a heart of social life for the immigrant communities of London. The patterns of assimilation of West African immigrants compared to others including Asian immigrants, were quite dissimilar. For the Asian communities, the pattern was accommodation with an intention to accumulate wealth and return home. The West African pattern was one of adaptation, where although the publicly stated aim was to return home, the outward behaviour indicated a desire to stay and adapt to British life. Accordingly, the West African population sought to integrate and adapt to the wider British society in varying degrees. This often was through marriage with white British women, although the chief reasons for such marriages would have been the basic desire for a mate and family, since most of these young men were single. These British women played a big part in the life of the immigrant communities. They acted as cultural facilitators and, as they were often ostracized by white society, integrated to different degrees into the immigrant communities, they had become part of. However, these interracial marriages were often fraught with difficulties and conflicts due to cultural differences. Oral testimonies of mixed heritage descendants of some of these Izon seamen confirms this.

The Black population were mainly of West African and Caribbean (West Indian) origin. In 1951, Among the 145 West Africans enumerated, 40 were from Nigeria and 15 of these 40 were Izon (Ijo, Ijaw) men. Most of the Izon were seamen. They along with most seamen were not very educated and so were sometimes looked down on by other, even students from their own Izon. One research article noted;

> As advocate for the Stepney seamen, Warama felt deserted not only by the Colonial Office but also, by the educated 'colonial' classes, who arrived in the UK to study. After visiting one well-known central London student hostel, Aggrey House, to invite its inhabitants to visit East London and speak with the seamen, she bitterly reported, 'the educated ones would cut themselves off. They wouldn't have anything to do with them. 'The EEWAC also saw the potential in connecting both groups of 'colonial' people. West Indian and West

African students at International House were approached in an attempt to interest them in their compatriots in the East End and the possibility of involvement in Toynbee Hall or with the Franciscan Brothers raised. These suggestions do not appear to have mobilised many into action, although Derek Bamuta's efforts to document the community in 1949 suggest there were at least isolated cases of engagement.[51]

In many ways, the social stratification that defined the wider British society was also evident among the immigrant communities. On some of the early Izon Seamen of East London, Michael Banton goes on to observe that:

A tribal group more representative of West Africans in Britain is that of the Ijo, who come from the western part of the Niger Delta. They have certain points of similarity with the Kru, for like them, many of their tribe are seamen and used to migrating in search of work; they are not advanced educationally and are sometimes looked down upon by other groups. Most of the Ijo in East London settled there just after the war, and for the first four to five years group loyalties steadily declined. This was owing partly to the individuals' personal difficulties, and partly to the fact that they were often let down by the men who appealed to their African loyalties. One Ijo who was acting as a landlord was at first unable to trust any but his fellow countrymen, and when a stranger came to him for a room he would reflect 'This man doesn't speak one language with me. No, I don't know how he will treat me,' and the would-be tenant was turned away. But after a while, he found that he had nothing but trouble from his fellow countrymen and began to think it might be better to avoid having business dealings with them. 'My people don't show you respect,' he said. It can be very much more difficult to collect the rent, or to recover a debt, from a man who claims to be your brother, and it is usually the less responsible person who appeals to the obligations of the relationship. The Ijo used to hold a 'meeting' when each man paid in two shillings a week and could borrow money from the fund when he was in need, but the number supporting it got smaller and smaller until the subscription had to be reduced to one shilling, and then after a while the surviving members wound it up. Men who failed continually to live up to their obligations were ostracized by the others so that the pattern came to resemble that of a core surrounded by a small number of isolates. Within the core no one was recognized as senior and a desperate equality prevailed; thus, while the collective sentiment was not dead, relationships between members of the group were on an inter-personal plane. Some stimuli would have evoked that sentiment: they would have gone to the help of most of their fellow countrymen if they were in trouble, and would have contributed to the expenses of a funeral for a member of their tribe no matter how much they disliked him when alive.[52]

Banton further states that;

In early 1952 group cohesion began to increase again. Some of the older men were in a better position to help others and were accorded a certain deference -

by the younger men falling into the category of 'Johnny Just Come.' A new 'meeting' was started with a membership of 13 and some of the local men who had been ostracized were not invited. One member of the group thought this decision wrong but he did not press the point. His un-willingness to come to judgment on a fellow tribesman was shown in the opinion he once expressed of a fellow countryman who spent much of his time gambling, who used to live a riotous life with women and gave no indication of settling down: 'I don't say he's doing wrong,' he said, 'London is a big place and there's room for all of us. He's been here longer than nearly all of us and he could have been sitting back giving advice. He's been unfortunate, but his way is completely different from ours.' At the same time as the new 'meeting' was started two new Ijo arrived and in a short space of time were provided with good housing accommodation and were drawn into a group life, which, as strangers to the country, meant a great deal to them. Making weekly contributions to a benefit fund is not only a form of insurance, but an incentive to saving greatly valued by some of the men; one of them explained that if he lent a man money and it was paid back in instalments, he was inclined to spend the instalments as they came in and thus the sum of these payments was not worth so much as the original loan.[53]

Through research into the Ijaw People's Association archives and oral testimonies, we can confirm that the Izon (Ijo) organisation Professor Banton was referring to was the Ijaw People's Association of Great Britain and Ireland, founded in 1948, through the efforts of ten dedicated young Izon men. But not all were seamen, and not all were limited in education. It is also noteworthy that the so called uneducated Izon seamen's organisation that they founded, became the long lasting community association that has impacted the most on the welfare of Izon people in London, and the United Kingdom, even providing welfare intervention and support to many of the students and better educated elite.

His other observation about European wives also tallies with what we know about the early Izon families of East London, many (not all) were mixed heritage or mixed race families, as observed in the paper:

The position of European wives in the tribal group is an interesting one. All the West African immigrants are males and whilst a few find wives among the United Kingdom-born coloured women, the majority marry or consort with white women, who frequently have come from the industrial towns of the North or from Ireland. The women make many concessions to the tastes and customs of their men folk and learn a great deal from them; they learn how to cook African dishes and often how to speak a little of their consort's language. They act as intermediaries for their men in dealing with officialdom and manage the correspondence of those who are not literate. The man instructs his wife in her obligations towards his kinsmen and countrymen, and being to some extent ostracized by the whites, she tends to identify herself with the cause of the coloured man and gradually obtains an honorary place in the system of tribal loyalties. In many ways, however, her influence operates against the immigrants' pre-migration values and is a means of adapting them to the expectations of the new society. As children grow up the father's obligations to his family may not harmonize to his fellow countrymen as well as they would. Conflict arises as a result of the control the English women have over some household matters, and was expressed in the words of a Nigerian who complained 'I'm fed up with all this business of "Missus say ..." I've lived in old-timers' houses in Liverpool not to know what it's like. These things should be man to man and woman. 'The sanctions which the tribal group can wield against wrong-doers may be extended to cover the wives of members of the group, for a man whose wife has disgraced herself in the eyes of the others, will not be able to take her with him when he goes to visit them. Where a group is fairly cohesive and some sanctions can be applied to enforce group norms, an element of social control is brought into the situation where the purely external means of control such as the police-are ineffective. Such sanctions, the refusal to help people, the withdrawal of recognition, etc., are not powerful, but in the long run they can have an 'important influence in bringing miscreants to heel'. [54]

Furthermore, Banton notes that:

> The small group among immigrants-such as that of members of the same tribe-has a very important function, in respect both to the individual members whom it helps to adjust to the new circumstances, and to the wider society. In Britain the barrier to the assimilation of the West African immigrants is not the unwillingness or inability of the immigrants to follow British modes of behaviour, but comes from the reluctance of the British public to accept them socially. Thus, the small tribal group is not the obstacle to assimilation which it is sometimes thought; for lack of organization on the part of the immigrants does not aid assimilation when the principal obstacle is created by the other group. Immigrant organization can help the men to fight for social equality and it is the only way by which effective means of social control can be developed. [55]

In summary, according to Professor Banton's observations, although there were larger identity groupings among these immigrants, the tribe or ethnic nationality identity was the strongest source of identity for many of them. He described a pattern he called segmentary opposition, where both the ingroup and outgroup were quite elastic. The broadening of the in-group was largely a function of shared experiences of racism. However, the narrowing of the ingroup to the tribal level also occurred. To illustrate, the Izon saw themselves as a group and others (including other Nigerians) as outsiders (based on the reality of ethnic nationalities of colonial Nigeria). However, in certain matters, Nigerian identity became more salient, for example, when in opposition to immigrants from other West African countries. In the same way, Black identity became salient when in opposition to white society.

Ethnic nationality associations or unions, were often important in building society among West African immigrants. These associations mirrored such associations that had already been established in their home countries. Two of the more well-organised associations in 1951, belonged to the Kru tribe with Sierra Leone/Liberian ancestry and the Izon of Nigeria. The Izon formed an association which nearly wound up due to weak commitment by its members. However, by 1952, as members became more settled, employed and economically buoyant, a stronger association was formed. These associations served three main purposes: adjusting new members of the community to British life, improving the welfare of its members and as a form of social cohesion and building lasting relationships of group loyalty between its members. We will see that the Izon community association named the Ijaw People's Association of Great Britain & Ireland, did indeed do its best in this regard.

For many of the immigrants from West Africa, social acceptance was important. The desire to be socially accepted had the effect sometimes of moving immigrants away from ethnic and group loyalties. However, the experience of prejudice in this pursuit also helped to draw them back to their traditional loyalties. Professor Banton noted that while many immigrants were open to following British modes of behaviour, the strongest barrier to assimilation was "the reluctance of the wider British society to accept them socially. There was a disconnect between the aspirations of 'Empire' where the colonial people were citizens of Britain and welcomed to the United Kingdom, and the cultural attitude of the masses of British society who were just encountering peoples of different cultures from around the world the first time.

We can identify some of the earliest young Izon men, who came and settled in East London Stepney "London Harlem" corresponding to the time of the study done by M. Banton in 1953. They came either as sailors or men seeking a better education. They include, but not limited to the following persons:

Mr Young Ogetti Kpiaye who was from Ayamassa, was living in Liverpool in 1945 in a Seaman's hostel but by 1947, he was living in London at 32 Brushfield Street. He was a merchant seaman. He is mentioned in a 1947 police report where he was a victim of a racist attack along with Mr Vincent Akenkide;[56] Mr Moses Kantel (Kantele), time of arrival is not known, but it is believed to be in the late 1940s. Mr Henry Adams (Adamson) Ofoniama from Kaiama, arrived in the 1940's and first lived at Liverpool before moving to settle in London. Mr Joseph Okoro, from Patani, whose time of arrival is obscure, but is believed to be quite early in the 1930s. Records show he was living in London by 1951. Mr Laurence Peretubo G. Okorodudu, from Esanma. Records show that he was living in London by 1947, while family testimony state that he arrived in the UK by 1939 and had previously sojourned in the

USA, as a merchant seaman. His first city of abode was Liverpool, and from Liverpool he made his way to London.[57] Mr Morris (Morrison) Benatarigha Oguoko, from Toru Angiama, is known to have lived in Stepney East London by 1947.[58] He was not a merchant seaman. He came to England for further education. Mr Albert Jitubo (Zitubo), from Abare, was known to have lived in London by 1947. He was a merchant seaman. Mr Stephen Kpakulukpa Okpokpo, from Odi,[59] time of arrival is not known but believed to be in the late 1940s. Mr Peter Norman, from Western Ijaw in Warri, his own time of arrival is not known, but is believed to be in the late 1940s. Mr James Ingobor (Ngobo), from Gbekebo or Ayakoromo, with time of arrival not known, but believed to be in the late 1940s. Mr Vincent Akenkide from Tuomo, family testimony and records show that he was living in London between 1947 and 1949.[60]

All these men at the time, came together and formed the Ijaw People's Association (IPA) of Great Britain and Ireland in 1948 with gradual build up to ten persons by 1951. A good number of these early young pioneers of the IPA married from the local white community of London while others went back to Nigeria to marry Izon women that they brought to London. Most of the children of these marriages have grown-up and become full adults with their own children and grandchildren, and formed what is now known as the British born Izon (Ijaw) community in London and other places. These families and other Izon immigrants, began to disperse from the East London area of Stepney when it was targeted for redevelopment and mass urban housing, and with it came local population replacement:

> Edith Ramsay and slum clearance in Stepney...Despite Ramsay's and others' efforts, the area was targeted for slum clearance in the late 1950s. Slum clearance schemes were generally initiated either by local authorities, in this instance by Stepney Borough Council, or by the London County Council (LCC). Sometimes people were rehoused locally in new estates, otherwise there was a tendency for people to migrate eastwards to Essex to new LCC estates being built there or private housing. Generally, at this time, slum clearance schemes were welcomed by local residents. In Stepney, this clearance resulted in the displacement of much of the local population, including many African and Caribbean immigrants. Although there was a continued growth of the African, Afro-Caribbean, and Asian presence, via seafarers settling, into the 1950s, the dramatic increase in Bengali immigration to the area in the 1960s and especially in the 1970s, meant that the remaining black population was demographically over-shadowed and the brief life of a small community of people of African origin came to an end.[61]

Edith Ramsay, (1895-1983) was an English educator and community activist who served on the Colonial Office Advisory Committee. She worked to improve social and housing conditions for immigrants arriving in Stepney, London during the mid-20th century. In 1951 Edith Ramsay was part of the campaign group which successfully fought for the re-opening of 'Colonial House', a Colonial Office hostel and recreation centre for members of the African-Caribbean community in Leman Street, Stepney.[62] The intimate connection between Edith Ramsay social welfare crusader and the early Izon community in Stepney, East London is demonstrated by the fact that one of the early Izon young men who lived in the area by 1947, Mr Vincent Akenkide, married an English woman, and one of their daughters was named Edith after Edith Ramsay, who was her godmother.[63] So, it becomes clearer that young Ijo families made up of mixed heritage relationships between Ijo men and white English women, encountered the social welfare activities of Edith Ramsay, and personally honoured it by naming their children after her.

REFERENCES

32. *This House is Africa - Accounting for the Hostel for 'Coloured Colonial Seamen' in London's East End*, p. 2. Milne_This House is Africa_IRIS, https://discovery.ucl.ac.uk/id/eprint/10062039/3/Milne_This%20House%20is%20Africa_I RIS.pdf, accessed between 01/08/23 and 31/11/23.

33. *This House is Africa - Accounting for the Hostel for 'Coloured Colonial Seamen' in London's East End*, pp. 1-2. Milne_This House is Africa_IRIS, https://discovery.ucl.ac.uk/id/eprint/10062039/3/Milne_This%20House%20is%20Africa_I RIS.pdf, accessed between 01/08/23 and 31/11/23.

34. Black History Month: Commemorating WW1 West African Merchant Seamen. Grave registration report for Glanadda Cemetery listing John Thomas and Isaac Peppell. Reproduced with kind permission from the Commonwealth Colonial War Graves Commission. https://rcahmw.gov.uk/commemorating-wwi-west-african-merchant-seamen/, accessed between 01/08/23 and 31/11/23.

35. Crew List: Agreement and Official Logs for Ship Nembe Official Number 114427, sourced from the Royal Museums Greenwich website https://www.rmg.co.uk/collections/objects/rmgc-object-646734 accessed on 06/12/23.

36. https://www.rmg.co.uk/collections/objects/rmgc-object-646734 accessed on 06/12/23.

37. Ancestry.co.uk, accessed between 01/08/23 and 31/11/23.

38. Ancestry.co.uk, accessed between 01/08/23 and 31/11/23.

39. Ancestry.co.uk, accessed between 01/08/23 and 31/11/23.

40. *This House is Africa - Accounting for the Hostel for 'Coloured Colonial Seamen' in London's East End*, p. 19. Milne_This House is Africa_IRIS, https://discovery.ucl.ac.uk/id/eprint/10062039/3/Milne_This%20House%20is%20Africa_I RIS.pdf, accessed between 01/08/23 and 31/11/23.

41. *This House is Africa - Accounting for the Hostel for 'Coloured Colonial Seamen' in London's East End*, p. 14. Milne_This House is Africa_IRIS, https://discovery.ucl.ac.uk/id/eprint/10062039/3/Milne_This%20House%20is%20Africa_I RIS.pdf, accessed between 01/08/23 and 31/11/23.

42. Coleman JS (1958, 1971) *NIGERIA - Background to Nationalism*, pp. 218-227.

43. Ancestry.co.uk, accessed between 01/08/23 and 31/11/23

44. https://honestjons.com/label/artist/London_Is_The_Place_For_Me/release/
3_Ambrose_Adekoya_Campbell, accessed 06/12/23,
https://reader.exacteditions.com/issues/9257/page/31, accessed 06/12/23.
45. Electoral Registers access via Ancestry.co.uk, accessed between 01/08/23 and
31/11/23.
46. Ancestry.co.uk, accessed between 01/08/23 and 31/11/23.
47. Ancestry.co.uk, accessed between 01/08/23 and 31/11/23.
48. https://www.ideastore.co.uk/local-history/outreach-and-education/local-history-online-
exhibitions/the-afro-caribbean-community-in-post-war-stepney, accessed between
01/08/23 and 31/11/23.
49. https://www.ourmigrationstory.org.uk/oms/seafarers-and-stowaways-in-londons-
harlem, accessed between 01/08/23 and 31/11/23.
50. MICHAEL BANTON 1926-2018: ONE YEAR ON After Michael Banton: some
reflections on his contributions to the study of race by John Solomos,
https://www.tandfonline.com/doi/full/10.1080/0031322X.2019.1619914, accessed
02/06/2024.
51. Milne_This House is Africa_IRIS, p. 19,
https://discovery.ucl.ac.uk/id/eprint/10062039/3/Milne_This%20House%20is%20Africa_I
RIS.pdf, accessed 02/06/2024.
52. THE SOCIAL GROUPINGS OF SOME WEST AFRICAN WORKERS IN BRITAIN,
also by MICHAEL BANTON Department of Social Anthropology, University of
Edinburgh, September 1953 Man © 1953 Royal Anthropological Institute of Great Britain
and Ireland, pp132-133. https://www.jstor.org/stable/2793947?read-
now=1&seq=2#page_scan_tab_contents, accessed on 02/06/2024.
53. MICHAEL BANTON (1953) pp. 132-133.
54. MICHAEL BANTON (1953) pp. 132-133.
55. MICHAEL BANTON (1953) pp. 132-133.
56. https://www.ourmigrationstory.org.uk/oms/seafarers-and-stowaways-in-londons-harlem
In the report Young Kpiaye is spelt Young Epiae, while Vincent Akenkide is spelt Vincent
Akankide.
57. Ancestry.co.uk and personal family testimony by Larraine Okorodudu, daughter of
Laurence Okorodudu.
58. Ancestry.co.uk and Ijaw People's Association archives regarding founding members of
the association, and family testimonies.
59. Ancestry.co.uk and Ijaw People's Association archives regarding founding members of
the association.
60. Ancestry.co.uk and personal family testimony of Edith Akenkide, daughter of Vincent
Akenkide. Accessed between 01/08/23 and 31/11/23.
61. https://www.ourmigrationstory.org.uk/oms/seafarers-and-stowaways-in-londons-
harlem, accessed between 01/08/23 and 31/11/23.
62. "The former 'Colonial House', 17 Leman Street, Whitechapel." UCL, The Survey of
London. Retrieved 2021-01-04. "Idea Store - The Afro-Caribbean Community in Post-war
Stepney". www.ideastore.co.uk. Retrieved 2018-10-31. Wikipedia
https://en.wikipedia.org/wiki/Edith_Ramsay#cite_ref-4
63. Personal Testimony of Ms Edith Akenkide, Oral History Interview 20/10/2023.

BIBLIOGRAPHY

Banton, M P. *The Coloured Quarter: Negro Immigrants in an English City* (1955, Jonathan Cape Thirty Bedford Square London)

Banton M P. *THE SOCIAL GROUPINGS OF SOME WEST AFRICAN WORKERS IN BRITAIN,* Department of Social Anthropology, University of Edinburgh, September 1953 Man © 1953 Royal Anthropological Institute of Great Britain and Ireland

CHAPTER 7: THE IJAW COMMUNITY ASSOCIATIONS OF LONDON AND RELATIONS WITH OTHER CITIES

The Ijaw People's Association of Great Britain and Ireland

The Ijaw People's Association of Great Britain and Ireland (IPA) is a social/cultural, non-governmental organisation (NGO). It is also an unincorporated community association, and has functioned in this capacity since its foundation from 1948 to the present. The motto of the association is SERVICE BEFORE REWARD. The following historical narrative of the Ijaw People's Association of Great Britain and Ireland, is compiled from the archives of the IPA, and the personal testimonies of foundation members such as Pa Stephen Okpokpo, Pa Laurence Okorodudu[64] and other members.

The early Ijaw community in London was centred around Tower Hamlets East End of London, home to the London Docks and not far from Tilbury Docks where Ijaw (Ijo, Izon) merchant seamen would spend their shore time. Many of the foundation members, if not most of them lived in this East London Stepney area, so it is not surprising that the early IPA condensed around the young Ijaw men living in this neighbourhood at the time.

The IPA was founded in 1948 through the collective effort of various Ijaw (Ijo, Izon) men residing in London at the time. They may have been inspired by the foundation of the Ijaw People's Union (later called Ijaw Cultural Union) in Liverpool in 1945. Liverpool was also an early city for Ijaw settlement from the 1920s onwards.

Through the enlightened efforts of a few outstanding young Ijaw men, the IPA was established in 1948. The main impetus came from Mr Young Ogetti Kpiaye, an illustrious son of Ijaw who hailed from Ayamassa (Tarakiri clan of Ijaw) situated in present day Bayelsa State. Mr Kpiaye was elected as the founding President of the IPA, and because of the trust in him he continued as President up to 1967, a total of 19 years.[65] According to the personal testimony of Pa Stephen Okpokpo, Ogetti, as he was fondly called, was not the bookish type, having not attended any formal higher education college, but he was extremely intelligent and had a keen sense of Ijaw cultural unity and political awareness. He felt the need for an organisation that could bring the individuals and their families under one community umbrella. The example of the 1945 foundation of the Ijaw People's Union in Liverpool, where many Ijaw men had stayed before coming to London, and communicated regularly with, would have inspired him to replicate likewise in London three years later. This is the birth of the Ijaw People's Association (IPA) of Great Britain and Ireland, starting out as an idea in the mind of a visionary. Mr Ogetti Kpiaye went around rallying, mobilising and convincing many of the Ijaw men living in London, both East and West at the time, on the need for an Ijaw organisation that could act as a cultural and social/welfare focus. Most of these young men had arrived London either from Liverpool or directly from Nigeria, as merchant seamen/sailors or seekers of better education and training.[66]

The original ten foundation members are as follows;[67]

1. Mr Young Ogetti Kpiaye (Foundation President up to 1967, 19 years), from Ayamassa.

2. Mr Moses Kantel (Foundation Vice President up to 1969)

3. Mr Henry A Ofoniama (Foundation General Secretary up to 1965), from Kaiama

4. Mr Joseph K Okoro (Foundation Treasurer up to 1967, 19 years), from Patani

5. Mr Laurence Okorodudu (18 years as President and 7 years as Vice President), from Esanma

6. Mr Morris Benatarigha Oguoko (one-time assistant secretary and interim chairman 1964, long serving member), from Toru Angiama I.

7. Mr Albert Jitubo (Zitubo), from Abare

8. Mr Stephen Okpokpo, from Odi

9. Mr Peter Norman, from Western Ijaw

10. Mr James Ingobor (Ngobo), from Gbekebo

According to Pa Stephen Okpokpo, the initial meetings started in Bethnal Green East London, at the home of the late James Ingobor (Ngobo). From the house of James Ingobor, meetings moved to the 4 Buross Street, Stepney Green, London E1 home of the late Mr Joseph Okoro and then on to his new home 40 Grove Road, Bow, London E3 and finally ending up at 18 Strahan Road, Bow London E3 5DB, which was purchased by the association. Often, the meetings would be held in members houses.

Other early members who registered and joined before 1957 include the following:

Mr Y.K Mieboh, (Yorkman Kamasa Miaboh) from Western Ijaw Warri LGAs, records show he got married in Liverpool in 1945, 1949 still living in Liverpool, and by 1953 lived in London.

Mr Walter Oloula, not recorded, in London by 1954.

Mr Donald Appiah, from Abare

Mr Moses Suwari, not recorded

Mr Isaac Alagoa, from Amassoma

Figure 24. Some Founding Members of IPA: From L to R, Mr L. Okorodudu, Unknown, Mr J. Okoro, Mr H. Ofoniama, J. Ingobor, Mr Y. Kpiaye.

Figure 25. Mr Morris B. Oguoko, IPA Founding Member, *left.*
Figure 26. Mr Vincent Akenkide, IPA Founding Member, *right.*

Figure 27. Mr Paul Kalabeke, IPA Founding Member, *left.*
Figure 28. Mr Moses Kantel, IPA Founding Member, *right.*

Mr Michael Eyedogha Abeki, from Amassoma, records show he was in Stepney, London by 1951.

Mr Paul Oyede Kalabeke, not recorded

Mr Lawrence Enekeme, from Amassoma

Mr Lawrence Eddy Okudu, not recorded

Mr Collins Ijebu, not recorded

Mr Vincent Akenkide, from Tuomo, in London by 1947.

After the initial meetings that took place at the home of Mr James Ingobor, the home of Mr Joseph Okoro 4 Buross Street, Stepney, London E1 was the popular meeting venue for the IPA. 4 Buross street is fondly remembered as one of the first houses in East London to be owned by a Black person and for this reason, the IPA were able to assemble there for meetings and other social activities. From 4 Buross Street meetings were moved to 40 Grove Road, Bow, London E3, when Joseph Okoro purchased it as a bigger house. The meetings, gatherings, parties, and get-togethers continued at this venue until the Ijaw People's Association members purchased a house in the Bow area of East London E3.

The Purchase of a House in Bow Area London E3

In 1951 Mr Michael Abeki, an early member of the IPA, who hailed from Amassoma town in present day Bayelsa State Nigeria, wanted to sell his house in the Bow area, and move to Manchester. The other foundation members decided that the IPA would collectively purchase this property, to be used to accommodate visiting Ijaw merchant seamen and students, as they often complained of lack of accommodation when they were onshore and in London. The House decided to approach Barclays bank, sometime in January 1951 for a mortgage loan of £700.00 to purchase this property.

Three members of the IPA being Henry Ofoniama (General Secretary), Joseph Okoro (Treasurer) and Stephen Okpokpo acting on the decision and directives of the association, approached Barclays bank and became the guarantors to the loan of £700.00, which was used to purchase the property. This loan was paid off by the membership of the IPA between 1951 and 1976. Or in other words, between 1951 and 1976 all members of the IPA through their contributions and levies contributed to paying off the mortgage of the Bow property. Originally, the weekly contribution was One (1) Shilling.[68] This was how the Strahan Road House was purchased and used as an accommodation for merchant seamen and students, and as a meeting house. It thus became known as IPA House. This property is still owned by the association, under Trusteeship. The initial plan was to have properties that could be rented out to students and seamen, in London, Liverpool and Manchester, but this plan was dropped due to practical challenges.[69]

Figure 29. Strahan Road, London E3 IPA Meeting House.

Figure 30. Mr Benaebi Oguoko standing in front of IPA HOUSE in Strahan Road, London E3, during a recnt visit in 2023.

Figure 31. Mr Henry Ofoniama (2nd right) with other prominent Izons in the 1960s.

Other Ijaw people continued to join and leave the IPA from the 1960's onwards that included a wide cross section of Ijaws from all walks of life. This has continued up to the present time. In the late 1950's and early 60's, younger Ijaws began coming to the UK either as students or young professionals seeking a better life. They formed the Western Ijaw Students Union and the Rivers State Student Union in the 1960s. They were followed by young professionals who came in the 1980's and 1990's. More young Ijaw people continued to arrive in the UK for various economic, education and social reasons, especially during the massive flight of educated professionals during the later stages of military rule in Nigeria. The latest group of Ijaws arriving in the UK for study and professional opportunities, are students on masters programmes sent by the Bayelsa State, Rivers State and Delta Governments, as well as, those on Federal Government Agency scholarships of Nigeria.

For reason of the aforementioned, the Ijaw People's Association increased from a small membership of about ten initial foundation members in the 1950s, to about seventy plus members by 1968.[70] Many of the student members who came from Nigeria in the late 1950's and early 1960's returned to Nigeria and became government officials, University Lecturers and business executives.

Figure 32. Young Izon men in the 1960s.

Figure 33. Some founding members, such as L. Okorodudu. L. Enekeme, and M. Kantel with young members of the IPA in the 1960s.

Good examples include Chief Edwin Kiagbodo Clark, Chief Ernest Iseru (Eseru) and Chief Alaowei Broderick Bozimo. All were embraced by the IPA and supported whilst in the United Kingdom. Chief Edwin Kiagbodo Clark went on to become a prominent minister and politician in Nigeria, while all three of them were the foremost Western Ijaw Law graduates, with Chief Earnest Iseru being the first, Chief E. K. Clark being the second and Chief A. B. Bozimo being the third. All of them played important roles in advancing the rights of Ijaw people in Mid-Western Region of Nigeria at the time.[71]

The 1960's and 70's records of the Ijaw People's Association, show a wide cross-section of Ijaws residing in London. They include the following persons (some with families): Y. Kpiaye, J.K. Okoro, L. Okorodudu, M. Kantel, S. Okpokpo, D. Appiah, A. Jituboh, M.B. Oguoko, S.A. Oki, F. Agugu, S.B. Ayaoge, B.A. Eneberi, F.B. Akpanari, L.A. Oki, L.O. Dorgu, L.E. Okudu, C.A. Okoro, A.L.T. Gagariga, J.A. Tokoro, P. Norman, A.O. Soroh, J.M. Aseh, M. Ofiniama, S.P. Edonya, K.E.J. Torunariagha, B.O. Kansese, J. Ingobo, J.B. Weigha, G.A. Epe, M.K. Amakoromo, T.L.J. Koko, W.M. Cotterell, M.I. Obi, E. Sawacha, J.I Kieribo, C. Ijebu, D.D. Narebor, J.A Eseimokumo, S.M. Momah, R.O. Angiama, H.A. Ofiniama, H.I. Bekeowei, P. Daobry, N.A. Igali, J. Tombofa, E. Dorgu, K. Brambaifa, Miss H. Ayaoge, H. George, E.K. Edaba, A.S. Odumo, K. Lawson, B.I. Alagoa, I.C.I. Tarigha, B.E. Zige, N. Fubara, T.K. Amachree, O. Numbere, G.A. Ekiyor, C.O Agbabi, B.C. Bozimo, B.F. Amasoye, M. Suwari, I.J. Benjamin-Stowe, V. Ekiye, L.Youdeowei, Y.K. Mieboh, J.O. Dinobewei, P. Kalabeke (outside London), F. Ogun, J. Okpongba, G. Nagberi, P. Okosi, S. Ebiye, E.F.S. Erefa, Mr Abeki, S. Akraka.[72]

Activities Through the Years

INTEREST IN IJAW POLITICAL WELFARE: The IPA has always been interested in the political welfare of the Ijaw people, especially in Nigeria. Very keen to make sure that the Ijaws achieve a befitting place in the newly emerging New Nigeria, in 1957 the membership played host to the great Nigeria and Ijaw Nationalist/Ijaw Leader Chief Harold Rowland Dappa Biriye, as chief representatives of the Ijaws and Niger Delta People's, and representative of THE RIVERS PEOPLE & CHIEFS CONFERENCE representing the Ijaws and Niger Delta Peoples, attended the 1957 constitutional conference held in London. Elders of the IPA recall that the late Pa Laurence Okorodudu was sent to meet him at Victoria Station. This implies that there was constant and regular communication between the IPA in London and Ijaws in Nigeria. It is noteworthy that, IPA was the only Pan Ijaw organisation that Chief Biriye met in London to discuss and brief about the independence talks. It is clear that Chief Biriye had a working knowledge about the organisation at the time and felt that they were in a position to support the work of securing a better place for the Ijaws in a Post Independent Nigeria. The IPA then hosted and met with him at 40 Grove Road, London E3 (Tower Hamlets East London), where a strategic meeting was held and he briefed them on the conference discussions, mainly 'Why the Ijaws in Nigeria should rise up and claim their rights in the New Nigeria being formed'. They furthermore discussed the general underdevelopment of the whole of Ijaw land and how to develop the homeland. He urged the Ijaws of London to sit up and play an active part in developing their homeland.[73] From the discussions they had, it appears that the members acted on them and following through the years sponsored a number of young Ijaw men in their education in the UK and contributed funds to welfare relief. Chief Dappa Biriye was again hosted by the IPA in the early 1990's, when he returned from Brazil (Rio De Janerio) after attending the international environmental conference.

The 1966/68 records show that during the 12-day Revolution/Uprising in the Niger Delta carried out by Major Isaac Jasper Adaka Boro and his Niger Delta Volunteer Service, the Ijaw People's Association as an NGO took a special interest in the whole affairs of the Niger Delta, the Niger Delta Development Board, NDDB and the detention & trial of Boro, his two lieutenant associates Samuel Owonaro and Nottingham Dick. When Isaac Boro died on the war front, the IPA took a special interest in his death and all Ijaw sons and daughters who had died as a result of the Nigerian Civil War. Members held a wake-keeping for the late Major Isaac Boro on 3 August 1968, in honour of his contribution to the emancipation of the Ijaws.[74]

In the 1970's, the Ijaw People's Association set up the Special Committee for Ijaw Action at home. It had as its members N.G. Inkuba, V. Ekiye, J.M. Aseh, B. Zige and F. Agugu. Mr Fred Agugu, long standing member and general secretary of IPA eventually returned to Nigeria as a technocrat. He was to become the Secretary of the Bayelsa State Movement. Thanks to his contribution and those of many other outstanding individuals, Bayelsa State became a reality at 7.15 am on the 1st of October 1996.

From the early 1990's the IPA in London and Ijaws of Liverpool were in constant interaction with Ijaw and Niger Delta organisations back in Nigeria. The Ijaw People's Association was also actively engaged in the humanitarian rehabilitation of the victims of the various community conflicts and government abetted human rights atrocities that took place in Nigeria, through the Ijaw Relief Fund, sending relief material and financial help to the Arogbo community, the Ogbe-Ijo community, Kaiama and Odi respectively. One of the IPA members at the time, Ms Sokari Ekineh played an important role in delivering relief materials to affected communities such as Odi, during the period.

The IPA, along with other Ijaw organisations, organised a number of conferences in London in support of the Ijaw community in London and to highlight the Niger Delta struggle against the violence of the Nigeria State. Mention can be made of The Niger Delta People of Nigeria Weekend Remembrance Activities, held in London on the 19th & 20th November 1999. The 'All Ijaw Meetings to deliberate on the Situation in the Niger Delta,' held on 1 April 2000, and 20 May 2000 Demonstrations organised in London in support of the Niger Delta struggle. Other events such as the Ogele Club/IPA awards, and Boro Day served as vehicles to sensitise the international community on the plight of the Niger Delta peoples. They have written letters and petitioned the British Government to put pressure on the Nigeria government concerning the Niger Delta.

The IPA was very active in regards to communiqués issued by the Ijaw community in the UK, which were aimed at directly influencing political events in Nigeria, especially the Niger Delta. These include the following: *Position of the Ijos on the Proposed Constitutional Conference* issued 1st May 1994. *Environmental Sustainability and Resource Control in the Niger Delta- An IPA Position Paper* 19th November 1999. *The Communiqué of the Ijaw Peoples Resident in the UK & Ireland* 1 April 2000. *Ijaw Peoples Resident in the United Kingdom & Ireland Matters Affecting the Ijaw Nation* 28 May 2000. And in association with other Ijaw organisations abroad, and under the umbrella of Council of Ijaw Associations Abroad (CIAA) *The State of Affairs in Bayelsa State.* In association with other Niger Delta organisations under the form of The Niger Delta Peoples Movement for Self Determination and Environmental Protection, NDPM (now wound up) several communiqués were issued from 1998 to late 1999 on the Niger Delta situation. It was under the umbrella of the IPA and the NDPM for Self Determination and Environmental Protection that letters were written to the British government, Nigeria public, and the Obasanjo administration and public demonstrations carried out against injustice and oppression in the Niger Delta. This included the government killings associated with the Kaiama Declaration, Odi Invasion and the proposed declaration of a State of Emergency in Bayelsa State. The IPA sent a delegation to the Eminent Persons conference of the Ijaw National Conference held on 27-29 November 2003 in Port Harcourt Nigeria. Delegates helped put together the communiqué that came out of that event. Lastly, the IPA actively corresponds with the UK Prime Minister's office, and The All Parliamentary Committee on Nigeria regarding matters that affect the Ijaw people of the Niger Delta.

Thus, the Ijaw community, mainly through the organisational efforts of the IPA, have been consistent in articulating the opinions, aspirations and humanitarian concerns of the Ijaws abroad, as it affects their ancestral homeland in Nigeria, the Niger Delta.

The IPA is an unincorporated community association serving its Ijaw members that abides by the laws of the United Kingdom. On the strength of the IPA's political welfare and community involvement with Niger Delta affairs, the IPA was invited by the Nigerians In Diaspora Organisation (NIDO) to submit a position paper and participate in the pre-conference forum which took place at the Nigeria High Commission London on Saturday 10 February 2005, in preparation for a Diaspora position for the Political Reform Conference held in Nigeria. The main highlights of the position paper were as follows: *Title - National Dialogue & National Rebirth: Executive Summary, the Rape of Africa and the Resultant Birth of Nigeria: The Structural Defects of Nigeria - The Illegitimacy of Government, Arbitrary Administrative Units, Fictitious Population Figures, Citizenship and Ethnic Ancestral Kinship, Resource Control & Resource Allocation, Sovereign National Conference or National Reform Conference?* Out of that endeavour, the IPA hosted Justice Nikki Tobi when he visited the UK after the conclusion of the political reform conference in Nigeria. He briefed the IPA and others on the inner workings of the political reform conference and the reasons why certain decisions were arrived at.

On Saturday 22 July 2006, The Ijaw People's Association organised the Isaac Boro day 2006 Commemoration at Lambeth Town Hall, Brixton London. Guest from the three States of Rivers, Bayelsa and Delta attended, as well as guests from the Ijaws living in the USA and Europe. It was a successful event. A conference was held during the afternoon of the event with the theme *BEYOND OIL AND GAS.* This theme was critically examined through the presentation of various papers such as *Isaac Boro - Life and Times & Challenges,* by Dr Amba Ambaiowei (Chairman Board of Trustees Isaac Adaka Boro Foundation). *Beyond Oil and Gas: Options for the Development of a Robust Ijaw Economy* by Mr Moffat Ekoriko. *Health Implication of Oil and Gas Exploration in the Niger Delta* by Prof Nelson Brambaifa (Member of Isaac Boro Foundation). *Shared Challenges That We Must Tackle Together to Position the Future* by Mr Ken Lewis Alagoa (President of the South People's Assembly Europe). And, *Beyond Oil and Gas Wealth Accumulation - Diversification through Globalisation* by Sterling Ellis (Managing Director Sterling Ellis & Co Inc). Ideas generated by the conference, are aimed at positioning the Ijaws in a sustainable future that is diversified from dependence on oil and gas resources. There were many top government functionaries from the aforementioned states, as well as traditional rulers and foundation members of the Ijaw People's Association UK. It was a well-attended event, attracting participants from the Niger Delta community in the UK in general.

Other Activities

The Ijaw People's Association, has functioned fairly consistently through the years in keeping the Ijaw community together and cohesive. On welfare and cultural matters, the IPA provides its members with financial, community and moral assistance. It renders help during the celebrations of births, and marking of death/funerals, marriages and weddings, immigration advice and court & legal assistance, educational assistance, from its foundation to the present time. The Ijaw House at Strahan Road was let out to mostly Ijo persons (mostly students) at reduced social affordable rent. Ijaw persons who found themselves homeless for various reasons were given temporary accommodation at Ijaw House, until they got themselves back on their feet. The IPA organises yearly fundraising, social awareness, seminars and general celebration events. Its members have taken part in the organising of various local and international events such as Ogele/IPA Awards Night in honour of the journalist Ms Ibiba Don Pedro (CNN African Journalist of the Year, 2003), several annual Boro Days in London and other events to the general delight and satisfaction of its members and visiting Ijaws from Nigeria.

The Ijaws living in the United Kingdom through the Ijaw People's Association, have created avenues for networking and meeting up on a formal or informal basis to socialise and address issues affecting the Ijaw community in the UK and Nigeria. For example, on 10 December 1967, the IPA held a Joint Executive Meeting of Niger Delta Area Organisations. At this executive meeting it was decided to call a mass meeting of all Ijaws in the United Kingdom and Ireland. The IPA was asked to convene this gathering. Accordingly in 1968 the Ijaw People's Association in London organised The All-Ijaw General Meeting, which took place on Saturday 24th February 1968. Delegates were invited and attended from Birmingham, Liverpool, Manchester and Leeds. At the All-Ijaw General Meeting, the IPA was given the function of 'being the central Ijaw body' which would coordinate all activities of the entire Ijaws in the United Kingdom and Ireland.'[75] The IPA seems to have performed this role very well, and is still the main organisation to call Ijaw sons and daughters together whenever the need arises.

The IPA has gone on to organise other events regularly such as fundraising events, the annual Foundation member's party, the End of Year and Boro Day events. An example was the 1st and 2nd Izon Conference held on 24 August 1996 at Dulwich Town Hall London UK. The main aims of that conference were;

1. To highlight some of the problems Ijaw face in the UK, in Nigeria, and elsewhere in the world, to the awareness of the public.

2. To educate Ijaw children born in the UK and some adults on Ijaw culture.

3. To encourage dialogue in order to moderate opposing views.

Figure 34. Izon Community condolence visit to late Kay Williamson's family.

Seminar topics discussed include the following: The importance of the Izon language to the Ijaw people, presented by Prof Kay Williams. The Traditional marriage customs of the Ijaw, presented by Flora Oki. Is the Izon language becoming Extinct? Presented by Dr M. Narebor. Female Circumcision in Africa presented by Chief (Mrs) C. A Awala. Sickle Cell Disease - A Family Centred Approach, presented by Chief (Dr) R E Akwagbe. Ijaws and the Miseducation Syndrome, presented by Dr R. Angiama. Unity presented by Mrs E Oluwole. And lastly Izons (Ijaws) In Contemporary Nigeria, presented by Chief E. K. Clark.

The various organisations and individuals, especially in London, attend each other's events such as births, deaths and funerals, launchings, fund-raisers, end-of-year parties, naming ceremonies and weddings. The Ijaw community in the UK is predominantly Christian, but most people have a cultural respect for traditional spirituality and belief systems. They seek to preserve the beneficial culture and customs of the Ijaw, as much as possible.

The IPA continues to provide social/and cultural welfare needs to its members, and also takes a special interest in Ijaw-land back home in Nigeria.

Figure 35. Some IPA Executive Committee Members in the early 2000s.

The Community in London also has close links with the Ijaw Community in the USA, mainly through the organisational networks of the Ijaw National Alliance of the Americas (INAA), The Council of Ijaw Associations Abroad (CIAA) and others. There are quite a lot of exchange visits between the two main Ijaw communities abroad. On an individual level, many families take time on holidays to visit their relatives in Nigeria. The United States is also a favoured destination for family visits, since quite a few Ijaws have immigrated to the US from the UK.

In 2018, the IPA celebrated 70 years in existence, being the oldest Ijaw organisation in the UK that continues to exist and function as a community association dedicated to the overall welfare of Ijaw People as citizens of the United Kingdom.

Records show that several other Ijaw and Niger Delta organisations existed in the 1960's such as the Western Ijaw Student Union and Rivers State Union, but they recognised the IPA as the main foundation body.[76] The leadership of the IPA duly recognising this, reaches out on a permanent basis to all the Ijaw community organisations based on town or clan affiliation, to get a broad consensus when important decisions or matters affecting the Ijaw Nation are discussed and action taken. This takes the form of holding All-Ijaw conferences or meetings. Furthermore, the IPA tries to keep up-to-date information on all Ijaw community organisations operational in the UK.

IPA Close links with Other Ijaw Umbrella Organisations Outside London

In Liverpool: Ijaw People have been living in Liverpool from the 1920's or even earlier. Most of them came as merchant sailors and economic migrants just like their counterparts in London. By 1945 the Ijaw People's Union was founded, later on to be called the Ijaw Cultural Union.[77] Some of the founding members include Messers Tom Agoro, Mark Favour, J. Anderson, D.A. Tonkumoh, David Dibbo, Author Tiwei, James Ojourun, P. Enagberi, A. Douglas, T. Enamu, S. Tonprefa and T. Tangaemi. Others who joined later in the 1950 and 60's include Kenny Ebuwei, Johnson Yekwe, Mrs M. A. Yekwe, Chief W. I. Okuboh, Mrs Okuboh, Mrs Koffah, Pastor Peter Opomu, Captain F. Sokare. The later immigrants came as students or seamen and engaged in various professions such as printing, catering, nursing, railway workers and engineers. Starting from the 1960's, the Ijaw Cultural Union (ICU) developed closer cultural affiliation with the Ijaw People's Association in London. The ICU operated on the basis of self help and collective welfare of its members. It maintained formal links with the IPA. From time to time, the IPA used to organise visits to Liverpool to socialise with the few remaining ICU members living in Liverpool. Members of the ICU of Liverpool actively participated in the life of Liverpool. For example, the late Mr Kenny Ebuwei was an active member of the Liverpool Labour Party as well as, being on the Board of Governors of his local primary school.

Many of the original members of the Ijaw Cultural Union (ICU) and Ijaw community have passed away or returned to Nigeria on retirement. Their children and grandchildren continue to live in Liverpool, London and other parts of the UK as active professionals contributing to the economic growth of the United Kingdom.

In Manchester: During the 1960s the Ijaw of Manchester formed the Ijaw Welfare Association to cater for the welfare needs of the small Ijaw community at the time. The association membership fluctuated and was up and down. Of the early Manchester Ijaw community, we can name Mr Edward Koko, Mr Toun who was a Shell (oil firm) official working in the UK, Mr Francis Obu, who worked in the steel industry, Mr Wilson Enisuoh, who was a high ranking United Africa Company UAC, official working in the UK, Mr David Kentebe (early 1970's), and Mr Moses Kantel, who originally lived in London and was

Figure 36. IPA's visit to the Ijaw Cultural Union of Liverpool in the Year 2003.

a foundation member of the IPA. There were others whose names have now been forgotten. The individuals worked in such professions as engineering, Inland Revenue, the Steel Industry and the Post Office, while some were students who have since returned to Nigeria.

The early Ijaw Welfare Association was in constant communication and cooperation with the Ijaw People's Association of London. The organisation cooperated fully, along with other Ijaw organisations in raising funds for aid during the Nigeria civil war. Members attended the various meetings and All Ijaw meetings organised by the IPA of London.

Many Ijaws returned home to Nigeria, and the Ijaw community of Liverpool and Manchester dwindled to a very small group of elders and their adult children. Since the late 1990's up to the present period, Manchester has again become a destination of opportunity for young Ijaw to better their lives and get a higher education. Many Ijaw recently arrived from Nigeria, have begun settling in Manchester to make a living and study. But they are not organised into any union, as was the case previously.

The IPA also keeps in touch with other Ijaws who have settled in Birmingham and Bristol, while isolated Ijaw persons living in smaller towns such as Leeds, Leicester and Reading to name a few, can be found. These individuals are usually highly skilled professionals such as nurses, medical doctors, scientists and bankers as well as newly arrived immigrants from Nigeria. All in all, they consider the Ijaw People's Association of Great Britain and Ireland as the Father organisation.

Figures 37 a & b. The late Pa Kenny Ebuwei of The Ijaw Cultural Union in Liverpool Meeting with then British PM Tony Blair and Miss World Agbani Darego in 2001.

Figure 38. Izon people attending a conference.

Figure 39. IPA Elders with some founding members such as Pa Stephen Okpokpo and Pa Laurence Okorodudu.

Figure 40. Izon cultural classes, 2017.

PRESIDENTS OF THE IJAW PEOPLE'S ASSOCIATION FROM INCEPTION
Mr Young Ogetti Kpiaye (Foundation President)
Mr Laurence Okorodudu
Mr Moses Kantel
Chief Lawrence Oki
Mr David Ayaoge
Dr Edwin Sawacha
Mr Rowland Ekperi
Mr Isaac Namabiri
Rev Francis B. Akpanari
Mr Morris B. Oguoko served as a caretaker chairman
Mr Beni Kansese served as a caretaker chairman
Patrons have included the following persons;
Mr Laurence Okorodudu
Mr Stephen Okpokpo
Mr Aliyi Ekineh
Mr Lawrence Okudu
Mrs E. Agugu

Mrs C. Narebor
Mrs G. Tombofa

MEMBERS OF THE COUNCIL OF ELDERS OF THE IJAW PEOPLE'S
ASSOCIATION 2023/4
Mr Edward F. Dorgu
Mr Patrick Doabry
Mr Lawrence Dorgu
Dr Edwin Sawacha
Mr Beni Kansese
Mr Tonbra Tonibor
Mr Christopher Sampoh
Mr Alex Sampoh
Rev. Francis B. Akpanari
Dr Richard Angiama
Mr Stephen Okpokpo
Mr Lawrence Okudu
Chief Lawrence Oki
Mr David Ayaoge
Mrs Victoria Esugunum

REFERENCES

64. Archives of the Ijaw People's Association of Great Britain & Ireland Testimonies of the late Pa Laurence Okorodudu (1999) and Pa Stephen Okpokpo. April 2006
65. Testimony of Pa Stephen Okpokpo April 2006.
66. Although most of the Young Ijaw (Ijo) men were merchant seamen, others came specifically to get a higher education or further vocational training.
67. Ijaw People's Association (IPA@70) 2018 Brochure, p7 and IPA archives.
68. TESTIMONY OF PA STEPHEN OKPOKPO ON 8TH DECEMBER 2019 in response to the question of "How did the 18 Strahan Road property come about", and 2006 Testimony
69. There were small Ijaw communities in Liverpool and Manchester at the time, and the onshore seamen tended to avoid the hostels. Ijaw Community testimonies 2006.
70. 1967/68 Membership list contained in Minutes of the Ijaw People's Association of Great Britain & Ireland - General Meeting minute book.
71. Fiofori, T., Daminabo A. O. and Ayotamuno, Y. (2009) *Ijo Footprints - Ijo Contributors to Nigeria and the World*, p. 38. Ijaw History Project
72. 1967/68 Membership list contained in Minutes of the Ijaw People's Association of Great Britian & Ireland - General Meeting minutes book.
73. May 2006 Testimony of Pa Stephen Okpokpo of London, a foundation member, as recorded by Miss Eva Amgbare/Benaebi Oguoko.
74. Minutes of the Ijaw People's Association of Great Britian & Ireland 2/6/68, 7/7/68 & 11/8/68

75. Minutes of the Ijaw People's Association of Great Britain & Ireland 3/3/68, 7/4/68 & 5/5/68

76. Minutes of the Ijaw People's Association of Great Britain & Ireland 3/3/68, 7/4/68 & 5/5/68

77. Testimony of Pa Kenny Ebuwei of Liverpool April 2006, as recorded by Mr Benaebi Oguoko.

CHAPTER 8: OTHER IJAW COMMUNITY ORGANISATIONS IN LONDON

Ijaw Women's Association founded 1987

Ijaw women have also been coming to the United Kingdom from at least the 1950s. We have records of some Ijaw women arriving in the United Kingdom in the 1950s onwards, mostly as students or wives of Ijaw men. Some of the students also got married to their fellow Ijaw men in London. These women formed themselves into informal Ijaw Women's network and met on a regular basis. According to Mrs Edna Knight (nee Ofoniama);

> When my mom was alive, she was part of the Ijaw community. So she was with my father, when he came here. He was in the Ijaw Peoples Association. He is one of the founding members of the Ijaw People's Association, and this association is still running up till today. And he was very much committed to that organisation. And when my mom was alive, she was in the Ijaw Women's Association. And I remember when she was alive, she used to take me to those meetings. And these were cultural meetings where the women would all get together. And basically, it is women living in the UK, London, mostly, they would get together once a month, they would basically talk about the things happening in you know, their villages back home. They would talk and welcome new members that have come from Nigeria, you know, acclimatised them, get them used to where things are about finding jobs. It was just basically, everybody networking and supporting each other. And then they used to do classes, like Ijaw lessons. We used to do Ijaw lessons, they used to give us lessons on tying, for example wrappers. And, you know, headscarf, and then you know, once a year, at least we would have a party, where we would invite other different Nigerian groups.[78]

It was in 1987 that this informal Ijaw Women's network was organised into a formal association with the establishment of the Ijaw Women's Association. Listed as 10 Foundation members are the following women;
Mrs Gladys Tombofa (Deceased)
Mrs Tonye Edonya (Deceased)
Mrs Clara Torunarigha (Deceased)
Mrs Celina Seikegba (Deceased)
Ms Veronica Jombo (Deceased)
Mrs Agugu

Figure 41. IWA members meeting.

Mrs Molara E Tarigha

Mrs Ogbomah-Zoradey

Ms Barbara Oki

Mrs Izonebi Vivian Apanari (Akpanari)

Other early members include Mrs C. A. Awala (nee Prefa), Mrs Claire Akpaere Narebor and Mrs Florence Ebiere Ayaoge

The reason for the creation of the Ijaw Women's Association, according to their brochure,[79] was to have an intellectual space where Ijaw women living in London could discuss matters important to them. The primary goals include empowering women, promoting social integration, fostering community development and preserving/teaching the Ijaw language and culture to their children and youth. The IWA motto is KENI WENIMO, in Ijaw language, which means (Walking or Working in Unity). The IWA has been involved in a number of community initiatives through the years.

The Presidents of the Ijaw Women's Association have been the following women:

Mrs C. A. Narebor, Pastor Mrs Molara E. Tarigha, Mrs Agugu, Chief Mrs C. A. Awala, Mrs Izonebi Vivian Akpanari, Dr Mrs Anthonia Garner, Mrs Cecelia Thomas, Deaconess Mrs Esther Tarre Oki-Akinlade.

Kalabari Central Organisation

The Kalabari Central Organisation is a Social, Educational and Economic Development Charity that works with local, national and relevant international Organisations in reducing poverty. It is positioning itself in cultural development and welfare amongst its members in a multi-cultural Britain. Its membership is made up of persons of Kalabari-Ijaw heritage. The charity commits to active promotion of equal opportunities and utilise the full potentials of members in order to benefit the society. The organisation has been active in London for over two decades. The current trustees of the organisation are Dr Boma Douglas, Dr Ibim Alfred and Dr Fubara Princewill.[80]

Nembe-Ibe Association UK

The Nembe-Ibe Association UK is a community organisation that is open to all persons of Nembe-Ijaw origin either by birth, marriage or settlement, that are resident in the United Kingdom and Northern Ireland. It has been in existence for over two decades and is an active community association that caters for the welfare of its members.[81]

Figure 42. Kalabari Central Organisation Group.

Figure 43. Wakirike Community Members.

London Tari Club (LONTAR)

The London Tari Club was founded in 1997 and is an exclusive private members club, whose aim is to promote the social and fraternal relationship amongst its members and respective families. It carries out its activities and social programmes in a non-political and non-governmental manner. It is a UK based high profile social networking club that caters for its members. Lontar is an Ijaw-oriented club, being that all members are of Ijaw Heritage.[82]

Other Ijaw welfare organisations that exist or existed and contribute to the welfare of Ijaw Community in London include the following:

Abari Development Association UK
Abonnema Society UK
Agbere Community Association Of Great Britain And Ireland
Arogbo Community
Bayelsa Union UK And Ireland
Bonny Improvement Association
Buguma Internal Affairs
Kabowei Ogbo UK
Odoni Community
Odoni Development Association Of Great Britain And Ireland
Opobo Community Association UK
Wakirike Community UK(Founded In 1953)

REFERENCES

78. Interview with Edna Knight 04/09/2023
79. Ijaw Women's Association UK, 36th Culture & Anniversary Celebration 16/09/2023 Brochure
80. https://www.facebook.com/KalabariCentralOrganisation/about, https://register-of-charities.charitycommission.gov.uk/charity-search/-/charity-details/4014397/charity-overview accessed in February 2024.
81. https://m.facebook.com/100075922397016/ accessed in February 2024
82. https://londontariclub.com/ accessed in February 2024

PART 4

**THEMES FROM THE ORAL HISTORY
INTERVIEWS, ORAL TESTIMONIES,
COMMUNITY FIGURES & ACTIVITIES,
PROFESSIONALS, RELIGIOUS LEADERS,
ARTISTS AND PUBLIC SERVICE**

CHAPTER 9: STORIES OF ARRIVING, RETURNING, STAYING AND OVERCOMING

In this chapter we capture narratives of arrival in the United Kingdom, the decision to stay or to go home, and for some, the decision to return to the UK after going home. We capture the motivations to leave the Ijaw homeland and the push and pull that many Ijaw immigrants faced. Some of these are stories common to many immigrants, some have a unique resonance to the Ijaw communities of the UK. Following this, in a latter section, the challenges faced by the Ijaw in the London on their road to settlement are explored. As much as possible, their own words are presented. This helps to paint a more vivid picture of both the times as well as their experiences. The first question that arises from the narratives is the contested nature of the word "migrant". This notion is not new and perhaps reflects participants' contact with the use of the word in the press and politicised discourse. As one of the interviewees remarked,

> I have a problem with that word 'migration'. Migration means, you intentionally leaving your place of birth and decide to settle in the UK. I find issue with the use of that word. I will tell you why. If you ask me for the reasons why I came to the UK, I'll tell you and the reasons why I came to the UK is for studies. (Rowland Ekperi)[83]

> The word immigrant didn't actually affect me really, because the time I came (1962), we were still a British colony. I came like a British person; I was given a British travelling certificate to come here and when I came here, the job was ready. (Rev Francis Akpanari)[84]

This notion perhaps highlights a key theme in the stories of people, who leave their countries for foreign lands. For many, the plan is often to stay for a while and return. But many times, life circumstances turn temporary migration into permanent settlement (von Koppenfels, 2014). However, it is pertinent to trace what underpins the original decision to leave.

While many migrants moved directly from Nigeria to the UK, for some, the UK was not the original country they moved to. However, for some reason, they found their way to the UK and settled here. One of the foundation members of the Ijaw People's Association, Lawrence Okorodudu, is said to have moved to the UK from the Deep South of the United States (interview with his daughter).[85] Furthermore, speaking about his father, another interviewee who was born to Ijaw parents in London in 1967 observes:

> I do not know what year, but he left for Germany. He went to Germany. From Germany, he came into the UK as a civil engineer and was working on the underground and from the underground, he went on to the Thames Water, till he retired. (Eneilayefa Edonya)[86]

Patterns of Arrival

While there is documented evidence of Ijaw people in London dating to the early 19th century,[87] the 1940's saw a steady influx of young Ijaw men into the UK. Some of these migrants were seamen who came here for work. The intention of many of these seamen was often to stay for a while, save some money and then return home. They often arrived at Liverpool where a buddy community of seamen developed. Some of them then found their way to London. Some of these seamen had some education, while others could not read or write. This presented some challenges as we discuss later in this chapter.

> They were just working in shipping, Elder Dempster Lines, like stewards in the ship and most of them are not educated but, they could serve. My father was one of them, my uncle that I grew up with was one of them. (Rev Francis Akpanari)[88]

> My dad is an Ijaw man. He left Nigeria in the 1940s. He got on a boat, as a lot of people did back in those days did and made his way to the UK. His plan was that he would come here for five years, and then make enough money and go back to Nigeria. (Edith Akenkide)[89]

At about the same time as these seamen came to the UK, other Ijaw men whose sole purpose was to get a UK education and return home, also arrived.

> My father, he is from Abonnema. And he came to the UK after the Second World War; I think it's 1947/48. And he came to study law. So, he came to study law, he met my mother, and they got married. And I was born in London in 1949. And then, when he completed his law degree, and his bar exams, he returned to Nigeria in I think it was 1952. And then my mother and I joined him in 1953. (Sokari Ekineh)[90]

Another respondent, Archbishop Doye Agama was born to Ijaw parents in London in 1956. He goes on to recount how the economic downturn of the 1980's in Nigeria and the steady erosion of the Nigerian middle classes,

Fig. 44. Edith Akenkide as a young girl. (Photo credit. Courtesy of Edith Akenkide photo album, used with her permission).

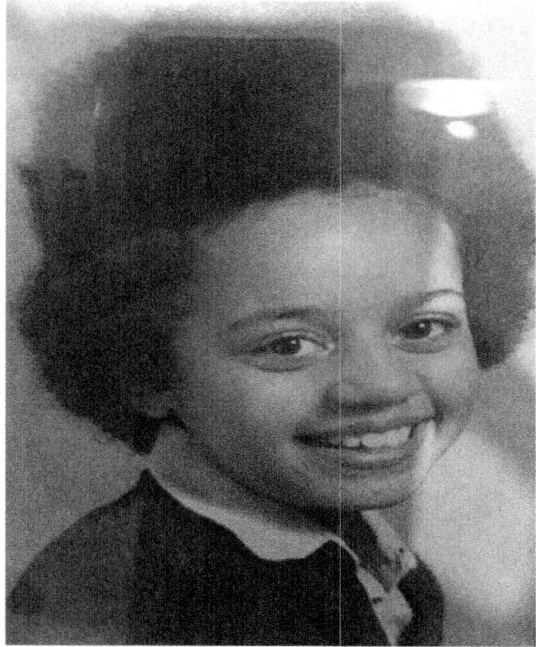

resulted in "the syndrome that today people call immigration."

> At the time, I was born, I think very few people from African nations generally had any intention of coming to the UK to stay in the UK. For most young people who came here, they came for the education. And that was it. And in those days, and up until a few years after the civil war, anyone who successfully completed a university degree became a professional in one area of skill or the other, could be assured of a reasonably good life in Nigeria. You have a house, a car, and a job until you retired. (Archbishop Agama)[91]

Another early wave of Ijaw migration to the UK occurred with the introduction of the voucher scheme for Commonwealth citizens in the 1960's. Lawrence Dorgu was a trained carpenter and joiner in Nigeria and arrived in the UK in 1963, using the voucher system.

> So, when I applied to my surprise, I got it within seven months, because we are classified as working artisans. (Lawrence Dorgu)[92]

Although, there is evidence of young Ijaw women in the UK in the 1950's, (see Archbishop Agama) records show, migration was mostly a male endeavour in the 40's and 50's. The seamen as would be expected, did not

Figure 45. Mr & Mrs Akenkide, parents of Edith Akenkide in the 1940s. (Photo is used with permission from Edith Akenkide).

travel with their wives. In addition, the young men who came to study often came alone and stayed for the whole of their degrees. As such, it was not unexpected that several of the young men from these two groups married white British woman. While many of the seamen stayed on and built lives in the UK, many of those who had come for education returned to Nigeria, sometimes with their British wives. These marriages of those who arrived after the second world war means that mixed-race identity is a prominent theme in the migration stories of some UK Ijaw who were born in the late 1940s to 1960. Some of the experiences of these mixed-race Ijaw permeate our discourse in different chapters of this book.

> The generation before them, they got married to white women and settled down. Because they've been serving the white men in the ship, they could speak English. (Francis Akpanari's wife)[93]

> I have also got memories of on a Sunday, we'd get dressed up in our best clothes, and going to meet other family members who looked like us. So, the mums were white, and the men were Nigerian. There was a lot of mixed races, people within the Ijaw community back then, I do recall a sense of belonging. (Edith Akenkide)[94]

> The foundational President, Mr Young Kpiaye, he married a white lady. Mr Okorodudu another foundational member, he has a mixed-race family as well.[95]

In understanding the original decision to move to the UK, there is also a theme of escape for some. This might be escaping difficult cultural, family issues or economic problems.

> She told me that the main reason that they came to the UK, was that my mother was extremely worried if she had daughters, that they would be circumcised because in our village that was still going on. Luckily for us, my dad was a very educated man. And he agreed with my mother, and he also didn't want that to happen to any of his daughters. And so, my mom says this was the main reason why they came to the UK. (Edna Knight)[96]

As we have mentioned earlier, for many, the decision to make the UK a permanent home was not often one that was thought out in advance. The desire for many was to return home. What factors then combined to create the accidental migrant? It is often a combination of factors: roadblocks back home and starting to raise family in the UK during this "temporary period" are common factors. One of our interviewees first came to the UK on honeymoon and started thinking about further education. While pursuing their degrees, they started a family:

> And, you know, by the time we knew it, you know, we already had two children. And so, we decided you know, there was no point of new beginning to move children from the UK back home. (Dr Boma Douglas)[97]

Returning to the UK

There are also poignant narratives of going back to Nigeria and returning for a second time to the UK. These play out in many ways. Often it is finding out that there are significant roadblocks to achieving career ambitions. This scenario plays out more clearly for later waves of migrants to the UK, from the late 1970's onwards.

> You have a wife; you have children and I wanted to back go to settle in Nigeria, but my wife wasn't prepared to go back with the girls. So, I had to make a choice. Must I be this highflyer, pursue money at the expense of the kids I brought into this world. I said no. I brought these kids to this world; Nigeria is uncertain. And some of my friends who went back to Nigeria many of them were killed practising their profession and that shook me. I said for me with a strong activist tendency, always fighting against injustice; professionally I'm not going to survive. So let me stay here to look after my children, to build a family and that's what I did. I still have the desire to go home. I want to make

sure to work with the people on ground to transform my place the Ijaw land. (Rowland Ekperi)[98]

Yes. There are few that went back, became lecturers, worked in the oil companies. As Rivers people, we thought will be opportunities for us, but it wasn't happening. In fact, I tried my best to see that I get a place not going back to NTV, but going back to the oil sector, but it wasn't going on well. You know, after spending time in the UK, you want to go back home, stay within your own area in Rivers State and for me to think of going back to Lagos, working in Lagos, my wife wasn't that interested that we should go to struggle in Lagos again. (Datoru Paul Worika)[99]

For some, it is the gradual decline of the security situation in Nigeria. This excerpt is from a daughter's perspective of how her Ijaw father (Aliyi Ekineh) and white British mother who had moved to Nigeria in 1953, returned to the UK.

So, my father, you know, was a corporate lawyer, and then some circumstances happened once when my mother and father were on holiday in the UK. This was around 1986. Their house at Ikeja was burgled by armed thieves and according to the staff that was looking after the property, the cook, he and his wife, they hid in the boys' quarters.[100] So, he said there was a gang with machetes. So, that happened on the night my parents were flying home. So, when they got to Lagos, they just missed it by one night, it could have been a massacre. So, my mother who had been there from 1953 to 1987, I think it was, and she just said, Okay, I can't do this anymore. So, she came back to England. And my father continued to practice. But eventually, he retired. And then he retired to UK, which is how he came back to the UK. (Sokari Ekineh)[101]

Aliyi Ekineh refers personally[102] to these circumstances of coming back to the UK as returning "without preparation".

Still for others, returning is about an opportunity to forge a new beginning, to make a fresh start:

I had gotten divorced. So, I decided to come to the UK. Because I felt it was easier for me to become independent, so to speak and work and continue my education and so on. (Sokari Ekineh)[103]

Challenges Faced by the Ijaw Community in the UK

After tracking the stories of decisions to come, to stay and to return, we capture the experiences and challenges of Ijaw migrants over the last 80 years. The United Kingdom of 2024 is a different country to what it was 80, 60 or even 20 years ago. The vibrant, inclusive multicultural society that we see today was in its foundational stages, when some of the actors in our stories arrived or were born the UK. As such, the varied experiences of our respondents carry the idiosyncratic hallmarks of the different time periods they have witnessed.

Central to many stories, is one of finding space in a new country. This search for space often comes with roadblocks. For many whose journey began long before the 1990's, these roadblocks were more difficult to overcome. The roadblocks are not only observed for the first-generation migrant. There are also poignant depictions of roadblocks for the second-generation and particularly those who grew up in mixed-race homes. However, alongside these stories of challenges are heartwarming depictions of triumph against adversity. Accordingly, this section is as much about the roadblocks as well as how Ijaw migrants navigated these roadblocks and forged new paths for themselves. Some of these new paths created new opportunities to make significant contributions to UK life.

First, we discuss some the hurdles and then we discuss how these hurdles were navigated. We frame these challenges under some key categories:

Literacy and Educational Challenges

As we have documented, while many Ijaw migrants were educated, there were some who did not have much formal education. Navigating the United Kingdom with very little education, presented a significant hurdle for these people. For some, the lack of education came with significant economic costs. Two stories capture this issue quite poignantly. The first is a story about one of the seamen who arrived in London around 1950:

> Yes, he cannot read and write, but he's very clever. He lives in Hackney. When he's going to work, he goes by train. When he goes to the train station, when he gets down to where he would wait for the train, he will stop at a particular place and put a mark on the wall of that station, so that when he's coming back, he will see that station. "Oh, that's where I am stopping", then gets off. So, that's how he's been going up and down like that. One day, the mark had been rubbed off, the train took him to the last stop, brought him back, took back, brought him to the last stop. So, the attendant said "Hey, there's something wrong". So, they approached him and said "Where are you going? He says, "I'm lost". They say "Where is your station"; he said "I don't know". This man was lost for almost eight, nine hours. He's supposed to be home for five o'clock, 12 o clock, he hasn't gotten home. The train attendant went to report to the police station and through vigorous interview, they managed to get where he was staying. That was how illiteracy was killing them.[104]

While this story is serious, it may also seem like a scene from a comedy and so the reader might be inclined to laugh, the next one is significantly more harrowing:

She was about 50 years when she died. So, she was born in 1942 and died in 1990. My father passed away in 1962, and I was 12 years old. So, from that age, my mother was looking after five of us. And it was a big struggle for her. Because she'd never been anywhere out of Nigeria. She came from the village of Kaiama, she couldn't read, she couldn't write. Yes, when my dad came here, he was a learned man, he acquired few properties as a landlord here in the UK. But obviously, when he passed away, my mother because she couldn't read or write, she didn't understand anything about wills, property, money. And unfortunately, all of those properties that were in my father's name got lost. Yeah, they got lost. And at that time, we were staying in one of those properties. And then the Housing Association moved us to a housing association property. So yeah, we only found this out, because about 20 years ago, some company, court contacted us about deeds, which were in my dad's name. And so obviously, with research, we found out that my dad owned three properties. But obviously, because of the time and because of my mom's education, she couldn't read or write, we lost those properties. And we couldn't get those properties back. But we did get a little bit of compensation. Because obviously, the deeds were in my dad's name. And those were the deeds. And so obviously, other people have now bought those properties. 20 years plus. So, we couldn't regain the properties, but we did get compensation. (Edna Knight)[105]

Educational challenges also feed into work. For those with little education, they had to take on multiple jobs. This clearly impacted on many aspects of family life and perhaps on the health of some of these people.

My mom struggled, she was a cleaner in a hospital, St. Charles Hospital, in London. And she also did other cleaning jobs. And I think altogether, she did about four cleaning jobs in one day, looking after all of us. And still we were always fed, we were always dressed, we all went to school, we all got educated to secondary education. (Edna Knight)[106]

Prejudice and Racism

The interviews also include moving depictions of racism, discrimination and struggles with immigration. Such struggles are not by any means limited to the Ijaw. They are the sort of struggles faced by early and even more recent immigrants of black origin. Some of the experiences of racism and discrimination documented by our interviewees are overt, some reflect the more disguised forms that still can be found in pockets of British society. For the mixed-race children, it appears that there is a more discernible impact of racism on identity formation and maintenance. John Ogetti Kpiaye is a musician who was born to a Nigerian father and white British mother in 1948. He suggests that the experiences of racism experienced by his mixed-race family, may have contributed to the breakup of his parent's relationship.

I think the other reason was at that time, late 40s, early 50s, there was so much racism. My mother later on, she told me of incidents where she would walk down Poplar High Street with me in the pram and people would stare at her. What do you do with that n******, you n****** baby ?. Right you know, and I think those pressures can bear on the relationship. (John Kpiaye).[107]

There is also a police record[108] of his father Mr Young Kpiaye, who was the first IPA President, being the victim of a racially motivated attack alongside Mr Vincent Akenkide in 1947.

Lawrence Dorgu arrived the UK in 1963 and recounts looking for a place to rent. He recalls being told by landlords that they did not want "blacks and no children, no wife, or no dogs or anything." The solution for him was:

Fortunately, some Nigerians had houses for rent. And the first room that I rented was owned by a Yoruba woman.[109]

Another interviewee who moved to the UK in 1975 also recounts an experience.

As a student on the train, I was beaten and attacked by the National Front. (Paul Worika)[110]

A final story from a former President of the IPA whose UK journey began in the 1980's as a student. This happened in Federal Avenue Meshach, Surrey:

My cousin had an Irish girlfriend, so that attracted racist attack. Two weeks after my arrival here in the UK, I was sleeping in the living room area that is very close to the road with the doors; these racist guys petrol bombed the house. There I was trapped; my cousin and his girlfriend were on the top floor while I was on the ground floor in the living room area. They couldn't come down from the staircase because fire had taken over the stairs and I couldn't come down from the living room door to go outside. I had to smash the glass window out. Then, those who were staying upstairs, they had to tie blankets, bed sheets as ropes to come down. That was my experience in the UK. Before the fire brigade came, many of the things were burnt down but I was lucky I did not sustain any cut apart from glasses that cut my toe. I managed to come out of that place unscratched. (Rowland Ekperi)[111]

Career Challenges

For some, a reason for moving to a new country is to advance one's career. Even when that is not a key determinant of the decision to move, there is an expectation of finding work that is rewarding and fulfilling. For some, the story is straightforward, their skills are appreciated and their ascent up the career ladder is smooth. For others, the story is much more complicated, involving meanders, rerouting and often, a redefinition of what success entails.

> If you go for interview, the job is there and they will be telling you, "Oh no, it has been taken, it has been taken" and in order to maintain my home, my family, I have to accept a job with the local government ... not directly in the field that I will have loved as well.[112]

> And so, whilst my father was here, Of course, he studied but he worked plenty of jobs. So, like, there's a time when he had 2 jobs: He worked in McDonald's, but he also, worked as a train driver. But he was actually educated, he's actually training to be a lawyer. So, that's quite interesting in itself, the fact that he was well learned, he had qualifications, but those qualifications weren't respected in the UK. (Joshua Garry narrating his father's experience of UK in the 70's and 80's)[113]

> Despite the fact that I was trained as a telecommunication engineer, I didn't actually work in that profession for long, you know, so, and that was how so many people survive here. You know, I knew a friend of mine, when I was in the post office, he was a PhD holder, you know, and he was sorting letters with us, you know, he couldn't just get that proper job that he wanted in this country. (Rev Francis Akpanari)[114]

Cultural Challenges

The Ijaw culture is a rich, collectivist one. As such, just like any other culture, when pitted against a different cultural system, conflicts occur. These conflicts or hurdles, often present themselves in wider interactions in society. But sometimes, they play out in the family unit. For Ijaw people in the UK, there exists this challenge of maintaining their Ijaw values, identity and UK family culture. The IPA played a central role in helping Ijaw migrants ease themselves into UK society. As has been mentioned earlier in this chapter, a number of the founding leaders of the IPA had mixed-race households, a fertile ground for culture conflicts. Recounting the role her father played in settling Ijaw arrivals to the UK, Larraine Okorodudu had this to say:

> Yeah. They (Ijaw people) just arrived from Nigeria, at Heathrow airport because people in Nigeria used to give them my dad's phone number. When you get to Heathrow, phone Mr Laurence Okorodudu and he'll come and pick you up and take you home.[115]

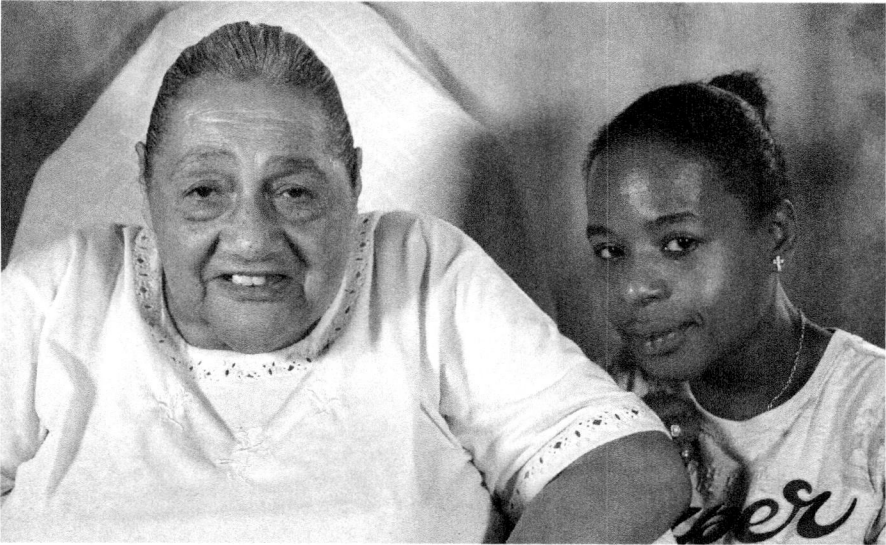

Figure 46. Laraine Okorodudu and daughter Ibukun.

And some of them literally came from Nigeria with absolutely nothing. My dad had to look after them you know, feed them and get them clothes and stuff like that because they used to land here, a lot of them with absolutely nothing.[116]

Actions like these, are mentioned in different interview excerpts and reflect the communal culture of the Ijaw. However, they often conflicted with expectations from family members. Recounting the impact of this on her British mother, Larraine Okorodudu once again:

She hated it. She used to complain about it. Yeah, because she said, ''The house is not my house, is it? This house is just nothing, but a free hotel for your people''. She was moaning, ''I go to work all day, every day. And they will come in here. Right? Getting free food, they've got no clothes. You're buying them clothes. And none of them are contributing a penny towards anything. I'm sick of it.''[117]

This notion of culture clash is not limited however, to mixed-race households. They permeate recollections of the interactions between first-generation Ijaw migrants and their children. The two narratives below, detail clashes related to guests and discipline.

Growing up you had this thing called an open-door policy, where at any given moment, an auntie and uncle could come and stay and visit for one month, and they could stay for a year. And that was it. And in that moment, where like an auntie and uncle will just come to the UK, your bedroom is no longer your bedroom. You know, and I think that traumatised quite a lot of people in my generation, they didn't like it, you know. Suddenly, you've got a stranger living in the house and suddenly, you've been displaced from where you live. Of course, there are some aunties and uncles who are great, you absolutely love them. But still, there was that lack of stability and balance and that's something that's quite difficult for my parents to reconcile, because that's the way it works. You know, I think those boundaries, I do recognise that you just need to explain, okay you know, you're not gonna have a situation whereby people can just come and stay, but equally, that we are one people, you know, you need to be able to help people, you need to connect with people. And I just think, communicating and educating might be a way of bridging that gap and staying connected. But I think equally from the perspective of Nigerians, is understanding that people in the UK, operate slightly differently. You know, there's some aspects of the British culture that's gonna seep into us. And a British man is really quiet, reserved, they step backwards. Nigerians are quite friendly and outgoing, that works very well with people in the United States. People in the United States are exactly the same. British people know, they're very, very reserved, and they stand back. (Joshua Garry)[118]

My mom, as I said, was bringing up five children. So yeah, I think looking back on it now, probably, it (her style of punishment) was a little bit too much. But obviously, my mum did what she knew how she was brought up in the village. And obviously, she didn't want any of us to go astray, you know, regarding getting into trouble with the police or anything like that. So, she put her rules on what she knew, as a child from her parents, and, you know, brought that with her to the UK. But obviously, nowadays, we can't practice that kind of punishing your children like that. (Edna Knight)[119]

Family Challenges: Ijaw Children and the UK Care and Foster System

One of the issues that crops up in the interviews is that, some of the children of the early Ijaw communities in London spent time in the care and the foster system. For some, this happened because single-race Ijaw families sometimes handed out their children to be raised by white families:

A lot of Nigerians would farm their children out to white families. So even though they were black, there was a lot of identity issues and racism played a major role. And for some people now, working in mental health, you know, studying, knowing about trauma and knowing how that has an impact. (Edith Akenkide)[120]

My mother used to visit me on her days off. She trained as a nurse and a midwife and worked in the NHS. These were the early black nurses in the NHS back in the 50s. And occasionally, she would even take me on a trip with her so I knew her. And she would try as a mother to explain to me that the lady I was calling mommy was not actually my mother, she was my mother. And my father is not the man I was calling Daddy, my father was a black man. And she later told me that I would keep on asking her well, what is a black man? Because, there were very few people that you could point to in Britain of those days. (Archbishop Agama)[121]

Okay, well I was born in London in 1965 to both Ijaw parents. I went from a very young age, where I was fostered in a white English family who lived in Sussex. So, I sort of spent my childhood commuting between the two. (Patience Agbabi)[122]

Other young children ended up in care. The reasons for these children ending up in local authority care, included family breakdown, one parent travelling back to Nigeria and the other working nights, death of one parent and subsequent collapse of family structure. The experiences of these children make for quite grim reading and are a reminder of how life was in the UK. However, they also help us question if as a society, the issues that we encounter in these narratives are confined to the past. Let us hear the voice of two people born to Ijaw fathers and white British mothers. John was born in 1949 while Edith Akenkide was born in 1964:

I think in 1954, me and my sister ended up in care. Because I think my mother had left and my dad couldn't work and look after us again. And for the next eight years, we were in care, you know. (John Kpiaye)[123]

My sister and I ended up in a children's home from the ages six to sixteen. So, from the age of six to 16, my mom would come and see us in the children's home. And that was it. There was a lot of trauma of you know, growing up in a children's home. There was a lot of sexual abuse in the children's home. There were children being sexually abused by the staff. I was just very angry, because I didn't have people that look like me. And it's interesting because the home is, you know, still not too far from where I live. In fact, this week, I've actually requested to get my file from London Borough. I was placed in a children's home from the ages six to 16. They were responsible for me up until the age of 18. I'm looking to write a book about my life. Looking back now, it was horrendous, but I had my sister there to support me. And like I say, as a child, you can't put a name to what it is, but, it was about being abandoned. It was about being racially abused on a daily basis, not only in the children's home, but also in school. I would get into fights because people would abuse me you know, racially. (Edith Akenkide)[124]

Figure 47. Lawrence Odiri Dorgu, IPA Member and Elder in the Community.

Other Ijaw children ended up in care, when one parent such as the mother, returned to Nigeria and the father working nights, could not look after the children during the night. In these situations, the Local Authority Social Services intervened and placed the children in Local Authority care with visiting rights and home time rights for the parent.[125] The other negative side of the dysfunctionality of trying to adapt to a different society was that some children ended up in a life of crime. The testimony of Tommy Jituboh (Jitubor) is a good example. One of the son's of the late Albert Jituboh, Mr Tommy Jituboh gave a YouTube testimony of his former life as an London Eastend gangster known by the nickname "The Bug". Later on in life Tommy Jituboh found salvation in the Christian faith and turned away from a life of crime.[126]

The Road to Citizenship

For Ijaw people previously and currently resident in the United Kingdom, the road to citizenship took various routes. Some was quite straightforward, from the British Nationality Act of 1948, and children born in the United Kingdom, having rights of citizenship. While for others, however, there are often tales of struggles with immigration authorities and others within the general immigration landscape. Two stories capture this succinctly. The first, is about an Ijaw man whose family was living in the UK, while he moved back and forth between Nigeria and the UK. He was asked to leave the country because, he had been found to have worked briefly while as a student. The intervention of church and community leaders prevented this from happening. The second is equally poignant:

> I think it took about actually two years because the lawyer handling my case later, after some time halfway through the process of getting my British citizenship, they found that that lawyer has been struck off from the list of practitioners, which she did not even tell me. (Lawrence Dorgu)[127]

Overcoming Challenges

Up till now, this chapter has focused on some of the key challenges faced by Ijaws in the UK. However, exploring challenges without a parallel narrative of how individuals and communities met and conquered those challenges, tells only one half of the story. There are interspersed with an acknowledgement of these challenges, inspiring accounts of overcoming. First, we tell some personal stories of overcoming. While these stories belong to the individuals, in many ways paint a picture of the resilient spirit that the Ijaw embody. The first excerpt from one of our interviews captures this spirit of a people:

> And so, I grew up seeing people of my parent's age, who when they arrived here, went and bought books to try to understand the culture. They went asking questions, "So, when you say this, what do you really mean" They were humble enough to do that, to make sure that they were able to communicate successfully to maximise the opportunity, so that they would leave something for their children. (Archbishop Agama)[128]

Another respondent provides a very personal and touching memory of her late mum. We have mentioned her earlier in this chapter; she came to the UK without any formal education in the 1960's:

> And I think altogether, she did about four cleaning jobs in one day, looking after all of us, and that we were always fed, we always dressed. We all went to school, we all got educated to secondary education. And yeah, my mom worked really hard. And one of the things she did when she was here, she learned to read and write. So, she went to remedial classes herself, took it upon herself to learn to read and write. So, by the time she died, she was able to read the

newspaper and I remember the first day I came home, and she had the Mirror newspaper and she said, look at that, I can read this. And she was reading it to me. And I was so proud of her. Yes. Honestly, she really did a good job. And, yeah, unfortunately, she died when she was 50 years old on her way home from work. But no, she was an absolute fabulous woman. (Edna Knight)[129]

Career hurdles were also dealt with resiliently:

Yeah, after my degree in accounting and business management, one of the barriers I faced at a time was that cultural difference, my accent was quite different at the time. And most of my experience of my schooling, both primary and secondary was in Nigeria. So, it was quite a difficult time for me to break into professional work at the time. So, what I did was, I had to volunteer for an accounting firm. I went to them, and I said, I want to work for you for free. I want to volunteer and they said, okay, come on board, what can you do and all that? I said, Well, whatever you give to me, I'm going to do. So, I started then as a normal desk man, a desk boy 17 and all that and hmm, gradually started learning, shadowing various accounting staff at the time. And that really helped me break into the industry, the accounting industry at that time. And after that, once I built myself, when I got the experience required, I then moved to various industries. (John Eperebofori Opuogulaya)[130]

I expanded it (my skills) by going to evening classes because I couldn't afford full time schooling because I've got to work hard for my living to look after my family. So, I did all evening classes to attain my ambition. I did in continuation to my carpentry and joinery; I attended evening classes to study building construction. (Lawrence Dorgu)[131]

Racism is an issue we have addressed several times in this chapter. The scars run deep. For many who are mixed-race, the fight is different, reconciling two equal parts of one's identity is hard work. But, there are stories of fighting and evidence of a path towards victory. Edith Akenkide remarking on her journey from being racially harassed and bullied as a child:

But I overcame all that. And, you know, it's interesting, I've gone into professional social work, I provide support to people with challenging mental health difficulties. (Edith Akenkide)[132]

These narratives of overcoming hurdles are expressed in many ways; but woven into the fabric of some of them, is the acknowledgement of the role that community played in overcoming challenges:

You know, they got involved in the Ijaw People's Association and the Ijaw Women's Association. And they're able to kind of form connections and relationships with people and over time, you know, they eventually get citizenship etc. And yeah, you know, yeah, their social mobility increases. And now, Mom is a homeowner in Brixton, which is quite expensive, to be fair. (Joshua Garry)[133]

I think about all my generation or my generation personally, of the Ijaw people, I would say about 95% of them went to Uni. So, that message has clearly come from somewhere and of course, that message kind of coincided with the Labour government's message the time of going to Uni as well. So, that's one thing, but I think in terms of our parents is, it's a means of survival, isn't it? Like, let's call a spade a spade, we weren't, especially in the UK, we weren't from affluent, highly successful backgrounds. And education provides, in some cases, the best safety, because one, it means you can work. You can take care of the children, you can end up not doing the job that they needed- that they want you to do, and you could survive. (Joshua Garry)[134]

Sliding Doors: The Road not Taken

The movie *Sliding Doors* shows two paths the central character's life could take depending on whether she catches a train. When recounting migration journeys, there is often a reflection on the path not taken. What would life have been, if the protagonists had remained in Nigeria? For some, they believe that moving to the UK has made a huge difference. Lawrence Dorgu is 84, at the time of our interview. He reflects as such:

As nature would have it, I am in this country but if I were living at home, I don't know what would have happened. I may have been dead because of the medical facilities in Nigeria. The medical care that I receive here, I can never get it in Nigeria. So, with my sort of ailment, because everybody has got some sort of ailment. My mates of the same age there is none, there is none remaining. There is none in Asamabiri (his hometown in Nigeria) anymore. All are gone. All gone. So, a lot of time, when I get home because I go to Nigeria every two years, I always feel the difference. I always feel it because there is no age group.[135]

There is also for some the realisation that there are costs to moving to a different country, that the dreams do not always come to pass the way they were dreamed. Yet, somehow, there is often a realisation that new paths have been forged and while some may have regrets, at the end for many, there is some sort of quiet satisfaction or perhaps acceptance. So, we hear again from our interviewees. First, an interviewee, whose mother we have spoken of previously.

Yeah, well, for my mom's perspective, I think that if she hadn't come to the UK, she may still have been alive. Because obviously, she was working so hard to look after all of the children. Now, had she been in Nigeria, she would have had the help of her family, her parents, her siblings to help her bring the children up. And I don't know if they would have had so many in Nigeria, but definitely, you know, I think, then her life experience of living would have been better. Obviously, she came here. And she did benefit because she learned to read and write. She learned to do a lot of things that she wouldn't have got the opportunity to do in Nigeria, because I don't even know if girls went to school in the village. So, you know, for her coming here had its pros, and it also had its cons as well. (Edna Knight)[136]

But in everything, you know, we have the pros and cons. People back home, they might not have the security that we enjoy here, but they have that family orientation, they have that togetherness, and they have according to research, it says Nigerians are one of the happiest people in the world. So, you know, they are benefiting that while here, you find out that we don't really have that. (John Eperebofori Opuogulaya)[137]

Conclusion

As we close this chapter, it is pertinent to reflect on the contributions of three different entities that assisted the Ijaw communities of UK, navigate many of the challenges they faced. First the associations and particularly the IPA and IWA. These organizations ensured that a community could form out of many different people who came into the UK. They helped to showcase a distinctive Ijaw flavour in the UK. The pioneers of these associations were very committed to building a strong cohesive community. Our interviewees provide vivid recollections of meetings, parties, food, and music in each other houses; using community as a force in combating the effects of isolation and discrimination.

It is fitting to read the words of the daughter of one of the foundation members and former President of the IPA:

(Many people) would have suffered a lot more because they wouldn't have had anybody to go to, would they? Because not everybody used to do what he used to do. If he hadn't come the time he came, the whole Ijaw People's Association, many things would have been completely different. It might have even collapsed altogether, or it may not have even existed because he was one of the foundation members and everyone came to him. Yes, they come, they integrate; they move out. They make their own families. But if Dad hadn't done all of that, then they wouldn't have had sponsorship to maybe come here and create a life. (Laraine Okorodudu)[138]

Even when some may not be currently embedded within these associations, there is a recognition of the role they play:

> I don't go to the meetings. Yeah, I haven't been for many years. When my mom died over 10 years ago, the Ijaw community came together, they came to see me at my home, and they were really supportive. So, they're there. I may not be in regular contact, but I know they're there. (Edith Akenkide)[139]

It is fitting also to recognise the many, white British women who lurk like shadows in the background of many of the stories in this project. Their perspectives; their stories and feelings are often presented by their children. Many have died; others are very old. We may not be able to fully capture their motivation to adventure into mixed-race marriages at a time when deep-seated prejudice was rife in the UK. What we know however, from second-person narratives is that they faced many challenges too. Many suffered greatly. They are not just a peripheral part; they are a key part of the tapestry of Ijaw history in the UK. A daughter of one of these women speaks of her mother:

> My mum was definitely a trooper. To go against society, to go against her family, as a white woman to marry a black man, it wasn't fashionable to have mixed race children back in the 40s and 50s. Not like it is now with the Kardashians, who have got mixed race kids, it wasn't. So, I believe my mom was really, you know, as they will say, faced a shoot, she really was a fighter. And I think that had an impact on her mental health. (Edith Akenkide)[140]

Finally, it is also pertinent to recognise the role of allies in the Ijaw story in the UK. Telling a people's history is never complete without remembering the work of allies who often at their own risk, shaped the evolution of the community. Some of our respondents have mentioned her; so, it is fitting that we highlight the role played by Edith Ramsay towards the integration and settlement of the Ijaw in London and the larger immigrant communities of London. Edith's work has been captured in both film and book, so we conclude with testimonies about her from two of our interviewees who interacted with her. First, Edith Akenkide and then Rev Francis Akpanari:

> Edith Ramsay, I think she was given an OBE by the Queen. So, she was an advocate. She was a real pioneer. And she helped us. I haven't got this particular photograph, but I do remember a picture of my mum and my godmother. So, I was named after my godmother and I think it's quite interesting because she was really, she stood up for justice, which I do. She stood up and supported the Nigerians in Whitechapel, back in the day and that wasn't easy for a white person to do that. But, now I can put a label to it, that she was definitely a fighter for equality and justice. And she supported the Ijaw People's Association and she really supported my dad, so much so that my

mom and dad named me after her. And I know I sent you some information because when we were researching, I didn't know that even now today, White Chapel they've honoured her, I think planting a tree. And again, a part of my own research, I'll be getting more information. But in Tower Hamlets, they know her and they've honoured her as well. I was named after her. (Edith Akenkide)[141]

Especially one lady called Edith Ramsey. Edith Ramsey was a white woman, a politician that was looking after all the black people in the East End. And during my first time in this country, she was a first lady. I was going to bring my wife from Nigeria. And they needed a guarantor to sign and my uncle said, let us go to Lady Edith's place and (imitates sound that suggests speed) she signed the thing, invited me for coffee, 7:30pm at her house. Always helping black people, you know. (Rev Francis Akpanari)[142]

REFERENCES

83. Interview 12/11/2023
84. Interview 22/08/2023
85. Interview with Laraine Okorodudu 05/09/2023
86. Interview 09/10/2023
87. See section on Early Ijaw persons living in London.
88. Interview 22/08/2023
89. Interview 20/10/2023
90. Interview 14/09/2023
91. Interview 16/08/2023
92. Interview 13/11/2023
93. Interview 22/08/2023
94. Interview 20/10/2023
95. Interview Edith Akenkide 20/10/2023
96. Interview 04/09/2023
97. Interview 14/10/2023
98. Interview 12/11/2023
99. Interview 13/10/2023
100. Living quarters for domestic staff
101. Interview 14/09/2023
102. Interview of Aliyi Ekineh with his daughter, Ms Sokari Ekineh sent in 14/09/2023
103. Interview 14/09/2023
104. Interview with Rev Frank Akpanari 22/08/2023
105. Interview 04/09/2023
106. Interview 04/09/2023
107. Interview 27/10/2023
108. https://www.ourmigrationstory.org.uk/oms/seafarers-and-stowaways-in-londons-harlem, courtesy of Tower Hamlets Local History Library and Archives, accessed on 10/09/2023

109. Interview with Lawrence Dorgu 13/11/2023
110. Interview 13/10/2023
111. Interview 12/11/2023
112. Interview Datoru Ben Paul Worika 13/10/2023
113. Interview 29/08/2023
114. Interview 22/08/2023
115. Interview with Laraine Okorodudu 05/09/2023
116. Interview with Laraine Okorodudu 05/09/2023
117. Interview 05/09/2023
118. Interview 29/08/2023
119. Interview 04/09/2023
120. Interview 20/10/2023
121. Interview 16/08/2023
122. Interview 05/04/2024
123. Interview 27/10/2023
124. Interview 20/10/2023
125. Personal testimony of Benaebi B. Oguoko
126. Tommy Jitubor tells his story,
https://www.youtube.com/watch?v=OQylz5qWCAs&t=1877s accessed 20/05/2024
127. Interview 13/11/2023
128. Interview 16/08/2023
129. Interview 04/09/2023
130. Interview 23/08/2023
131. Interview 13/11/2023
132. Interview 20/10/2023
133. Interview 29/08/2023
134. Interview 29/08/2023
135. Interview with Lawrence Dorgu 13/11/2023
136. Interview 04/09/2023
137. Interview 23/08/2023
138. Interview 05/09/2023
139. Interview 20/10/2023
140. Interview 20/10/2023
141. Interview 20/10/2023
142. Interview 22/08/2023

CHAPTER 10: MAINTAINING AND TRANSFERING IJAW CULTURE IN THE UK

Introduction

Identity is a key theme when tracing the history of a community, whose ancestral roots lie in another "home". For first-generation migrants, living in a different country creates challenges to one's identity and requires adaptation. For the second generation, issues of identity take on a different shape as these children of two "homes" simultaneously inhabit two identity spaces. Where other factors such as race and mixed-race identity come into play, it gets even more complex. The first part of this chapter focuses on the UK-born Ijaw, who we define as those who were born to at least one Ijaw parent in the UK. We trace their initial awareness of, and their definition, construction and reconstruction of both Ijaw and British identities. This chapter also addresses how they maintain connection with and enact both identities and how they resolve any identity conflicts. The second part of the chapter focuses on how culture transfer has occurred within the Ijaw community in the UK and some of the challenges inherent in trying to maintain and transfer Ijaw culture across generations in the UK.

PART A: STORIES OF UK-BORN IJAW PEOPLE: FORMING, MANAGING AND MAINTAINING IDENTITY

Original Connection with the Concept of Being Ijaw

Our interviewees have different recollections of the incorporation of the Ijaw identity into their perception of themselves. For some, these memories are rooted in Ijaw community life in the UK, as well as home life. Joshua was born in Nigeria to Ijaw parents but, moved to the UK at two. He recounts how both events at home and cultural events organised by the Ijaw associations were central to connecting him to his Ijaw identity.

> I remember growing up, I was first learning how to swim. It's funny. My uncle just threw me into the swimming pool. He said, Yeah, like an Ijaw person will never drown. So, you know, that concept. To him, the point of it was, you know, Ijaw people, recognise our connection with the water. We've recognised our connection to that aspect of nature. (Joshua Garry)[143]

> I think I first realised I was an Ijaw person, it kind of came to my attention during, I can't quite remember the exact date, but it was an event of the Ijaw People's Association and the Ijaw Women Association, they had a party. For a part of this party, they created a calendar and on this calendar, you had various pictures of you know, dignitaries, etc. But there was one picture that was captioned the Ijaw people of London. It has all of us sitting down, all of our cousins and family friends, and you know, I was wearing a wrapper. And so, at that point, you know, I was quite clear that okay, I'm Ijaw, because I knew the purpose of the photograph was to capture us young people wearing these wrappers. So, that was when I first realised that okay, I am Ijaw. (Joshua Garry)[144]

Another interviewee who was born in the late 1940's to an Ijaw father and British mother, recounts the more domestic aspects of life as central to creating a connection to his Ijaw identity. He recounts his early days living with his Ijaw father. In these excerpts, food and music play a big part in the memories.

> No matter how early I woke, first thing it's him making his food, cooking, and then his music. And then he would be singing along, and I would say to him, I said Dad, what's the song about and he was, "it's about this man and his wife and they're having a problem, and they broke up and they're trying to, he wants to get her back." (John Kpiaye)[145]

> I have memories of me dancing in, like, brightly coloured, so I'm assuming it was Nigerian cloth, and dancing to Nigerian music. (Edith Akenkide)[146]

For some, this connection occurred by visiting Nigeria and their ancestral Ijaw homelands. One of our interviewees (Archbishop Agama) was born to Ijaw parents in the UK in the 1950's, but spent the early years of his life in the UK. As a child he visited the Ijaw heartlands in Nigeria and remembers rivers, sacred fishing ponds, communal housebuilding and rites associated with growing into manhood. He recounts his experiences of his earliest connecting with his Ijaw roots.

> I paid my very first visits to what is now Bayelsa in the early 1960s. What struck me was the abundance and the freedom. By using these two words, I mean, apart from the fact that everything was big, you know, the rivers were big, the trees were big, much bigger than what you saw in Europe, what they call rivers here, were little streams. In most of the places I visited, even little children paddled canoes on these big rivers freely and went fishing and so on. There are several things that I noticed. I mean, I'm not, you know, umm so familiar with maybe some of the traditions and culture, but I could see certain things, certain patterns that really struck me to make me understand in my, youthful thinking that, here was a people who were highly sophisticated, in the organisation of their community, but also in their relationship with the natural environment around them.[147]

Cementing the Connection

Visiting Nigeria has also served to cement the connection with Ijaw identity and resolve a weak sense of identity.

> So, I made my first trip to Nigeria when I was 18, when I was old enough to get on a plane. I made links with the Ijaw People's Association, and a few people were very supportive and helped me make links with people back home. Mr Doyle was one of them and Mr Paulo, both have now passed. So, when I went to Nigeria, they helped me go to the village and I met my family and I'm still in contact with many of my cousins now. And then when I got back, I then joined the Ijaw People's Association. At some point, I was very active, and I was the welfare officer as well over the years.

> So, that was really a positive experience and when I came back, I felt I knew who I was. I felt, you know because I felt that I was Nigerian, and I was British. And that was the beginning, I think for me, coming into my own. I wasn't confused about my identity after I got back from Nigeria, and I had a plan what I was going to do. So, that was a really positive one. (Edith Akenkide)[148]

Pride in the Ijaw Identity

The connection with this identity sometimes led to a sense of pride, a feeling of belonging and accordingly a desire to enact this identity within the UK society. This also involves trying to showcase the distinctiveness of Ijaw culture when juxtaposed against the dominant ethnic groups of Nigeria;

> I am an Ijaw girl born in the UK. As far as I am concerned, I am 100% Ijaw, I love my culture. And, you know, I identify with my culture. For me, when I wear my Ijaw clothes, and I'm going to one of our cultural events, I'm very happy, I feel very proud to be Ijaw. When I send the pictures to my friends, when I post them on WhatsApp to my friends to say, Oh, I'm at this event, or I'm at that event, the first thing they say is, Oh, my God, look at your outfit. I can't believe it, you know, and couple of occasions, I've taken my English friends to some of our events, and they're just so impressed with the food and fashion. And they just keep coming. Oh my God, look at how the men dress, it is so smart. They just didn't believe that, you know, we have fashion. And yeah, so I'm really happy about that. (Edna Knight)[149]

> There's no way on earth. You could get me in a group amongst Nigerians and I will not say I'm Ijaw, I'll make sure they know, it has to be known" (Joshua Garry)[150]

Embeddedness within Ijaw Culture: Language, Identity and Connection

Language is a central part of culture, often a tool to achieve total immersion in a culture. For some of the UK born Ijaw people, there is a sense of pride at being able to understand the language;

> So, when I go to the meeting, in my IWA, I'm a member now, they speaking Ijaw and I can translate that into English. So, I'm quite happy about that. Even though I can't speak it fluently. I can understand it fluently. So, if you spoke to me, I would be able to tell you what you're saying. (Edna Knight)[151]

For others, there is some sadness at not being able to participate fully due to their lack of fluency in the language;

> So, I can't speak and I'm the youngest of seven, none of us can speak it. And if anything, I can multiply that across the Ijaw people, like all the young Ijaw people I know and speak to in this country, few of them, can speak Ijaw. So, there's no way I can be fully connected and fully immersed in the Ijaw culture, if I can't speak the language. (Joshua Garry)[152]

And still for others, a struggle to claim the identity because of a lack of knowledge of the language and culture.

> You know, I've always been kind of proud to say no, I'm not Jamaican. I'm Nigerian. My father's from Nigeria. I did struggle with saying, I'm Nigerian. For what? Because I didn't feel Nigerian. I didn't feel that because I couldn't speak the language. And I didn't know their culture. Really. It seemed very strange that I will call myself Nigerian. But I've always thought of myself as Pan African. (John Kpiaye)[153]

Managing Ijaw and British Identities

For those who migrated from Nigeria, ethnic identity is often central. For those born in the UK, the reality is different. The UK born Ijaw are simultaneously British and Ijaw. This potentially requires some internal coordination about where, when, and how to enact these different identities. This has sometimes caused some tension especially in youthful stage of life.

> When you're young, when you're in the UK, you're embarrassed, you want to assimilate as much as possible. So, that kind of desire to assimilate meant that, I didn't take my mother's language seriously. I didn't want to listen to it. But equally, and this is something that you know, I'm quite critical of Ijaw people

in comparison to maybe Yoruba people, I don't think my mother or father actually made an effort to teach me Ijaw. (Joshua Garry)[154]

I never really got involved, with the Ijaw meetings and so forth, you know, young, born in England. You know, my head was in other things, you know, and I remember 1967, when the civil war started in Nigeria, and then my Dad, he would come home from work and sit and watch the news. And he would have tears in his eyes, you know, he would say, you know, I want to go home, I want to go home, and fight and you know, that he obviously couldn't and I became very hurt about that whole Biafran thing. (John Kpiaye)[155]

It appeared many Ijaw parents understood this tension and in their own ways tried to help. On the one hand, they wanted to keep the essence of Ijawness alive in their children. But they also realised that, their children must adapt and succeed in the wider UK society. So, we see concerted efforts to create a combination of both worlds. From some narratives, this attempt often has mixed outcomes. Edna Knight recalls her mother's efforts to raise children that were simultaneously Ijaw and British, and talks about her very Ijaw approach to discipline and a nuanced appreciation of the need to fit into British society.

I remember that my mother used to be concerned about making sure that we fitted in, as they would say, into the English lifestyle. And so, she learned how to cook English food. I remember that very well, because she wanted to know how to cook the pies and the soups. And she didn't want us to go to school and not know what these things were. So, she made a point of learning how to cook English foods. And, you know, at least three times a week, we had English foods, and then the rest of the time, we'd have Nigerian foods. (Edna Knight)[156]

Stand firm, tell them you are born here. This is your home; you are lucky to have two cultures. So, make use of it properly. So, my children learn both Nigerian ways of life, and English way and use them to help themselves to achieve their goals today. (Datoru Paul Worika)[157]

Balancing the Assertion of an Ijaw Identity and the Nigerian Identity

There is also some evidence of tension around Ijaw and Nigerian identity in our interviews. For instance, for some, there is the desire to assert Ijaw identity while at the same time, refraining from placing too much emphasis on it and embracing the larger Nigerian identity.

When you look at Nigeria, you understand that it is made up of so many ethnicities. So, growing up, I was very, very clear that, you know, growing up in this context of, a heavy dominated Yoruba culture, the Igbo didn't dominate as much but, you knew about them. It became apparent to me that in some ways, I'm different. And I'm Ijaw. And for a long, long time, I called myself Ijaw before I called myself Nigerian. However, as I've become aware, and as I become more learned, and I've done more reading, I've come to the understanding that ethnic and tribal division is somewhat what's holding us back. So, for me, I put being African above everything else, and I put being Nigerian above everything else. (Joshua Garry)[158]

Stepping outside our interviews, a young Ijaw lady who grew up in the UK wrote a thought-provoking article (https://www.aljazeera.com/features/2021/7/8/being-ijaw-in-the-uk-an-oddity-among-fellow-nigerian-youth) about bringing Ijaw identity into the conversation about Nigerian Identity in the UK. She perceives that the Ijaw culture within the Diaspora exists in an "endangered culture zone" and so feels the need for her Ijaw identity to take primacy.

Igniting wider dialogue about Ijaw tribal erasure and ethnic cultural preservation, is the first step to getting us out of an endangered culture zone. But, these conversations amongst diasporic Ijaw are few. (Stephen-Diver, 2021)

Living in Two Worlds

Some of the UK Ijaw, have interesting experiences of living in two worlds. As we capture in another chapter, there are a number of stories of "Coming, Departing and Returning". Some of the interviewees who were born in the UK, have experiences of living in both Nigeria and the UK. Bishop Agama was born in the UK, lived his early life with white families in London and then moved back to Nigeria as a child. As an adult, he returned to the UK. Here, he recounts adapting to life in Nigeria as a child:

I had a lot of problem adapting to Nigeria. I suppose nowadays, it's not easy to take a kid like that. But in those days, the difference was huge. Even with us being quartered where we were, we were one of the first black families to live in the Amadi flats in the Shell quarters in Port Harcourt, Nigeria. I remember having my very first encounter with a snake there. I didn't know that snakes are dangerous, I thought you could play with them and talk to them as you've seen in cartoons on the television. Then, we moved into the Rumukrushe Camp, which at that time was very small. All the foodstuffs and so on, were being flown in for the benefit of the expatriate community. And it was an international community, with people from Venezuela, from Royal Dutch Shell, and from the UK. My parents, my mother in particular, wanted me to now learn about the food and so on and would make some of the African dishes for me. My problem was more when I went to Nigeria. And when I came back.[159]

I had a British education; we had the British and the Dutch education stream. So, if you spoke Dutch, you went to the Dutch side. We spoke English, went to the English side and I think eventually we were about six black kids including my eldest sister and a couple of other black kids who by that time, had also joined us. But, we were very few and my parents felt that again, I needed to have a taste of Nigeria. So, for one year they sent me to a local primary school. It was an experience I did not want to repeat. I arrived there, they asked me, ''Where was my...? They call it something, that's a knife they used to cut grass. "What do you mean?" And somebody gave me one and said I should cut. They were highly amused by my effort. But, you know, it wasn't a good experience. (Archbishop Agama)[160]

Sokari Ekineh, who is mixed-race, lived in Nigeria and the UK simultaneously for large parts of her childhood and into adulthood;

Growing up of mixed race in Nigeria was always for me, challenging. For my brother, he would always say, it wasn't challenging. And I think that has a lot to do with the fact that he's male, and I'm female. I think that because as a man, as you well know, you can negotiate and be out and about, whereas, you know, I was not allowed to be, you know, galivanting here and there, obviously. So, my, my experience of being of mixed race in Nigeria was not very good. And my experience of being mixed race in England was not that much better, because it was just the opposite. You know, in Nigeria, we were always called half caste, which I found really offensive. Then, once you got to England, it will be "go back where you came from." (Sokari Ekineh)[161]

Identity and the Mixed-Race Ijaw of London

For the Ijaw who were born in the UK to mixed-heritage (race) families, the intersection between race and culture often meant that issues of identity were particularly salient. The early Ijaw communities of the UK had a reasonably large mixed-heritage population. We can now identity the families of Akenkide, Okorodudu, Jituboh, Kpiaye, Okoro, Enekeme, Okudu and a few more to have been mixed heritage. This meant that for some of the children born to these families, there was a sense of belonging within the Ijaw community.

There was a lot of mixed-race people within the Ijaw community back then. I do recall a sense of belonging. (Edith Akenkide)[162]

This sense of belonging (at least for some) can often be contrasted with a general sense of "not belonging" within wider UK society. This often manifested in a very complicated relationship with the UK.

> So, after my dad died, I grew up in a children's home, I was racially abused, which was quite common for black and mixed-race people or people that look different in the UK as it was in the 70s. So, I believed, and I felt I never belonged in this country. (Edith Akenkide)[163]

> I'd say all this time I was probably eighteen, nineteen, twenty, I didn't like white people. I hated the English country in a sense, right? I hated Englishness because it was always about, we were the best in this, we are the greatest in this, we had an empire … and I hated, you know, anything to do with them. So, when in 1966, England was playing Germany at the World Cup, I desperately wanted England to lose. Yeah, me and my Dad were watching it. And he also didn't want them to win, right? This is just the whole experience of being black in England. Yeah? And even though Germans are white, I didn't care, right? I just didn't want the English to win. When England won, I was so upset. It's a weird thing isn't it? That, you're born in a country … (John Kpiaye)[164]

The family circumstances for these mixed-race children, were different. Some maintained connections with their mothers' families, while for others, there was no connection with their mothers' families. This may have led to a greater sense of isolation. However, it appears that experiences within wider society were often similar for both those who were connected and those who were not connected to their mothers' families. Sokari Ekine recounts her experiences of Boarding School in the 1960's in the UK;

> So, when they had the half term, I will go to stay with my grandmother because my grandmother lived there. And then she would sometimes come and visit me at the school. I can't really say much about the school except I didn't like it, put it like that. Yeah. I mean, there were not … I was the only black kid in the school. I was the only person from another country outside of Britain, so it was very weird. Because I played a lot of sports that helped me get through. I played hockey and basketball, netball and athletics. (Sokari Ekineh)[165]

Many of our interviewees from mixed-race families are now in their 60's and 70's and have found ways to reconcile their Ijaw, Nigerian and British identities. The issues they talk about still exist, but the UK has grown into a more tolerant society today than in the 40s, 50's, 60's, 70's and 80's. For some, reconnecting with their white British roots has been very beneficial. Edith Akenkide reconnected with her mother's family in her late 50's. Earlier, she recounted how visiting Nigeria at the age of 18, helped in her journey towards understanding herself. Here, she weaves both stories into a heart-warming narrative;

> So, in 2020 in lockdown, I wasn't in my office from March till September. So, when I went back to my office, I found a letter. And that letter said, "Dear

Edith, I believe that your mom and my mom are sisters, and I'm doing my ancestry.com research. And I really would like to explore more about our family". It was my first cousin from my mom's side. So, since 2020, till now, we've been having communication, building up to when we're physically going to go and have a family reunion. And we did that. In June 2023, my sister flew over from Canada. So, we went to Liverpool and then we went to St. Helens, my mum was actually born in St. Helens. I went to her house where she grew up, went to her school and the area that she grew up in St Helens.[166]

That was really emotional, knowing that we've got a family this is from my mom's side, my mom's family because she married a black man. And that was very common in the 1940s. So, to have this reunion this year, they all knew about us, but they also knew that my mom had married a black man. It was very emotional, but it was happy. And I've made wonderful reconnection with my cousins. My mom's got two sisters. At one point, all the sisters were pregnant at the same time. So, I've got a cousin, Michelle, who was born the same year, but due to racism, we never knew each other. I always say you know, it's never too late. And so, we're building on that from this year. So, both experiences, going back to Nigeria meeting my family, my mom, and my dad's family was wonderful.[167]

Maintaining the Ijaw Culture and Identity in the United Kingdom

Is the Ijaw culture endangered? The word ''endangered,'' connotes a culture on the brink of extinction. This is not the case with the Ijaw. The Ijaw are a prominent tribe in Nigeria. In recent years, they have even produced a President in Nigeria. Outside Nigeria, for those versed in the geo-politics of crude oil, the Ijaw maintain their association with the oil-rich Niger Delta region of Nigeria. But in terms of their culture, their customs, and values, outside Nigeria, and perhaps within the UK, there seems to be less knowledge of the Ijaw among ordinary folk. Is this a case of the Ijaw not promoting and transferring their culture effectively in diasporic communities? Some seem to think so and advocate for greater visibility in the diasporic public sphere.

And in fact, to add to that identity thing, we the Ijaw, we're always taking a backseat, we are never at the centre of things. And, you know, I just said to myself, back in the day, at the High Commission, you know, you don't see the Ijaws freely, but you see others, the Hausas, Yorubas and the Igbos in and out freely, and so on. And so, my wife and I, we got involved at the centre. And eventually, when it was time to take leadership, I put myself forward to be the Chair of the Nigerian community, the very first time an Ijaw person has taken up a position like that. Yeah. So, I had this vision where I could also go on the podium and say, "Aahn Ijaw",[168] you know, those sorts of thing. That is the identity thing and wanting to put that stamp, and I succeeded in doing it. (Dr Douglas Boma)[169]

I do like, go back to the point of making ourselves more visible in the Diaspora. As you know, this country called Nigeria is not just one group of people or two groups of people. (Sokari Ekineh)[170]

Keeping a culture alive, vibrant and visible requires not just engagement in the diasporic public sphere, but also transferring the culture through the generations.

But as our people here, it is very, very imperative that we keep the culture going. We should continue to instil our culture in them, especially our language, because our children, if they can't speak our language, it will be a major problem going forward. (Eperebofori John Opuogulaya)[171]

The next sub-section addresses two salient challenges of culture transfer and maintenance for the Ijaw in the UK. Following this, some of the ways the Ijaw of the UK have historically attempted to keep the culture alive and relevant, are highlighted and current efforts to maintain Ijaw, language and culture in the UK are explored.

Challenges of Culture Transfer: Keeping the Language(s) alive in the Diaspora

The question of language pops up severally in this project. From the narratives, many feel this aspect of keeping the language alive among younger generations, is one where there have been missed opportunities. There seem to be many angles to this issue. A younger UK-born Ijaw man sees it this way:

As for myself, honestly speaking, I think at the time, and it's not a criticism, I don't think our parents immediately recognised the importance. But apart from our not recognising the importance, I think our parents were bombarded with so, many challenges. So, many layers of injustice in the UK, that really, they didn't necessarily have the headspace for that. Some of them had immigration challenges. So, that's a tension. You know, they've got to find work, but some are working menial jobs. They're confronting racism, discrimination, in addition to, you know, situations that are happening within the family. So, I think of course, if my mother could turn back the hands of time, she would have had a much more concerted effort to teach the language to me. But I think, at that time, in context of all the stuff that was going on, and what they did, in what they placed importance on, they just simply didn't place it on, learning language. That's my opinion. This is not a fact. I can't say that you know, this is the case, just what I think from observation. (Joshua Garry)[172]

But, there are possibly other issues to consider here. One is the multiplicity of Ijaw dialects. The Ijaw see themselves as one people, but among the Ijaw people there are many dialects, which are sometimes not mutually intelligible. This means that in certain areas where Ijaw conversations might be relevant, there is likely to be a reverting to English.

> Although, we are the same but because we have Ijaw-Okrika and we also have Ijaw Sagbama, we have Ijaw-Kalabari. (Paul Worika)[173]

Another challenge to keeping the language alive, is the limited opportunity for transfer, especially through the family unit. One main reason for this is that the number of Ijaw marriages have dwindled over time. Transferring a language that does not have a wider societal presence is difficult when none or only one parent speaks or understands it.

> Because of my marriage to a non-Ijaw person, my children cannot speak the Ijaw language. They can speak their mother's language; the Ijaw language they can understand but they cannot speak it. But the good thing is they understand Ijawness, and they are reading Ijaw books, the provisions they have, they have these tapes now. They still read Ijaw books often, but they make sure their own children don't make the mistake I made. (Rowland Ekperi)[174]

> I think the continuity is non-existent. I think it's dying if I'm being honest. The last Ijaw wedding[175] I remember was in like, 1998. So, for almost two or three decades there hasn't been any Ijaw marriages. And you've got to remember that many of our parents came to this country with Ijaw partners. I've only seen one Ijaw wedding in this country and in the UK. I'm one of seven. None of my siblings married Ijaw people and they live in Nigeria. So, of seven people from just my parents' lineage, none of us have married Ijaw. So, of course, there are salient and worrying questions about continuity, because not only do you have a situation where none of us could speak our language, they are not as connected with the Ijaw Peoples and the Ijaw Women's Association as I was. (Joshua Garry)[176]

Joshua Garry suggests that the issue of no marriages among Ijaw UK, stems from ideas passed on by parents that sometimes blurred the lines between members of the community and family. In essence, in a bid to keep the community cohesive, everyone was seen as family.

> I'll give a lot of credit to the IPA and the IWA, the parties that they held were amazing and the community it created. I call them my cousins.[177] I think we kind of made a mistake, calling everyone our cousins, because that's why we don't have any Ijaw weddings anymore. So, first thing first, I'm gonna set up when I have kids, unless you are a bonafide blood relative, it's all fair game, you can marry them. I'll let them know that this person here, they are not your family, they're not your cousin. (Joshua Garry)[178]

Figure 48. Ijaw children in London performimg in honour of Ms Ibiba Don Pedro, the CNN African Journalist of the year, 2003.

Keeping the Younger Generation Engaged in the Associations.

The pioneers of many of these Ijaw associations are gone. Others who are very active now are getting older and there are sometimes fears that the culture within the UK will suffer or disappear, if increased participation from the younger generations is not achieved.

> The elders were a bit scared that the community might be extinct because the youngsters were not joining or showing interest. (Eperebofori Opuogulaya)

There are also concerns that part of the reasons for dwindling participation is that some view aspects of Ijaw culture as incompatible with Christianity.

> I think some people think the tradition, our culture is not relevant, that sort of attitude has come into the mind. Before we used to play masquerade[179] and all those things. Nowadays, anytime, even if you sing a song, some will take it as if you are singing to an idol or you are not a believer. (Paul Worika)[180]

The Role of the Associations in Maintaining Izon (Ijaw) Culture

Central to culture transfer within the UK, has been the role of the Ijaw associations. Prominent among these associations are the IPA, IWA and other related associations. Although there is a perception that the Ijaw Associations are not as influential as they used to be, those who grew up with these societies and for whom participation in the associations' events[181] was at some point a fixture of their lives, understand the impact of the associations.

> I would say for me, personally, the most important thing the two organisations did was connect young Ijaw people who may have never been connected before. In fact, just yesterday, I had several people here for a barbecue, you know. So, it means that I've got friends, cousins, I've got people that's the biggest thing it's given us. It's given us people. And it's given us a sense of identity. We know that we're Ijaw. And we know what in some capacity, we know what it means to be Ijaw. (Joshua Garry)[182]

> There were cultural meetings where the women would all get together. And basically, it's women living in the UK, London, mostly, they would get together once a month. They would basically talk about the things happening in, you know, their villages back home. They would talk and welcome new members that have come from Nigeria, you know, acclimatised them get them used to where things are about finding jobs. It was just basically everybody networking and supporting each other. And then they used to do classes, like Ijaw lessons. We used to do Ijaw lessons, they used to give us lessons on tying wrapper and, you know, the headscarf. And then you know, once a year, at least we'd have a party, where we'd invite other different Nigerian groups. And so yeah, I mean, we kept the tradition. I know how to cook Nigerian foods; my mother taught me; I know how to tie wrapper. I know how to basically tie the 'gele'. And yes, you know, basically, the values were that, you know, we would help whoever we can, wherever we can, we also want to make sure we keep our tradition. (Edna Knight)[183]

Hopes and Plans

The Ijaw associations still operate today. Their role within the diasporic public sphere persists. While there is a prevailing sense that they are not as influential as they once were in the lives of the Ijaw people living in London or the UK, there are hopes, plans and engagements afoot, to keep these associations thriving and relevant to the Ijaw community.

> I think the Ijaw People's Association, I think it's so crucial. I think it's so relevant now. I think it's absolutely crucial it's still there. It plays a role in society, because a lot of Ijaw people, regardless of if you are mixed race, or you from Nigerian, or you British, British people, the culture, the language, the food, the dancing. And I would love to see just how you go to do ballroom dance and you do Ijaw dancing, you know, how you got Bake Off, you could have, you know, cooking classes of Ijaw food, Ijaw fashion. Because I do think what my Dad and other members started was really relevant. It was so important back then. And I still think it's so important in our culture and in our society today that it continues. (Edith Akenkide)[184]

Figure 49. Members of the Izon Community of London at the Burial of an Izon person.

Maintaining the language seems to be one of the top priorities. In that sense, there are plans and endeavours to keep the language alive.

> You know, our idea is to have an Ijaw school here to teach the children that are born here, to be able to speak the language. (Rev Francis Akpanari)[185]

> We have Wakirike language teachers here who are helping our children. We have a problem because we didn't start early. We have classes every Monday. I mean, Sunday month end as well. (Datoru Paul Worika)[186]

Improving participation and especially the participation of younger people in the community associations, is another key endeavour. Both younger and more senior members of the community are playing a key part in this;

> And when I joined, I now was able to influence and invite people within my age group to join, because most members were elders. So, when I joined, I started inviting my peers to join. And I was made the secretary at the time and whilst I was secretary, I used that to, you know, to help develop the

organisation, reach out to our members, put in place, welfare packages, that will help our elders, reach out to them, and help them in various areas, like members that require mobile wheelchairs, making contributions to help in those areas. So basically, my contribution here, even now as president, is basically bringing the Ijaws together, bringing the Wakirike people together, you know, for us to bring our various experience, knowledge and qualification together to help build ourselves. (John Eperebofori Opuogulaya)[187]

And I want to help, get the next generation to be involved in the Ijaw traditions and culture, learning how to cook. And, you know, also, wanting to go back home and see what that's all about as well. (Edna Knight)[188]

Conclusion

The Diaspora cultural transfer process involves a back-and-forth translation and reconfiguration of symbols, customs, traditions, and practices. This is certainly the case for the Ijaw community in the UK. As the community is slowly refreshed by new arrivals from Nigeria and as those born in the UK interact with these newer migrants, Ijaw culture in the UK will continue to evolve.

REFERENCES

143. Interview 29/08/2023
144. Interview 29/08/2023
145. Interview 27/10/2023
146. Interview 20/10/2023
147. Interview with Archbishop Doye Agama 16/08/2023
148. Interview 20/10/2023
149. Interview 04/09/2023
150. Interview 29/08/2023
151. Interview 04/09/2023
152. Interview 29/08/2023
153. Interview 27/10/2023
154. Interview 29/08/2023
155. Interview 27/10/2023
156. Interview 04/09/2023
157. Interview 13/10/2023
158. Interview 29/08/2023
159. Interview with Archbishop Doye Agama 16/08/2023
160. Interview 16/08/2023
161. Interview 14/09/2023
162. Interview 20/10/2023
163. Interview 20/10/2023

164. Interview 27/10/2023
165. Interview 14/10/2023
166. Interview with Edith Akenkide 20/10/2023
167. Interview with Edith Akenkide 20/10/2023
168. An Ijaw form of greeting in social gatherings
169. Interview 14/10/2023
170. Interview 14/09/2023
171. Interview 23/08/2023
172. Interview 29/08/2023
173. Interview 13/10/2023
174. Interview 12/11/2023
175. Among the Ijaw born in the UK
176. Interview 29/08/2023
177. Ijaw family and friends he grew up with
178. Interview 29/08/2023
179. Traditional Masquerade dances of the Ijaw
180. Interview 13/10/2023
181. We have discussed some of these events in the general history chapter.
182. Interview 29/08/2023
183. Interview 04/09/2023
184. Interview 20/10/2023
185. Interview 22/08/2023
186. Interview 13/10/2023
187. Interview 23/08/2023
188. Interview 04/09/2023

CHAPTER 11. THE IZON (IJAW) DIASPORA AND RELATIONS WITH THE IZON HOMELAND

There are many different definitions of the word "diaspora". However, one commonly accepted feature of the concept is that Diaspora assumes a homeland that can be returned to, even if this notion of return is virtual or metaphorical (Vardanyan, 2016). The concept of 'home' has always been an important one for Diaspora citizens as they think through how to relate to both to the home of their origins and the home where they live. This is certainly the case for the Ijaw of the United Kingdom. For many diasporic Ijaw, there is this simultaneous construction, shaping and definition of their relationship with the United Kingdom alongside a desire to connect and engage in issues in Nigeria. This process is evident both for those who left Nigeria for the UK as well as, for those born in the UK and for whom the concept of home may have different connotations. Indeed, even for many who have never visited Nigeria, this idea of Nigeria as home has significance;

> I definitely need to go and visit both my villages and my, you know, my maternal home as well. (Joshua Garry)[189]

This pull of the original homeland, often gives rise to Diaspora engagement with their home countries. The relationship between the Diaspora and home can often be seen as a two-way relationship; political engagement that link constituencies in one country with a homeland somewhere else (diaspora politics) (Adamson, 2016) and one where the home communities seek greater engagement with the UK Diaspora through Diaspora-oriented policies and programmes (diaspora policies) (Gamlen, 2006). In this chapter, while we note the inclusionary policies of the Ijaw community towards the Ijaw Diaspora, we focus predominantly on one arm of that relationship: the directional relationship between the UK Ijaw Diaspora and the Ijaw communities in Nigeria. While the focus is mainly on the Ijaw communities, many contributions and engagements are directed also at the larger Niger-Delta region and the country as a whole. We do not adopt a strictly chronological perspective in our discussion, but instead paint an overall picture utilising mainly interviews with Ijaw people in the UK as well as historical records to establish these narratives. Five main themes can be extracted from analysing these sources.

1. Diaspora Politics
2. Contributions to Institutions
3. Humanitarian and charity contributions to communities
4. Engagement with other Diaspora organizations and efforts
5. Contributions to family members and staying connected.

THEME 1: DIASPORA POLITICS

The issues that affect Ijaw land and the Niger Delta have implications for the world due to Nigeria's position as an oil producer. In that sense, Diaspora politics have significance beyond enlightened self-interest of the Ijaw peoples. Before we detail the ways in which the UK Ijaw community has engaged in Diaspora politics, it is useful to trace the history of the self-determination struggle of the Ijaw people of Nigeria.

The Ijaw (Ijo, Izon) people of Nigeria are the largest ethnic nationality of the Niger Delta Region (NDR) of Nigeria. There are also sizeable Ijaw populations in Ghana and Cameroon.

Before the Nigerian Civil War (1967-1970), there were four regions in Nigeria. The largest was the Northern Region. To the west of the river Niger was Western region, Midwest region, east of the river Niger was the Eastern region.

> Niger Delta was also split into two, one attached to the eastern region, the other attached to the western region. The Niger Delta has always struggled to be an independent region, but nobody allowed them to do that before the civil war, during the civil war and after the civil war (Aliyi Ekineh)[190]

This desire for self-determination in the Niger Delta, is linked to the Ijaw self-determination story. The quest for self-determination for Ijaw people can be traced to the 1950's. While the precise dates are contested, the discovery of oil in the region was a catalyst. Following the discovery of oil, this region which is responsible for producing much of Nigeria's wealth became and has for many decades been one of the most deprived regions in the nation. This deprivation led to the formation of political groups and movements in Nigeria, aimed at self-determination and greater control of the oil resources of the region. One of the central figures in the narrative of Ijaw nationalism and self-determination is Isaac Adaka Boro.

Shortly before the Nigerian Civil War began, Boro and his army annexed the Ijaw lands and declared a Niger Delta Republic, which some historians have referred to as a "desperate cry for some sort of political inclusion" (Watts 2003, p. 21). This uprising and the death of Isaac Boro is for many, the first key moment in the Ijaw self-determination history. Prior to this uprising, Boro had documented his anger at the Nigerian state for neglecting the Niger Delta remarking that:

> Year after year, we were clenched in tyrannical chains and led through a dark alley of perpetual political and social deprivation. Strangers in our own country [...] the day will come for us to fight for our long denied right to self-determination [...] If Nigerian governments refuse to do something drastic to improve the lot of the people, a point of no return will be reached. (Boro, 1982, p. 66)[191]

The second major turning-point in the narrative of Ijaw self-determination was the killing of Ken Saro-Wiwa. Saro-Wiwa's execution by the Nigerian State was seen not only as an Ogoni issue; the Ijaw constructed it as an event that affected them too, especially the young people in the Ijaw Youth Council (IYC) in Nigeria who launched their 'Operation climate change' in 1998, as they gathered to draw attention to their severely degraded environment through oil and gas exploration and production. This was the same issue earlier championed by Saro-Wiwa and the Ogoni people in the mid-1990s. Just as Ijaws in Nigeria responded to this, there was a complementary response from the UK Diaspora. In many ways, for a generation of UK Ijaw citizens who grew up after the Nigerian Civil War, this was a turning point.

> Yeah, I think I'm not sure. But I think that was probably from around the early days of Ken Saro-Wiwa, because my father talked about that a lot. And I think even for himself, that became a point when he became more active in the context of how the people of the Niger Delta, how they exist in relation to the Nigerian State, given the production of oil. (Sokari Ekineh: activist and writer)[192]

Throughout these times, Ijaw communities abroad have continued to engage with issues affecting the Ijaws in Nigeria. We detail these forms of engagement under three sub-themes.

• Diaspora role in homeland politics: support for homeland political institutions and political agendas
• Diaspora role in homeland politics: Diaspora citizens becoming active in homeland politics.
• Diaspora roles in consciousness-raising:

Diaspora Role in Homeland Politics: Support for Homeland Political Institutions and Political Agendas

> I'm still of the opinion that many of the decisions that affect places like Nigeria are taken outside Nigeria. And the Diaspora needs to be aware of their potential

when it comes to influencing what happens in and to the nations of their origins. (Archbishop Agama)[193]

Institutionally, Diaspora politics of the Ijaws in the UK has often been funnelled through the Ijaw Peoples Association, which was founded in London in 1948. Over time, perhaps highlighting the multiplicities inherent in Ijaw identity other organizations have emerged. For example, the Wakirike Community of the United Kingdom and Ireland have existed since 1953.

> Because at the time, we were not very keen on grouping ourselves under the IPA. So, the Wakirike, the Kalabari, and others in the Ijaw nation, came together and called ourselves the Federation of Ijaw Communities. And then from there, we later decided that the best way is to call ourselves the Ijaw National Congress, the name used in Nigeria. (Datoru Paul Worika)[194]

There are other clan-based associations such as the Kabowei Ogbo clan association which was formed in 1994. Other institutions have been formed in the UK with specific strategic goals and projects related to Ijaws in mind. One of such organizations is Izon Egberi. These organizations have become complementary avenues through which Ijaw people in the UK have engaged in Diaspora affairs and in many ways have enriched the Ijaw "diasporic public sphere" (Laguerre, 2005) in the UK.

Despite the presence of other associations, the Ijaw People's Association has often taken the lead role in Diaspora politics. As far the Ijaw associations in the UK are concerned, engagement in Diaspora politics dates back as far as the 1950's.

Diaspora Role in Homeland Politics: Diaspora Citizens Becoming Active in Homeland Politics and Issues.

Another key theme of engagement in Diaspora politics, is how citizens in the Diaspora became active in homeland politics and issues. For some, direct involvement in homeland politics has been the route. Some Ijaw in the UK have returned to Nigeria to take up public service appointments. Many of them have utilised their work experience and skills in these public service environments. One of the interviewees highlights this issue.

> I served as Senior Special Assistant on technical services with Goodluck Jonathan when he was a governor. Then, when he became vice president that's when I worked with the Niger Delta technical committee and contributed towards the initiatives that brought about the amnesty program. I also served under Seriake Dickson (another governor of Bayelsa State in Nigeria) as Senior Specialist Assistant in the same position, technical services. (Ombrai Oguoko)[195]

Others have used their skills to engage directly with institutions back home to affect change.

> That was at the time of Ken Saro-Wiwa, so, I just began to get involved with certain people in Port Harcourt, people like Oronto Douglas, I forget people's names now, Jennifer Pere, who was with the Niger Delta Women for Justice. So, I sought those people out, and then I built a relationship with them. And then I started working mostly in terms of using my knowledge of what was happening there and writing about it.[196]

Even when circumstances have conspired to derail such endeavours, many Ijaw citizens find ways to continue their efforts to engage:

> I had entered a PhD programme at Leeds University and what I wanted to look at was violence against women by the oil companies and the Nigerian state Unfortunately, I got sick, so I dropped out of my PhD programme, but I decided I still wanted to do the research. So, I raised some funds personally and then got in touch with Oronto and NDWJ. It was a huge project, Jennifer and I; we travelled throughout, Rivers State, Bayelsa and Delta State talking to different women who were impacted by oil and the Nigerian state. So that was an eye opener to both me and Jennifer. So, out of that I published a research paper.[197]

Diaspora Roles in Consciousness-raising

A third sub-theme of Diaspora politics is Diaspora roles in raising consciousness. Throughout the years, the Ijaw Diaspora in the UK have contributed significantly to increasing awareness about issues affecting the Ijaw communities specifically and by extension the Niger Delta region of Nigeria. These activities involve writing, education of foreign entities, lobbying, and protests and so on. Speaking about writing;

> I felt my role was to write in the Diaspora about what was happening. And I maintained contact with all the activists who were working in the Niger Delta, some were based in Port Harcourt, and some were based in Bayelsa as well. So, I maintained, regular contact with them. So, when something happened, I would write about it. So, the idea was that I was publishing this in the Diaspora. (Sokari Ekineh)[198]

Speaking about raising awareness on the international scene,

> We came up with the idea of a Boro Day and we internationalised the Boro Day event. Subsequently every governor, the 6 states of the Niger Delta, was represented in an annual Boro Day event here in the UK. What was the purpose of that event? We wanted to bring the Ijaw case, the injustice that the Nigerian

state has meted out to the Ijaw people, the crime of the oil companies against Ijaw people to the international scene.[199]

And through those events we were also able to bring the Ijaws all over Europe, the Ijaws in America to come here to share discussions. We had symposiums; we had conferences within those events to make sure we have a blueprint for Ijaw land. So, the events were to make sure we control the development agenda of Niger Delta and Ijaw land. (Rowland Ekperi, former President of the IPA)[200]

Protests have also been one method the UK Ijaw Diaspora have utilised, to raise public awareness of issues affecting the Ijaws and the Niger Delta;

Yeah, we were protesting against Shell, and we decided the best way to draw attention to ourselves was to chain ourselves up. And you know, so we're all chained together and padlocked. So, we sat across the road, the street, or is it Northumberland Avenue, I think we sat across there. So, we completely blocked the traffic. And, you know, we had placards, etc., etc., to highlight what was happening regarding the oil and Shell. (Sokari Ekineh)[201]

Where there are issues in Ijaw land, we will carry placards, in fact my children they love that. They are all grown up and are successful people, but they like to go and demonstrate with cousins and me. (Rowland Ekperi)

In addition to raising public awareness, there have been efforts to engage directly with the UK government and policy makers to act on issues;

We've educated the British policymakers on what's really happening in the Niger Delta. We made presentation to the parliamentary group for Niger Delta. We have been invited to Chatham House to speak about issues affecting the Niger-Delta and Nigeria. (Rowland Ekperi)[202]

Within these narratives there is a clear understanding of how various activities influence each other. For example, Rowland Ekperi speaking about events organised by the IPA in the UK suggest that programmes abroad had an impact back home;

It was one of those things that brought about the creation of OMPADEC. You most probably have heard about OMPADEC. OMPADEC gradually became what is now NDDC. (Rowland Ekperi)

While there is often a smooth relationship between home and Diaspora citizens, Diaspora views have sometimes conflicted with the views of Ijaw organizations in Nigeria. For example, in 2022, The IPA had to distance themselves from reports credited to its President regarding a popular amnesty programme for Ijaw militants. This perhaps highlights the idea that Diaspora views on issues affecting the homeland are not always homogeneous. Accordingly, sometimes, the claim to speak for diasporic opinion is sometimes contested in the diasporic public sphere (Laguerre, 2005).

THEME 2: HELPING AND STRENGTHENING INSTITUTIONS

One way the Ijaw people in the UK have contributed is collaborating and strengthening of institutions back home. These may be political institutions, public, cultural and professional institutions associated with Ijaw interests. Sometimes this effort is channelled through the IPA; sometimes it is channelled through other partner institutions. One of such institutions is Izon Egberi;

> With the collaboration of the IPA, now we're doing something as Izon Egberi. First, we have created awareness of the pains we are inflicting on ourselves first. That contribution is vital to me so, we don't repeat the same mistake that will undermine our collective interest when we come against external people outside Ijaw land. Second is bridge building, focusing on the unity and love for one another, instead of the divisiveness that politicians have brought. Through that promotion and awareness that we created, there's some sort of unity in some clans.[203]

This focus sometimes broadens to the wider Nigerian context, for instance, collaborating with and strengthening professional institutions. Dr Douglas Boma talks about how as an engineer in the UK, he has worked to improve the relationship between engineers of Nigerian origin in the UK with the Nigeria Society of Engineers. As a forum, they organised events that included the Nigeria Society of Engineers and presented qualified candidates for Chartership with the Nigeria Society of Engineers. Such endeavours have yielded returns:

> Now, one other point I have not been able to highlight was this thing about my relationship with the Nigerian engineers here in the United Kingdom. There is an organisation called the Engineering Forum of Nigerians. And I was the president of that body for nearly four years. A former Secretary of our forum was called up by OBJ to resuscitate the Nigerian railways. So that today, the railway is operational is because they pulled that man from here to Nigeria, and that's how the Nigerian railway came alive. (Dr Boma Douglas)[204]

THEME 3: ASSISTING COMMUNITIES

> And I think that now for me, what I want to do is I want to do things more to help people in my community in Kaiama. And that's what I'm going to be doing. (Edna Knight)

These words from an interviewee who was born to Ijaw parents who moved to the UK in the 1950's, captures the sentiments of many of the Ijaw people in the UK. Indeed, such contributions to communities in the homeland is central to how the Ijaw in the UK engage with the homeland. These contributions take many forms and often involve the channelling of both individual and institutional efforts. One prominent area of focus is supporting healthcare and water provision;

> Through Izon Egberi, we are contributing to the healthcare centres in various communities. We are doing it community by community; the government has health centres that the government don't fund. They don't even buy the drugs, but Izon Egberi is doing that as well. (Rowland Ekperi)[205]

> I'm currently in the middle of providing two boreholes for the secondary school in Kaiama. One will be accessed by the children in the school; the other borehole will be accessed by the whole community. So, the community is going to benefit. And then the next project I'm looking at is they've got a medical centre, they have the building, but they have no equipment. So that's the next project I'm going to be looking at. So, as far as I'm concerned, this is a way of giving back to my community. My mother and father helped their community when they were alive. And I just want to carry that on. So that's what I'm going to, that's what I want to be doing. That's the vocation I've got. (Edna Knight)[206]

Another area is flood. Floods are a recurring environmental issue due to the riverine nature of the terrain where the Ijaw live in Nigeria.

> Now, also in 2010, I joined the Ijaw National Congress, Europe, and then I was made the financial secretary. And one of the initiatives, one of the things we did was to help our people back home with, I think, in 2012, there was a major flood back home that affected a lot of people. And what we did, we came together contributed not just money, medical facilities, clothing, and all that, and shipped them to Nigeria. And we as members travelled to Nigeria went to various communities that were affected and distributed these medical equipment. (John Eperebofori Opuogulaya)[207]

Education is also a key avenue for engagement;

There was one time they (IPA) raised funds, and I went to Nigeria, I was given monies, and myself and my friend, colleague, Jennifer, we went and we bought different items, which we then distributed to schools Yeah, I think that was the time of the Odi invasion. (Sokari Ekineh)[208]

We (Izon Egberi) are also providing school desks to communities as well. We are also providing school uniforms to some communities. Then, we also tried to set up some scholarship fund for some persons from very poor background; to finance their education through to university level. We don't have enough resources to do as many as possible. (Rowland Ekperi)[209]

But what we're trying to do at the moment now is to promote something that probably you guys have been aware of. Back to farm, a concept that Oyakhilome promoted in Rivers State. We are trying to do that in our schools in Ijaw land. We're taking it one by one. Now from the primary school level, from primary five, and six, so on and so forth, we should encourage our younger ones to go back to farm to do farming.[210]

There is a project I want to do in the village, right now. My dad left the house in the village, and they are using it as a school. So, I want to sponsor the school properly. So, they can use the building, or we can get a bigger building for them. (Eneilayefa Edonya)[211]

Finally, there are also efforts to ensure the continuity of the Ijaw culture and language within communities in Nigeria:

Many persons don't know the strategic support that we give from out here … to make our people back home aware that Ijaw language must be preserved. We are doing all that. Now Gbaramatu is a typical case in Ijaw land. Patani, we're trying to do that in Patani as well. We are losing the Ijaw language Patani is now trying to emulate what is happening in Gbaramatu kingdom and see whether we can encourage all Ijaw local councils that they must promote Ijaw culture in schools.[212]

THEME 4: THE IJAW IN THE UK AND COLLABORATION WITH OTHER IJAW COMMUNITIES IN THE DIASPORA

The idea that a wider Diaspora exists, is not lost on the Ijaw of the United Kingdom. There is a realisation that collective efforts of the wider Diaspora, can drive change efforts more effectively. There are many diasporic organizations that Ijaw people of the UK are involved with;

I'm also a member the Ijaw Diaspora Council. I've been a member for the last two years in that organisation. And I think it's important to engage with other Ijaw people, not only in the UK, I mean, in Australia, in America.[213]

And, you know, last year when we had the floods in certain villages, even my own village, we helped, to fundraise to get water purification tablets, to get grain, food rice, with the help of the Red Cross, and that was done with the IDC. This year, we actually already put out things to tell people to be aware of, you know, the floods. Because, last year, they were really bad. And we're informing people about what they need to prepare for floods. So, that's a new venture that I've gone into, and I'm looking forward to, to working more with them. And then also the Ijaw women of America. I've was at a Day event, too, for the last two years. And the Ijaw women of America, they've projects to build solar panels in several villages, and I believe they've done at least 10 or 12 or so. Yeah, so I'm you know, I'm just a sponsor for them to keep funds so that that project can go ahead, and those projects are going ahead. (Edna Knight)[214]

Now, also is it in 2010, I joined the Ijaw National Congress, Europe, and then I was made the financial secretary. (Eperebofori Opuogulaya)[215]

THEME 5: CONNECTING WITH FAMILY

Maintaining a connection to home takes different forms. For some it is maintaining constant communication with families in Nigeria and sometimes offering economic assistance. For some, visiting home has become a key part of their relationship with home. Frequent visits home help to solidify the connection with families and communities in Nigeria.

I travel home almost every year. Every year I go, in fact, even last year, I went home twice. (Datoru Paul Worika)[216]

For some, visiting home may present more challenges;

There are a few of our people who find it difficult maybe because they think of accommodation back home, the life that they have here is not what they want it to be, so, they don't want to go home.[217]

Conclusion

The UK Ijaw community in London has become a powerful force for political and cultural mobilization and is expected to play even a bigger role as members continue to forge links with other Ijaw Diaspora communities and with the Ijaw communities in Nigeria. In the same vein, there is a concerted effort by Ijaw communities and associations in Nigeria to reach out in many ways to the Ijaw communities in London in search of economic and political support. This two-way process has often functioned well over the years. In the future, as the Ijaw community of the UK evolves and includes more people who may only know the homeland conceptually, managing this two-way relationship may require different strategies and approaches as the younger generation integrate more and more into the wider UK culture as British citizens of Ijaw descent.

REFERENCES

189. Interview 29/08/2023
190. Interview received from Sokari Ekineh on 14/09/2023
191. Tebekaemi T, Editor (1982) *The Twelve Day Revolution* by Isaac Boro, p. 66, Mai-Bornu, Z. (2020). *Dynamics of leadership styles within the Ogoni and Ijaw movements in the Niger Delta.* Journal of Social and Political Psychology, 8(2), 823-850.
192. Interview 14/09/2023
193. Interview 16/08/2023
194. Interview 13/10/2023
195. Interview 21/08/2023
196. Interview with Sokari Ekineh 14/09/2023
197. Interview with Sokari Ekineh 14/09/2023
198. Interview 14/09/2023
199. Interview with Rowland Ekperi 12/11/2023
200. Interview 12/11/2023
201. Interview 14/09/2023
202. Interview 12/11/2023
203. Interview with Rowland Ekperi 12/11/2023
204. Interview 14/10/2023
205. Interview 12/11/2023
206. Interview 04/09/2023
207. Interview 23/08/2023
208. Interview 14/09/2023
209. Interview 12/11/2023
210. Interview with Rowland Ekperi 12/11/2023
211. Interview 09/10/2023
212. Interview with Rowland Ekperi 12/11/2023
213. Interview with Edna Knight 04/09/2023
214. Interview 04/09/2023

215. Interview 23/08/2023
216. Interview 13/10/2023
217. Interview with Datoru Ben Paul Worika 13/10/2023

BIBLIOGRAPHY

Lampert, B. (2009). *Diaspora and development? Nigerian organizations in London and the transnational politics of belonging.* Global Networks, 9(2), 162-184.

Eberlein, R. (2006). *On the road to the state's perdition? Authority and sovereignty in the Niger Delta, Nigeria.* The Journal of Modern African Studies, 44(4), 573-596.

Mai-Bornu, Z. (2020). *Dynamics of leadership styles within the Ogoni and Ijaw movements in the Niger Delta.* Journal of Social and Political Psychology, 8(2), 823-850.

Tabar, P. & Jaulin, T. *Workshop 12: Diaspora Politics and Diaspora Policies.*

Demir, I. (2012). *Battling with memleket in London: the Kurdish diaspora's engagement with Turkey.* Journal of Ethnic and Migration Studies, 38(5), 815-831.

Mai-Bornu, Z. L., (2020). *Historical Narratives of the Ogoni and the Ijaw. Political Violence and Oil in Africa: The Case of Nigeria,* 85-128.

Gamlen, A. (2006) *Diaspora Engagement Policies: What are they, and what kinds of states use them?* Centre on Migration, Policy and Society, Working Paper No. 32, University of Oxford.

Adamson, F. B. (2016). *The growing importance of Diaspora politics.* Current History, 115(784), 291-297.

Sheffer, G. (2003). *Diaspora politics: At home abroad.* Cambridge University Press.

Laguerre, M. S. (2005). *Homeland political crisis, the virtual diasporic public sphere, and diasporic politics.* Journal of Latin American and Caribbean Anthropology, 10(1), 206-225.

Vardanyan, V. (2016). *Homeland and Diaspora: Connection Through Spaces.* Culture, 6(14), 75-84.

CHAPTER 12: CONTRIBUTIONS OF IJAW PEOPLE TO IJAW COMMUNITY AND LONDON SOCIETY: AN INTRODUCTION

This chapter seeks to highlight the outstanding contributions of some selected Ijaw persons from various professional sectors and social standing, an all-round view, through their professional and community volunteer activities, to the Ijaw community and the wider London society. It seeks to document how Ijaw people in the UK are utilising their talents, resources and impacting the wider society.

Contributing can be addressed in two complementary ways: first, from an objective perspective by measuring how actions of Ijaw migrants and their descendants have made a discernible impact on UK society, and second, from a motivational lens: by investigating the motivation to make some discernible impact in a sphere of society. Taking this into account, this chapter begins by extracting from interviews the motivations that underpin the contributions Ijaw people have made to the UK. Following this, the chapter includes brief portraits of some people who have contributed to various sectors of UK society. Beyond the people profiled in this chapter, there are myriad of other ways Ijaw people have participated in and benefitted UK society which cannot be captured in this book.

For the Ijaw person born in the UK, contributing to society occurs more organically as the UK is the first home. The motivation to contribute to the other home, Nigeria, comes with the increased connection with the home of their parents. We capture some of these in the chapter on Ijaw Diaspora-home relationships. For Ijaw people who have moved from Nigeria to the UK, the gradual redefinition of "home" is often a catalyst for the motivation to contribute to society. The narratives in our interviews suggest that engagement often starts with a realisation that the UK is now home, but also as a result of beginning to feel a sense of "home" in the UK. Sometimes, a key point in this transition to seeing the UK as home occurs when children are born, or other key milestones are achieved. The shift from stranger to citizen, is a core theme in our interviews and a key driver of the process of broader engagement.

> I don't say I'm a stranger here. I got involved with the people I call my local community and London in general. (Datoru Paul Worika)[218]

While this shift from stranger to citizen has been relatively easier for some, there is a perception that the transition is perhaps more difficult or challenging for some and one that limits their potential to contribute to wider society. This idea of seeing oneself as a stranger or visitor versus a citizen, is explored more by Bishop Agama:

> Ethnic identities are good, once they are kept in the perspective. Everybody needs to have an identity, but then you're also a citizen of this earth beyond that. So, you should not allow the ethnic identity to restrain you from contributing to and benefiting from the wider blessings. I say this because many of our people, not just the Ijaw people, but many people of ethnic minorities have made themselves permanent strangers, such that even their children end up not really know who they are. I think time has come when we have to be very clear. We have to be very clear. That yes, this is your ethnicity, but the world is your oyster. And if we don't do that, it will be a very long time before we start seeing maybe an Ijaw Prime Minister in the UK and what is wrong with that? Anyway, what I mean is, we should not because of the beauty of ethnicity start, inadvertently, self-excluding ourselves. And then we complain that we are being excluded, when sometimes our own mindset is part of that exclusion. (Archbishop Agama)[219]

In terms of motives, one important motivation to engage, is often to help the UK community better understand the Ijaw community, its culture, its art, and its values. Specifically, for the Ijaw in the UK, it is to make the Ijaw stand out as a distinct group of Nigerians in the UK and within the sea of various immigrant cultures.

Related to this, is a desire to improve intercultural relations. This often extends beyond the confines of Ijaw culture to Nigerian culture, African culture and to the broader minority ethnic community relations with the broader UK society.

> So, you have to be involved, get yourself involved. I got involved as a school governor for 10 years, I served as a school governor in Hackney. As a school governor, I have to make others to know that as black people, where they see us aggressive and so on, that is not aggressive. So, I know of a teacher who said because a father came and was raising his hands to explain things, you know, in our culture, where they talk and try to explain with their hand to emphasise the point. Like even me now, I am doing that. They said the person is aggressive and is trying to fight them, I said no, that's not true. And they later, the school come to understand that we are not fighting anybody, the parents are not fighting anybody, but they are trying to explain to them, (interviewer laughs) and they come to understand ... Okay, um, I would say, as I've hinted that, my effort has been towards the broader minority ethnic community, because I see these problems as being common to most of us and that if we approach it collectively, then probably it will be more effective. As one of the well-known or recognised minority ethnic leaders in the UK, I was asked at various times to attend high level meetings, to make contributions to discussions at city level at a national level. To interact with parliamentarians; visit No 10 Downing Street, as the case might be" (Archbishop Agama)[220]

But I came into Manchester; I met with some of the locally based ethnic minority church leaders. And from the conversation, they were telling me, you know, the problems that they were having, people don't recognise them and give them access to buildings, and so on and so on. They feel discriminated against and all of that. But by this time, I was a bishop. So, I went to the meeting of the bishops in the city. Again, I was the only black face, chatted with them and told them that this is a conversation I've had. And they said actually, they have also been looking for a way to reach out to minority ethnic church leaders and even some of the white church leaders who they're not so close to. So, I started trying to see how I could help with all of that. (Archbishop Agama)[221]

There is often a strong personal element to the intensity of the motivation to contribute, as well the persistence and the direction of this motivation. In that sense, experiencing or witnessing some or many of the challenges and roadblocks discussed in another chapter, often serve as the fuel for seeking to influence particular spheres of UK society. One of the Ijaw women profiled (Edith Akenkide), details how her experience of racism growing up as mixed-race Ijaw-British have shaped her choice of career and the initiatives she has chosen to contribute to:

So, I studied social work. And I trained and qualified as a social worker. And I worked in mental health. I progressed up to a manager, but I was also aware of equality. And I was aware that racism even as an adult, it was happening. I was aware there were a lot of nurses in the NHS that due to racism and discrimination, they weren't progressing. So, I set up networks to address racism and discrimination in the NHS and local authority. (Edith Akenkide)[222]

Some choices of avenues chosen to make contributions are framed in terms of ensuring minority ethnic representation in important aspects of UK society.

So yeah, at the moment, I'm a detention officer at Harlow police station, and looking after people arrested that come into custody. And then when I'm not doing that, I'm policing on the streets of Harlow, the streets of Essex, and that's quite challenging in itself, because obviously, there isn't a lot of black, or ethnic minority police officers. So, whenever anybody sees me, they always want to talk to me, and I try to encourage people to join. Because, you know, a lot of people say, "Oh, there's not a lot of people in the community that looked like me". But if we don't join, if we don't come and ask and see, then you know, we're not going to get more people that look like me. But I like to encourage more of our people to, you know, come and join the police because we can only make a difference if we're actually there. And so, I think it's really important. (Edna Knight)[223]

The idea of giving back, also comes up when discussing motivations. For many of the Ijaw we interviewed, and even for those who have had a complicated relationship with the UK, this theme of giving back emerges:

> And, you know, the volunteering is important to me, I've had a good life. I've had a community that I live in that has been good to me. And I just want to give back. So, I'm giving back to being a police officer, volunteer police officer in one way. (Edna Knight)[224]

Finally, there are also important acknowledgements of some barriers to effectively contribute to UK society.

> It wasn't easy, because I will say racism was there. You have to go a lot of way to walk yourself to any point even in the church, the schools and the workplaces, it wasn't easy. (Datoru Paul Worika)[225]

> So, I have had opportunities where there's been racism in some jobs, but I just brush it off and just carry on, because I'm not gonna let anybody stop me from what I want to do. (Edna Knight)[226]

In the next section, we profile the contributions of some Outstanding Ijaw People to UK society. These people cover a broad spectrum of careers, economic sectors, backgrounds, and ages, but because of space we could not cover as much as we had wanted to.

REFERENCES

218. Interview 13/10/2023
219. Interview 16/08/2023
220. Interview 16/08/2023
221. Interview 16/08/2023
222. Interview 20/10/2023
223. Interview 04/09/2023
224. Interview 04/09/2023
225. Interview 13/10/2023
226. Interview 04/09/2023

BIBLIOGRAPHY

Hack-Polay, D., Mahmoud, A. B., Rydzik, A., Rahman, M., Igwe, P. A., & Bosworth, G. (Eds.). (2021). *Migration practice as creative practice: An interdisciplinary exploration of migration.* Emerald Publishing Limited.

CHAPTER 13: OUTSTANDING IJAW PERSONALITIES OF LONDON

Mr Henry Adamson Ofoniama, 1922 - 8th May 1975: Entrepreneur and Real Estate Investor

The late Mr Henry Adamson Ofoniama hailed from Kaiama, of Kolokuma Ijaw in present day Kolokuma/Opokuma Local Government Area of Bayelsa State, Nigeria. Before coming to the Britain, Henry was a teacher and a clerk with the Nigerian Railways.[227] The earliest documentary evidence we have of Henry living in Britain is from 1952, where he is listed on the London Hammersmith and Fulham Electoral Register living in Fulham, West London.[228] This corresponds to family records.[229] But family records mention a period of arriving from Nigeria and first living in Liverpool, before coming to London. So, it is possible that Henry Ofoniama was in the United Kingdom by at least 1950. He is listed as one of the foundation members of the Ijaw People's Association (IPA) of Great Britain and Ireland that joined before 1954. Henry Ofoniama was one of the early members of the IPA who facilitated the acquisition of a property in East London, most probably because of his knowledge of Real Estate at the time. Quite a number of Ijaw men owned their own houses in London at the time, and one of them decided to sell his property to the IPA. Henry is fondly remembered for this and being one of the first Trustees of the IPA.

Ofoniama, an educated and learned person who worked in the Post Office and attended Balham College studying Commerce. Very early the entrepreneurial spirit manifested itself in him and he went into the property - real estate business, by the 1960s Henry had purchased a number of properties in West London and family members remember up to five properties. One such property was 192 Kensington Park Road, and was "the first African shop in London", selling ground rice, and what have you. Henry owned it. He lived above the shop, and rented the shop to a Nigerian man with his Caribbean wife.

By 1961, Henry had married his wife and Ijaw woman from Nigeria and returned to live in London with his wife and children. Later on, he was travelling back and forth from Nigeria doing business. Eventually he returned to Nigeria on his own to work with the Rivers State Government and sadly passed away in 8th May 1975. In his passing, his family lost control of his properties, because the children were young at the time, his wife did not

Figure 50. Mr Henry A. Ofoniama in his youthful days.

understand the property business, and estate agents swindled them out of their entitlement and inheritance.[230] According to his daughter Edna Knight (nee Ofoniama);

> Yes, when my dad came here, he was a learned man he acquired few properties as a landlord here in the UK. And but obviously, when he passed away, my mother because she could not read or write, she did not understand anything about wills, property, money. And unfortunately, all of those properties that were in my father's name got lost. Yeah, they got lost. And at that time, we were staying in one of those properties. And then the Housing Association moved us to a housing association property. So yeah, we only found this out, because about 20 years ago, some company, court contacted us about deeds, which were in my dad's name. And so obviously, with research, we found that that my dad owned three properties, but obviously, because of the time, and because of my mom's education she could not read or write, we lost those properties. And we could not get those properties back. But we did get a little bit of compensation. Because obviously, the deeds were in my dad's name. And those were the deeds. And so obviously, other people have now bought those properties. 20 years plus. So, we could not regain the properties, but we did get compensation.[231]

This was most unfortunate and sad, but Henry is an early example of the learned Ijaw man and African who saw opportunity and acted on this by trying to make a success of himself in London at the time, despite the hostile environment. He is an inspiration to the younger generation.

Mr Morris Benatarigha Oguoko, 1919 - July 1984: Electronics Technician

Mr Morris Benatarigha Oguoko hailed from Toru-Angiama of Ijaw in present day Patani Local Government Area of Delta State. Records show that by 1947, Morris (Morrison) Oguoko was living in the East End of London in the Stepney area.[232] He came to Britain to educate himself and eventually trained as an Electronics/Electrical Technician. He worked in several areas such as furniture, the railways and electronics technical field. He returned to Nigeria in 1958 and got married to an Ijaw lady and bought her back to Britain. He had a number of children with her in the UK.

Morris Oguoko was one of the founders of the Ijaw People's Association in 1948 and was a close friend of the Foundation President Young Ogetti Kpiaye, Laurence Okorodudu, James Ngobo (Ingobo), Vincent Akenkide and others. He was a long serving member (1948-1974) before returning to Nigeria, functioning sometimes in the capacity of Assistant Secretary and Caretaker Chairman. According to the testimony of one of his sons, Mr Ombrai Oguoko:

Figure 51. Mr Morris B. Oguoko.

... so, growing up in the UK the members of the Ijaw community that were my father's age, we used to refer to them as Uncle, even though they were not blood related and they were ... Everybody was Uncle, sometimes they had meetings in my father's house ... all of them gathered around, we used to go to another room, whatever the meeting was, sometimes they had the meetings in their own properties or in 18 Strahan Road. Or if we were lucky, we begged my dad to take us with him, we follow him down there and sit with the old men. These men were very way tight, they were tight. I do not think of any type of family or strong friendship like they had.[233]

Mr Morris B Oguoko's services to the Ijaw community in London includes being one of those members who consistently contributed to the purchase of a property in East London to accommodate visiting offshore seamen and students (welfare interventions and supporting their university education), and opening his house up to young Ijaw men who needed a few days, or some time, to stay at a safe place in London. Morris Oguoko returned to Nigeria in late December 1974. On his return to Nigeria, he was immediately appointed a member of the Council of Elders of Angiama, and was the secretary until he passed away in July 1984. Morris Benatarigha Oguoko embodied the Ijaw (Izon) spirit of truth and love for his fellow Ijaw man or woman, which he lived and demonstrated throughout his life in the UK and Nigeria.

Mr Laurence Peretubo Okorodudu, 1920 - October 2003: Merchant Seaman and Civil Servant

Mr Laurence Peretubo Okorodudu hailed from Esanma of Mein clan Ijaw in present day Bomadi Local Government Area of Delta State Nigeria. Family testimony maintains that he arrived in the United Kingdom in 1939 as a merchant seaman. Previously, he had sojourned in Alabama USA, before making his way to Liverpool (UK) and from Liverpool down to London. Records accessed from the merchant ship vessel, the Radcombe, dated 21 November 1942[234] tell us that by this date he was already in the United Kingdom. He is listed as a Fireman, aged 22[235] and a West African of British nationality. He was leaving Britain and arriving in the USA in 1942. Family recall that he spent some time in Liverpool. It is not clear that he intended to stay and settle in the UK initially on arrival, but once married to his English wife, he stayed. He is one of the founding members of the IPA, who did not return back to Nigeria.

Laurence (sometimes spelt Lawrence) was one of the foremost persons and early young Ijaw founders of the Ijaw People's Association of Great Britain and Ireland. He was one of the Presidents and held this office for many years. Laurence Okorodudu's major contribution is his keen interest in making sure that young Ijaw men, be they seamen or students had a place called home in London. His home was open to the Ijaw community, and many young Ijaws lived there, for periods of a few months up to three years or more,[236] while trying to find their feet settling into London life and eventually becoming citizens. According to his daughter Larraine regarding what she thought might have been the fate of Ijaw people coming to London if persons like her Dad were not around to assist them settling in:

> They would have suffered a lot more, wouldn't they? They would have suffered a lot more because they wouldn't have had anybody to go to, would they? Because not everybody used to do what he used to do. If he hadn't come the time he came the whole Ijaw People's Association, everything would have been completely different. It might have even collapsed altogether, or it may not have even existed because he was one of the first foundation and everyone come to him. Yes, they will come they integrated; they move out. They make their own families. But if Dad hadn't done all of that, then they wouldn't have had sponsorship to maybe come here and create a life.[237]

His other services to the Ijaw community in London include being one of those who contributed immensely to the purchase of a property in East London, to accommodate visiting offshore seamen and students (welfare interventions and support their university education), and opening his house up

Figure 52. Mr Laurence Peretubo Okorodudu.

to young Ijaw men who needed a few days to stay at a safe place in London. The Ijaw community in London has a special appreciation for the genuine welfare activities that Laurence and his friends engaged in that allowed many young Ijaws to feel at home in London, and also to become productive members of society with full British citizenship.

Laurence Okorodudu is recalled being sent to meet with the late Chief Harold Dappa Biriye in the 1950s at Victoria station, as a part of the Ijaw community interest in the constitutional talks that took place in London, regarding Nigeria. Later, the Young Dappa Biriye was brought back to East London to address the IPA members on the constitutional talks and the importance of taking an interest in the advancement of the Ijaw people in the proposed Independent Nigeria. Clearly, there were close links between Ijaw organisations in Nigeria and the IPA in London at the time, links that have been maintained up till today. So, Laurence Okorodudu is also remembered as helping to forge and maintain close links between the Ijaw community of London and Ijaw associations in Nigeria concerned with the political emancipation and progress of Ijaws in Nigeria. The late Laurence Peretubo Okorodudu died in London in October 2003. His funeral was attended by a large cross-section of the Ijaw community of London.

Mr Philip Seikegba, 1932 - 2020: Educator

Phillip Seikegba hailed from Esanma of Mein clan in present day Bomadi Local Government Area of Delta State. He was a teacher in Nigeria, before coming to the United Kingdom. In 1972, he was assisted by his cousin Chief Ojobolo, to immigrate to the United Kingdom. His first place of stay in

Figure 53. Mr Philip R. Seikegba.

England, was in Chelmsford. When he came, he already had six children, but he arrived by himself. His wife and children followed later on. As soon as he settled in, he returned to his profession as an educator and worked in the Youth education sector. He remained in education until he retired. His service to the Ijaw community in London, and London itself is that he was a long serving General Secretary and Housing Manager of the Ijaw People's Association of Great Britain and Ireland, contributing to the general welfare of the Ijaw community, and furthermore, as an educator contributing to the educational sector of London. Mr Philip Seikegba passed away in London 2020 and was buried in his home town Esanma Nigeria, according to Ijaw and Christian rites.

Dr Edwin Sawacha MBE: Engineer and Housing Executive

Dr Edwin Sawacha hails from Egodo of Mein Ijaw in present day Burutu Local Government Area of Delta State Nigeria. He came to the United Kingdom in 1966 on a Mid-Western State Government scholarship to study Civil Engineering and Construction, eventually settling in London UK, due to professional work opportunities. He is a highly qualified engineer and was in project management and construction management advice. He qualified at Herriot Watt University Edinburgh & Brunel University, and has an Uxbridge Master's Degree and PhD in Construction, Project Management & Human Behaviour & Safety 1982-1992. Life Coach at A.C.N. Dr Edwin Sawacha was awarded an MBE in 2010 for his excellent contribution to social housing in North-West London. Edwin joined the board of Westway Housing Association in 2007 and was the Chairman of the Scrutiny Committee. Now retired, Dr

Figure 54. Dr Edwin Sawacha.

Edwin Sawacha was also for a time, two time President of the Ijaw People's Association of Great Britain and Ireland. As a long serving member of the IPA, Dr Edwin Sawacha contributed immensely to the upliftment of the Ijaw community in London and the provision of affordable housing to the local community of North London. Currently, Dr Sawacha lives in London.

Prof Richard Ogoja Angiama, 1939 - 2020: University Lecturer and Author

Prof Richard Angiama (BA, BSc, MA, M Phil, PGCE, PhD) hailed from Odimodi/Aghoro of Iduwini clan Ijaw in present day Burutu Local Government Area of Delta State, Nigeria. He immigrated to the United Kingdom in the 1960s in pursuit of higher education. Prof. Angiama was an Educator who specialised in the teaching of Mathematics, and delivering adult education programmes that addressed Mathematical deficits in the adult population of London. He contributed immensely and significantly to the UK education system. He was based mainly at the Centre for Continuing and Community Education, Goldsmith College, University of London.

Publications published and unpublished:

◆ *Adults Re-Learning Mathematics: Mathematics Investigations* (See also ALM1-1 compiled by Diana Coben ISBN 0901542784 (1994)

◆ *Quality Assurance CVCP Academic Audit* (Hall Mark Bulletin for the students and staff of Goldsmiths' College university of London.) (1992)

◆ *School for Work* (1987)

Figure 55. Professor Richard Angiama.

• *Teaching Adult Students Mathematical Investigation* (see Proceedings of ALM-2 compiled by Diana Coben, Mathematics with a Human Face 1995, ISBN 090154989) (1995)

• *The Education Problems of West Indian Children in British Schools, A Critical Examination;* unpublished PHD Thesis

• *The Great Debate* (1986)

• *The Hand Shakes Investigation,* (see Proceedings of ALM-2 compiled by Diana Coben, Mathematics with a Human Face 1995, 090154989) (1995)

• T*he Philosophy of Adults Learning Mathematics & Bloom's Taxonomy of Educational Objectives* (1996): An Overview. Compiled by Diana Coben, Adults Learning Mathematics (1997).

Prof Richard O Angiama was a long standing member of the IPA and contributed his wealth of knowledge and experience in uplifting his fellow Ijaw people and the entire community in London, through making Mathematics more accessible within Adult Education.

Rev Francis B Akpanari: Religious Leader and IPA President

The Rev Francis Boss Akpanari was born in 1941 in Nigeria, he hails from Okumbiri of Central Mein Ijaw in present day Sagbama Local Government Area of Bayelsa State. He came to the United Kingdom 1962 to study Telecommunication Engineering. At the time of his arrival, he did not see himself as an immigrant, but just as someone who came to London to further his education. In his own words he says:

> Okay, I came here, not to come and stay. I came here to study. I came I think in 1962 and I studied telecommunication engineering. And my aim was that, okay, after the studies, we would all go back home. And one thing or the other, you know, these jobs, you know, getting married having children, by the time you realise you're here, you know. When you go back now, you don't want to even stay there, you want to come back here because you are used to here. During that time when I came, because it was very far away now, I met so many of the only Ijaw seamen that just after they're nearly nearing their seamanship contract, they just caught up at Liverpool, and they settled down here. Those are the people I knew. Only a few students from Ijaw that were here at that time, you know. So, then suddenly, by time we realised it, you've become an immigrant. The word immigrant didn't actually affect me really, because by the time I came, we were still under the British colony. I came like a British person; I was given a British travelling certificate to come here and when I came here the job was ready. Any job you want to do, just go to the job centre, get working, there is no wahala., like that … but we the Ijaws that were here at that time, few of them that were here, we are about 12, all students. So, the lawyers and doctors and all that. And when I came, people like E.K. Clark, he was just finishing his studies. We met each other here before he left. All of them were also students. When you call that name immigrants, it confuses me. Because that is always person looking for probably paper to stay permanently.[238]

Although trained as a telecommunication engineer, Rev Akpanari has done several types of work through the years, as a part of adapting to the local economy of London. He has been an engineer, building cars in Dagenham Car factory, worked in the Post Office and as a cab driver. Eventually, he went into his calling as a religious cleric and opened his own church, a branch of the Celestial Church of Christ;

> As a Reverend I had a church with congregation, which I prayed for. I've prayed to heal people, which I've prayed for people to get on in life, the church is called Celestial Church of Christ.[239]

Rev Akpanari has been a long standing member of the IPA. A member since the 1960's, he recalls meeting with the original founding fathers and other Ijaw students in London. As a member of the IPA, he has contributed to the welfare

Figure 56. Rev. Francis Boss Akpanari.

of the Ijaw community of London, and all who have benefited from such community assistance through the years, be it bereavement, education assistance and general welfare concerns. He was the Vice President from 2012 up to 2016, and became the President in January 2020 during the trying period of COVID 19. In his capacity as President, he has visited Nigeria and discussed investment opportunities with the Bayelsa state government. He has met with the Governor of Bayelsa State on several occasions, participated in various events that highlight the environmental pollution of Bayelsa State, buried the last of the Foundation members of the IPA, and overall presided over the Ijaw community in London, of which the community acknowledges the role of the IPA in this regard. As President he has further developed a cordial relationship with the INC-Worldwide and the Ijaws in the USA. He will be stepping down from his position as President of IPA in August 2024, as his terms come to an end. Rev Akpanari presently lives in South London with his wife, and is now retired.

Elder Pa Aliyi Sunjuye Ekineh, 1921 - 13th May 2021: Barrister, Author and Activist

Elder Pa Aliyi Ekineh hailed from Abonnema in Kalabari Ijaw, in present day Rivers State, Nigeria. He came to the United Kingdom just after the Second World War (1946) to study law. In the United Kingdom, as a student he was a strong member of the West African Student Union (WASU). He graduated and was a practicing lawyer until his retirement. During this time, he met up and brainstormed with other young West African leaders such as the late Kwame Nkrumah[240] and others such as Nnamdi Azikiwe (Zik) and Obafemi Awolowo. He was very much politically active at the time.

In 1948, Aliyi met his wife Mrs Florence Ekineh (nee Cheakley) and they got married. They had a number of children. When he completed his law degree and bar exams, he returned to Nigeria in 1952. Later in 1953, he was joined by his wife and children. This was the early days. Prior to him coming to Nigeria, he was at a school in Sierra Leone, where a lot of Nigerians actually attended Fourah Bay College.

The late Aliyi Ekineh was in Nigeria from 1953 to 1987, where he set up Cheakley Chambers and practiced law. Furthermore, Aliyi was appointed as a Director of Central Bank of Nigeria in 1970 by General Yakubu Gowon and he served with distinction as a Board member under the Chairmanship of Ogbeni Oja, Chief Adeola Odutola.

During the Nigerian Civil war, he was involved in the Nigerian government side in containing and defeating Biafra, collaborating with Col. George Tamunoiyowuna Kurubo in galvanising international support for the Nigerian

Figure 57. Aliyi Ekineh.

Government. On his return to the UK, because of the welfare of his wife and children, Aliyi Ekineh threw himself into Ijaw, Niger Delta liberation politics and engaged with the London Ijaw community, especially the Ijaw People's Association of Great Britain and Ireland, where eventually he was made a patron. He also worked in close collaboration with the late Godfrey Arumoh in campaigning against the injustice against the Ijaw people and Niger Delta Region of Nigeria. In this regards he wrote quite a number of books, and became a published author in his own right. In one of his interviews[241] he elaborates on how disappointed he was in then Prime Minister Gordon Brown, promising the political rulers of Nigeria, weapons to clamp down on peaceful agitations in the Niger Delta. He wrote a series of protest letters to 10 Downing Street and organised peaceful protests, to highlight the injustices meted out against the people of the Niger Delta in the name of exploiting crude oil resources.

Because of his contributions to the welfare of his people back in Nigeria and in London UK, members of the Niger Delta Peace Initiative and Development (NDPiD) paid a courtesy visit to Pa. Aliyi Ekine at his residence in London on 14 September 2019. In attendance were the President of the organisation Ms Annah Buseri, General Secretary Mr Martins Biu, NDPiD Patron and former President IPA, Elder Rowland Ekperi, Elder MacDonald I.J. Mopho, a lawyer and author; and Niger Delta Environmental Protection Activist Mr Benaebi Benatari Oguoko. The group was warmly received by Pa. Ekineh, while Mr Rowland Ekperi introduced the group and acknowledged Pa Aliyi Ekineh's immense contributions to the Niger Delta Region through decades of relentless advocacy and struggles for an independent Niger Delta, while based in the United Kingdom. In his word "I have known Pa. Ekineh for several decades, and one thing that brought us so close is his consistency in advocating for an independent Niger Delta, a cause he has been dedicated to since 1966. This he committed his time, personal resources and even engaged his family in the pursuit." An award of a plaque in his recognition of his noble contributions for the struggle was presented to Pa Aliyi Ekineh by the President of the organisation on behalf of NDPID, Ms Annah Buseri.

Esteemed Elder Pa Aliyi Ekineh Aliyi, Barrister at Law passed away on 13 May 2021 at his address in Beckenham Kent, where he had lived since relocating back from Nigeria in 1987. He is survived by his three children, six grandchildren and five great grandchildren.

Books Written by Pa Aliyi Ekineh

* *No Condition is Permanent: A Historical Novel on Nigeria* - 1989
* *Tears and Weeping of the Niger Delta: Struggling for Separation From Islamic Nigeria* - 2003
* *All about Nigeria: A Monster Created by Great Britain* - 2009
* *Commentary on IGBO World Convention, 1999 - 2000*
* *Nigeria: Foundation of Disintegration* - 1998
* *Southern Nigeria: The Case for Self-determination* - 1999
* *"Somewhat Artificially Created":* Essay on Nigeria and Africa's inherited Burden - 2001
* *Nigeria's Silent Holocaust: A Call to Save the Peoples of Divided Nigeria from the Never Ending Bloody Conflict* - 2000
* *Nigeria: The Grave Mistake of 1914: the Only Hope for Southern Nigerians* - 1998
* *JuJu Moon: A Miracle in Africa* - 2001
* *Nigeria: Foundations of Disintegration* - 1997

Reverend Oyinkariowei Dorgu, 27 June 1958 - 8 September 2023: Medical Doctor and Bishop

Originally a Medical Doctor by training and education, Reverend Oyinkariowei Dorgu bears the distinction of being a trailblazer following in the footsteps of another earlier Ijaw Bishop.[242] In 2017, he became the first Nigerian born Anglican (Church of England) Bishop to practice in London, and its first Black Bishop in 20 years. In recognition of his being the first Black Bishop to be consecrated since Archbishop (then Bishop) Sentamu in 1996, at his consecration, Dr Sentamu, and Bishop Wilfred Wood (the first Black

Figure 58. Reverend Oyinkariowei Dorgu.

Bishop in C of E to practice in the UK) placed on Kariowei's head the jeweled mitre that had been entrusted to each of them in turn. He is also the 13th Bishop of Woolwich. He has contributed significantly to the London local faith community and to the Ijaw community in London, of which he was a part. From 1979 to 1985, he studied at the College of Medicine at University of Lagos, Nigeria. He graduated with a Bachelor degree in Medicine (MBBS) and then worked as a general practitioner. In 1987, Dorgu moved to the United Kingdom. He studied theology at the London Bible College and the Evangelical Theology College from 1990 to 1993 in Northwood, Greater London. He completed a Diploma in Evangelism in 1991, a Diploma in Pastoral Studies in 1993, and graduated with a Bachelor of Arts (BA) degree in 1993. Reverend Dorgu trained for ordained ministry in 1993, at Oak Hill College, Southgate, and undertook his postgraduate theological research for MA Missiology at All Nations College, Ware (https://southwark. anglican.org/news-events/news/latest-news/death-announced-of-the-rt-revd-dr-karowei-dorgu/). Kariowei was ordained in the Church of England as a

Deacon 1995 at St Paul's Cathedral, and as a Priest in 1996. He served his Curacy at St Mark's Church, Tollington Park, and Islington in the Diocese of London from 1995 to 1998. He then joined St. John the Evangelist Church, Upper Holloway where he served as an assistant curate/associate vicar from 1998 to 2000. A team vicar from 2000 to 2012, and became the Vicar incumbent from 2012. On 6 March 2016, he was additionally made a Prebendary of St Paul's Cathedral, London.

On 20 December 2016, Dorgu was announced as the next Bishop of Woolwich, in the Diocese of Southwark. He was consecrated a Bishop by Justin Welby, the Archbishop of Canterbury, during service at Southwark Cathedral on 17 March 2017. As such, Dorgu became the first ever Nigerian Bishop in the Church of England in Woolwich. He attended and was responsible for the faith welfare of a significant portion of the Nigerian population, many of who worship in black-majority Pentecostal churches rather than the Church of England. Oyinkariowei Dorgu also the 13th Bishop of Woolwich. (https://en.wikipedia.org/wiki/Karowei_Dorgu).

Reverend Kariowei Dorgu's contributions to the Church of England

Reverend Dorgu identified with the evangelical tradition of the Church of England. He was always keen to share the good news of salvation through faith in Jesus Christ. He had a deep concern for mission and regularly led open-air evangelism in his parish, which saw his church grow remarkably. Bishop Kariowei also had a keen interest in training candidates for lay and ordained ministry, offering his expertise as a tutor on a number of training programmes. He was for many years Assistant Director of Post Ordination Training in the Stepney Area Dorgu's service to the Church of England was exemplary. He was a man of great faith, who served the Church of England with distinction until his death. He was the first-ever bishop of African extraction appointed by Queen Elizabeth II as the 13th Bishop of Woolwich in March 2017, succeeding Bishop Michael Ipgrave. He was responsible for the Woolwich Episcopal Area, which includes the boroughs of Greenwich and Bexley. He was the only black bishop to be consecrated in the Church of England since Sentamu in 1996. He was known for his humility, devotion, excellent service and commitment to his work and his dedication to his community. He was a man of great integrity, who was respected by all who knew him. Bishop Kariowei Dorgu died peacefully after a long struggle with his health on 8 September 2023 in the presence of his family at King's College Hospital London England, from pneumonia; he was aged 65. His death was a great loss to the Church of England and the Ijaw community in London, and he will be greatly missed by all who knew him.

Mr Young Ogetti Kpiaye, 1920 -1970: Ijaw Community Leader

Mr Young Ogetti Kpiaye bears the distinction of being the first Ijaw man in London to organise his fellow young Ijaw men into an association, which was named the Ijaw People's Association of Great Britain and Ireland (IPA) in 1948.

Young Ogetti Kpiaye hails from Ayamassa in present day Sagbama Local Government Area of Bayelsa State, Nigeria. Family testimony and historical records sourced from ancestry.co.uk, tell us that Mr Young Kpiaye, as a young man arrived in Britain as a merchant seaman and was living in a seaman's hostel in Liverpool in 1945. Young came to London where he met a young English lady from West Somerset in 1946 at a ballroom dance and eventually married her. They had two children together.[243] By 1946/47 while Young was in London he met up with other Ijaw men such as Morris B. Oguoko, Vincent Akenkide, Joseph Okoro, Albert T. Jituboh and Laurence Okorodudu.[244] By 1948 they had formed the first Ijaw organisation in London, the IPA. According to the testimony of his son, John Kpiaye, he recollects his father meeting with his Ijaw brothers:

> And when I came home to live with my father, he would on a Sunday, have these meetings. He used to call all his country members and they would come down, IPA members, Mr Lawrence, Mr Morris Moses, Joseph Okoro, Vincent. And they would come, but they would not speak English. They only ever speak in Ijaw. And I would listen to them. And I would say no, I am going to play football. I did not understand what it was about. And so, I kind of, you know, I was 12 then, you know, and as a big Arsenal fan. Yeah. And I believe they would take turns to go to other houses to have their meetings.[245]

Young Ogetti Kpiaye was the foundation President of the IPA and President from 1948 to 1969, a total of 21 years. During this time, he led the organisation to purchase a property in East London to help provide accommodation to visiting Ijaw seamen, who arrived at Tilbury Docks and wanted somewhere to stay during shore time. They also provided accommodation to young Ijaw men who came to London to study. Quite a few prominent Ijaw men who became government officials in Nigeria were beneficiaries of this welfare. As President, he also oversaw the collaboration of the IPA with Chief Harold R. Dappa Biriye in his attendance of the constitutional conferences that led to Independence of Nigeria, in London. Furthermore, he was still the President when Isaac Boro staged his 12 day revolutionary action, and the Nigeria Civil war broke out, with the Ijaws of the Niger Delta needing that international support. During his time, a lot of young Ijaw students joined the IPA in the late 1960s and the IPA provided a lot of welfare support for these young men in

Figure 59. Mr Young Ogetti Kpiaye, foundation president of IPA.

settling into London. Under his leadership the IPA provided a free community welfare support for young Ijaw men coming to London, who after settling in and finding their feet, moved on as self-reliant persons contributing to the economy of London.

Young Kpiaye is mentioned in a documentary of Tower Hamlets Local History and Library Archives, highlighting race relations at the time in the late 1940s, where both Young Kpiaye and Vincent Akenkide were the victims of a terrible racist attack, because Young defended his wife against insults by some white men as she passed on her way home. Mr Young Ogetti Kpiaye died in 1970 when he fell ill in London and was advised by his fellow Ijaw brothers to return to Nigeria to recuperate, which they facilitated. Sadly, he died in Lagos, Nigeria in 1970. He was honoured posthumously by the IPA in 2018 at its 70th anniversary of existence.

John Ogetti Kpiaye (Musician, Songwriter and Music Producer)

A befitting anchor for Mr John Ogetti Kpiaye's contribution to London and the United Kingdom is his tribute song called 'Ijaw Echoes' (For My Father)

Figure 60. John Ogetti Kpiaye.

published on the *Red Gold and Blues* Album, and released in 1996. This song was John's tribute to his father and Ijaw Heritage, being the son of Young Ogetti Kpiaye, one of the founding members of the Ijaw People's Association, and first Foundation President from 1948 up to 1969. During the interview for this book, John recalls what he knows about his father coming from Liverpool to London and meeting his mother in a ballroom dance.

John's mother was an English woman from West Somerset, who came to London during the Second World War as a young woman. His parents got married in the years before 1948, while John was born in 1948 and his younger sister born in 1952. They lived in the Spitafield area of Stepney East London during this time. Due to marriage breakdown in 1952 John and his sister was taken into care and spent time in the Countryside of Hornchurch Essex from the years 4 to 12. During their time in care, their father used to visit them. When he reached 12 years, his father took him out of care and from that time he lived with his father, where he had the opportunity to eat African food, observed his father and friends meet and discuss Ijaw matters, play Ijaw music and do other things relating to Ijaw culture. He recalls that they spoke mostly in Ijaw language. He mentions that because of the time spent in care, he did not get to understand the Ijaw language, but he was acutely aware of his Ijaw heritage. John lost his father, Young Ogetti Kpiaye to illness, when his father passed away in Nigeria in 1970. Because of this, he did not have the opportunity to get to know his father's people and was recently informed that his father hailed from Ayamassa Town, in Sagbama Local Government Area of Bayelsa State.

John attended Phoenix School for asthmatics in Mile End and Daneford Modern in Bethnal Green. He left school at 15 and began working as an apprentice welder. In 1966, his mother bought him his first guitar which he quickly taught himself to play. At the time the reigning Black music was Ska and Rock Steady (the precursors to Reggae music) as well as soul and jazz, so John naturally began learning these styles of music. Eventually, a year later he quit his job and formed a band called 'The Hustling Kind' that was later changed to 'The Cats,' and decided to try and make it as a musician. He was pretty successful in this regard since he has not looked back in regret ever since. This is how John got into music and became an influential musician. His musical contributions to London and UK society are largely within the sphere of the budding Black Music scene that was evolving during the 1960s right through to the 1990s. Although he is largely 'a hidden from sight musician', his influence is enormous. John, along with other notable musicians was responsible for creating what has become known as British Reggae - Lovers Rock. He also features prominently in the reggae genre of Dub poetry. According to one notable music commentary:

> Success was soon to come. In 1968 Kpiaye thought it would be a good idea to do a rock steady/reggae rendition of the classical composition *Swan Lake*. He worked out a piano melody line on his sister's piano at home and his band recorded the tune. They made history as the first British reggae group to have a top 50 entry in the UK singles chart. This led to tours in the UK and Europe but by 1971, the group had split up. Soon after Kpiaye joined 'In Brackets,' a popular reggae band on the club circuit who were also the backing band for most of the reggae singers doing live work, including Ginger Williams, Owen Grey, Winston Groovy, Dandy Livingstone and Joy White. After the band folded in 1973, John Kpiaye became totally involved in writing, producing and playing on numerous reggae hits. It was during this time that he earned his reputation as the leading reggae guitarist on the British reggae scene, developing his own distinctive style of playing. His main influences were Steve Cropper, Freddie King, Grant Green and Earnest Ranglin. From the latter, he learned that there was more to a reggae guitar than strumming and picking. Between 1975-77; John had his greatest success as a writer/producer, churning out countless hits for Dennis Harris' Lovers Rock record label. His production had a distinctively British feel and consisted mainly of female harmony groups like Brown Sugar, Fifteen Sixteen and Seventeen and many solo female singers doing the kind of romantic reggae that became known as 'Lovers' Rock'. Between 1977-82 John Kpiaye did a lot of session work, adding special touches to the productions of artists like I Jahman Levi, Georgie fame, Aswad, Eddie Grant, Linton Kwesi Johnson, Dennis Brown, Janet Kay, Dennis Bovell and others. Since 1982 he has been the resident guitarist in the Dennis Bovell Dub Band, touring the world with Linton Kwesi Johnson. Working with Bovell and

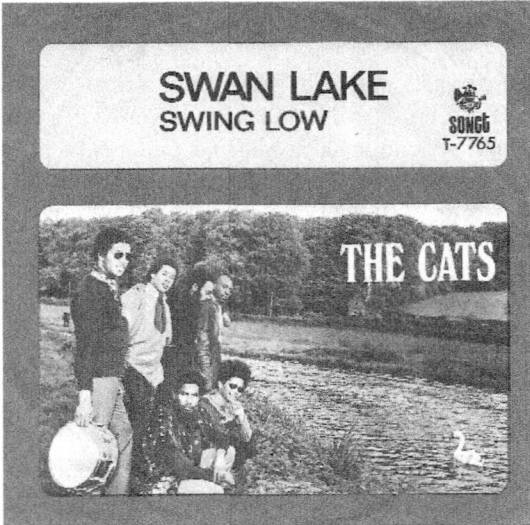

Figure 61. The CATS : John O. Kpiaye in the middle with tie and Michael Okoro, son of Joseph Okoro holding the drum.

Johnson gave John Kpiaye the freedom he needed to perfect his soloing style, the evidence of which can be heard on LKJ's recordings and on his own album, *Red, Gold and Blues.* This album combines the traditional and the modern, and taps into the breadth of Kpiaye's musical experience and knowledge of reggae, ska, rock steady, blues, classical, African, dance hall and jazz. The album reached number 2 in the Jazz FM album charts.[246]

Another commentary states;

A lot of musicians that were coming over from Jamaica around the late 70s who'd be recording in England, they'd say "give us that sound, that kind of lovers sound you got there" (John Kpiaye). Alongside Dennis Bovell, Kpiaye was also the in-house musician at Dennis Harris's Eve Studio in Lewisham. A well-documented part of the lovers rock story, the 8-track studio was the engine room for Harris's various label ventures since the mid-70s, namely his newly formed Lovers Rock label in 1977. The same year, Kpiaye graced the company with multiple hits from local singing talents, Cassandra and Brown Sugar - with three of his original songs swiftly becoming anthems - 'I'm In Love With A Dreadlocks', 'Black Pride', 'I'll Never Let You Go Out Of My Life' - "People would go in the record shop and say 'is there anything new on the Lovers Rock label?' And the guy would say 'yes, and we also got a couple of other tunes in the lovers rock style' and from that, people began to refer to all this kind of genre as lovers rock" (John Kpiaye). Kpiaye's output for the label was always credited to his alias Brownie "T" - That was because no one could spell my name correctly so we used that instead.[247]

John comments on how 'I'm In Love With A Dreadlocks was made;

On 'I'm In Love With A Dreadlocks': "One day he (Harris) came to me and said 'I've got some singers and I need some songs; do you have anything?' I said, 'of course', and I forgot about it. Then a week later, Dennis says, 'We're running the session tomorrow, can you bring the song down for these girls?' I said 'yeah sure' (laughing). So, I had to write something that night and he had this tune on the DIP label called 'Curly Locks' by Junior Byles. I said, "I'm gonna write a reply to that and that's what I did. We went down there the next day and rehearsed it with the girls and cut it. On vocals, we had Caron Wheeler, Carol Simms who became Kofi, and Pauline Caitlin who sang lead ... these were all young girls. They didn't write at the time; the lovers rock thing was very much a female thing when it started and none of them really wrote until later on. I had to write loads of stuff." As well as writing the song, Kpiaye also played most of the instruments: "Leroy Green played the drums and I played the bass, keys and guitar overdubs". Notably, a young Green was one of the in-house drummers at Eve who also went on to record the much-coveted street soul white label 'Love Is The Key' over a decade later. 1977 was also the year Deniece Williams 'Free' became No.1 in the UK Charts - a major soul hit suitably covered by Brown Sugar with Caron Wheeler on lead and released the following year. "What we were trying to do was add more melodic content - put the rhythm track down and then add keyboard lines, guitar riffs, little solos here and there... a lot of vocal harmonies, and that had the effect of softening the music" (John Kpiaye).[248]

John got into studio session music because it allowed him to be more creative. He did not really like being on the road for long periods of time, and so session studio music production suited him better. At one period during the 1970's John was the number one Reggae music guitarist, engaged in monthly session work, playing for and producing some of the best musical talent at the time.[249]

John also played other music genre such as soul music, and has played in different parts of the world, in Europe, South America, Africa and Japan. John mentions that he has toured i.e. played in Uganda, South Africa, Senegal, Tunisia during the period he was working with Linton Kwesi Johnson, being a member of his Dub Band. He started playing on all his records from 1979. In 82, he decided to tour and for the next 30, years, John toured with him. Kwesi introduced John to Pan-Africanism, and is credited with bringing to John's attention the Nigerian novel 'Things Fall Apart'. John has also played with Fela Anikulapo Kuti of Nigeria and Salif Keita at international 'World' music festivals. We can see that John Ogetti Kpiaye (aka Brownie T, John Matumbi, Lord John, although, he was not part of the Matumbi reggae group) played a phenomenal role in the music scene of Black Britain and directly impacting and influenced the wider British music industry today, since many of his musical compositions have been sampled by other upcoming artists, and Black music has had a heavy influence on the wider British music industry. Coming

Figure 62. John O. Kpiaye on the right with Michael Okoro 2nd right, The Cats Band.

back to the question of his Ijaw identity and African identity, asked about it, this is what John said;

> Interviewer: From your narrative, you knew very well, about that which is similar to other Ijaw families of that same period. They understood that they are from, a part of Nigeria, known as Ijaw . And maybe that's got to do with that. They know. They were constantly meeting up themselves, speaking the language.[250]

> Johns' Reply: "I've never gone with that. But I've always been aware that my father was Nigerian, and he was from a part of Nigeria. I wasn't sure of the name of the part, but I knew he was, his people from Ijaw, and that they spoke Ijaw language. And I've always been in a sense, very proud of that, because when I'm working with musicians, and a few of them say, your name, were you born here or were you born in Jamaica, I say, no, no, no, no, that I was born here. But I'm not Jamaican. And they said, well, where are you from? And I will say my father was Nigerian. And I said, Yeah, because they presume, because I was such a big name, that I'm Jamaican … I've always been kind of proud to say, ''No, I'm not Jamaican. I'm Nigerian. Yeah. Well, welcome. My

father's from Nigeria. I did struggle with saying, I'm Nigerian for a while, because I didn't feel Nigerian. I didn't feel that because I couldn't speak the language. And I didn't know their culture. Really, it did seem very strange that I will call myself Nigerian. But I've always thought of myself as Pan African.[251]

This sums up the matter of dual identity. Although John was well aware of his Ijaw roots from Nigeria, because of the circumstances of his upbringing, he did not understand the Ijaw language and was cut off from some of the culture. His father never told him which town or village in Ijaw he came from, and did not attempt to teach John the Ijaw language. Consequently, John's identity was molded as he grew up and embraced and contributed to the emerging Black music scene in London and the UK, and eventually he saw himself as Pan African. Did John reject his English identity? Although he mentions racism directed towards him as a mixed heritage child, and may have harbored resentment for the cultural imperialism exhibited by colonial British culture, currently he has come to terms with his English heritage from his mother's side. John Ogetti Kpiaye will always be remembered for his enormous creative contributions to Black British culture via music. As the son of one of the founders of the Ijaw People's Association of Great Britain and Ireland, his tribute to his father in the instrumental ''Ijaw Echoes'', is a befitting memorial of the journey from immigrant to citizen. John Ogetti Kpiaye currently lives in Royston, just outside of London and still is actively involved in the music business from his home music studio. He creates music that is used in advertisements and jingles and background music. He is 76 years old.

Ms Edith Owofiniere Akenkide: Social Worker

Edith Akenkide is a Senior Social Worker, and in 2019 was Essex Partnership University NHS Foundation Trust Chair of the Black, Asian and Minority Ethnic (BAME) networking group. Edith was born in 1964. Her father was the late Vincent Sawyer Akenkide and her mother was English, Mrs Irene Akenkide. Edith's father immigrated to the United Kingdom from Nigeria at least a year or two before 1947, while her mother Irene was an English woman from St Helens near Liverpool. Vincent Akenkide was one of the early foundation members of the Ijaw People's Association of Great Britain and Ireland.[252]

After her father passed away in 1970 and she was taken into care because of family difficulties, Edith lost touch with the Ijaw community. Later, as Edith became older and curious about her roots, she visited Tuomo her father's home town in Ijaw land Nigeria in 1982 at the age of 18, as a part of a journey of exploration of her Ijaw Identity. Through that journey, she had a clear idea as to what she wanted to do in life and chose a career in social work. After her

Figure 63. Edith
O. Akenkide.

initial training in 1996, Edith qualified as a Social Worker, and it is within this area of work that she has impacted most on London Society. She joined the National Health Service (NHS), working in various community teams as a Social Worker. As part of her career development, Edith undertook further training and studies to become an Approved Social Worker (ASW). This was converted to Approved Mental Health Professional (AMHP) in 2007. According to Edith, there were two main reasons why she decided to become a Social Worker. She had experience of growing up in the care system and felt that she could contribute to making the NHS and local authority, a fair place for all people using the service. Furthermore, due to personal reasons, she wanted to make a difference in the lives of people - particularly those suffering from mental illness and from Black, Asian & Minority Ethnic (BAME) backgrounds. In her own words;

My role involves working on behalf of the local authority to perform some responsibilities under the Mental Health Act (MHA). This includes the coordination of a mental health act assessment and making applications for the detention of individuals suffering from a mental disorder in a hospital. It's my responsibility to ensure that the MHA and Code of Practice are followed and that assessment is conducted in a suitable manner. I have worked in various senior leadership roles within the NHS and local authorities. I was previously a senior practitioner and later promoted to deputy manager. My role involved providing cover for the head of social care in their absence.[253]

In 2016, Edith joined the North Essex Partnership Trust as a Senior Social Worker, and within a short period had initiated a BAME Network within the Trust, supported by the Chief Executive and Board. She was elected the first chair of the BAME network and worked with members to ensure a fairer NHS. Edith then applied for the Ready Now Programme. In 2018, following completion of the Ready Now Programme, she was nominated for a BAME inspirational leader award at the 2018 Windrush Awards and she also won an award for Equality and Diversity RCN in 2018. Edith also worked as a Magistrate and chaired courts in East London. She would go to the Crown courts and sit in appeals, and worked very closely with Operation Black Vote to try and get more black and ethnic minority people to become magistrates. She was a magistrate for over 10 years.

Edith in all sense of the word, can be said to be a High Professional Social Worker who has contributed much to improving Social Work and Mental Health Care delivery within London. She lived up to her Godmother's name that she was named after - Edith Ramsay, who worked with immigrant communities in East London from the 1940s up to the 70s. Edith Akenkide's work within the Ijaw community of London involved being the Assistant Welfare from Officer of the Ijaw People's Association, volunteering her time to help out support the elderly community members, and other Ijaw persons, who had welfare needs that could not be provided by the government. Currently, Edith Owofiniere Akenkide lives in London with her family.

Mrs Edna Tokoni Knight (nee Ofoniama): Catering and Hospitality Manager and Special Police Constable

Edna Knight (nee Ofoniama) is an outstanding Ijaw lady who proudly identifies with her Ijaw heritage. Born in London to Ijaw parents, Mr Henry and Susanna Ayibatonye Ofoniama, she is married to her Australian husband and has one son. Her father, Henry Ofoniama was one of the early founders of the IPA.

Her early education was in Hotel, Catering and Hospitality Management, where she rapidly progressed into managerial positions, working with global

Figure 64. Mrs Edna Knight.

brands such as the Compass Group. From 1981 to 2006, Edna worked as a professional in the Hotel, Catering and Hospitality sector, before leaving and deciding to fulfil her childhood dreams of becoming a police woman. So, in 2006 she became a special constable. In her own words;

> So, I am what you call a special constable. I have a police warrant, I have the powers of arrest, I do everything a normal police officer will do. The only thing is, I do not get paid. So, it is a volunteer role. So that was my way of still being in the police. But, obviously not going against what my mother wanted. So, I kind of got the best of both worlds. So yeah, at the moment, I am a detention officer at Harlow police station, and looking after people arrested that come into custody. And then when I am not doing that, I am policing on the streets of London. Well, I mean Harlow, the streets of Essex, and that is quite challenging in itself, because obviously, as you probably know, there is not a lot of black or ethnic minority police officers. So, whenever anybody sees me, they always want to talk to me, and I try to encourage people to join. Because, you know, a lot of people say, ''Oh, there are not a lot of people in the community that looked like me''. But if we do not join, if we do not come and ask and see, then you know, we are not going to get more people that look like me. And to be quite honest, I have enjoyed it in the police, the force I work with, there has been no discrimination. I have got the role of Chief Inspector as a Special

Constable. And I have had no obstacles, put in front of me, and you know, I can go as far as I want to within the career ladder. But I decided to stop at that, you know, Chief Inspector. And yeah, I am happy with that. But, I would like to encourage more of our people to, you know, come and join the police because we can only make a difference, if we are actually there. And so, I think it is really important. So yes, so that is my history and training.[254]

Edna has contributed immensely to London society in general, as a top professional in the Hotel, Catering and Hospitality Sector, and later a Special Police Officer, at a lot of risk to her own personal wellbeing. Within the Ijaw community, she has volunteered her time, energy and money in contributing to the welfare of the Ijaw people for over 30 years, as one time treasurer of the IPA, member of the IWA and member of the Ijaw Diaspora Council. She is involved in several personal philanthropic projects in Kaiama, where her parents hailed from, and with which she strongly identifies. Edna Tokoni Knight currently lives in London with her family.

Mr Datoru Ben Paul Worika: Engineer and Civil Servant

Datoru Ben Paul Worika is a retired Senior Housing Officer and Engineer. He hails from Ogu Town of the Wakirike (Okrika) Ijaw of present day Rivers State. Born in 1951, he arrived in the United Kingdom as a young student in 1975, to study Electrical and Electronic Engineering, on a government scholarship. He returned to Nigeria and worked in Nigeria for three years, before returning to the United Kingdom in 1978 because of his young family who were living in the UK at the time. Later, he decided to make the UK his home and has since gained British citizenship and lives in London permanently.

Datoru Paul Worika quickly found work in several fields. He worked in the Transportation Department of the London Borough of Hackney, but eventually ended up in the Housing Sector of the Local Government Authority, as a top civil servant and Housing Executive, where he has made his biggest contribution to London life. He is also a Director for Hackney Alms House, (Social Supported Housing) where support is given for the accommodation of elderly persons (55 years upwards). This scheme makes decisions and also assists vulnerable young people to access housing needs. He has also been very active in the charity sector, supporting and contributing to the welfare of London society in this regard. Charities that he has worked with or is still currently works with include, Hackney Joint Estate Charity, as a Director; Trustee, South Hackney Parochial Charity; Trustee of St. John School Charity, and locally, the Treasurer of Victoria Community Association, and a School Governor. In his own testimony, Datoru states;

Figure 65. Datoru Paul
Worika.

Throughout my period as a school governor, I helped the school, the teachers
and as well as our people to get involved, to know what their children are
studying in the school, or what they are doing, how good they are. When they
say, "Oh no exam, don't set it, test them". No, you don't just test. You have to
test. Let all of them do it. Don't just say, "Oh this person is good at sports, is
good at doing something outside during exercise and so on". Let them all
participate, let them get involved, So that, they show themselves which we did.
So, gradually, we get involved and for them to know us and us to know them
that this is how they are, and they too come to know this is what we are. Well,
I have exhausted myself as a British Nigerian, I'm very proud to tell you that,
I am a proud Rivers Ijaw, Wakirike Ijaw person.[255]

Datoru Paul Worika's contribution to the welfare of the London Ijaw
community, has been through his active membership of the following
organisations, the Wakirike Community Association, the Federation of Ijaw
Communities (FEDICOM), now defunct, and the Ijaw National Congress
(INC-Europe). As a member of the Wakirike Community, he helped organise
the Wakirike Community School which was held every Sunday. Currently
Datoru Paul Worika is retired and lives in London with his wife and adult
children.

Mr Joshua Tamunopreye Garry: UK, National Diversity Awards 2022 Winner, Educator and Historian

Mr Joshua Tamunopreye Garry is a Teacher, Educator, Historian and Public Speaker. His parents hail from Akugbene Town of Mein Ijaw Clan. He was born in 1991 in Lagos, Nigeria, and came to the United Kingdom with his parents in 1993 as a child. Since then, he has lived in London, and gained UK citizenship. Joshua undertook his higher educational studies at Queen Mary's University London and graduated in History. Narrating his pathway to studying history and teaching, Joshua talks about this in his interview;

I wanted to do a joint honours degree in English literature and history, but I didn't pass the English literature. I only passed history well. I didn't get the grade I needed to get in English literature. But my A levels and I went to Queen Mary University of London I went there because my father- So, whilst I'm a Garry, on my father's maternal side I'm a Narebor (native name) and Narebor are quite well known people and one of the Narebor's studied in Queen Mary's. Then I was like, Yeah, I want to study at Queen Mary University. So, I went to Queen Mary's University. When I went to the Mary's University, like I did history, because I could do it, I was good at it. But whilst in there, I harboured ambitions of working in the City of London, becoming a banker, because I always wanted to be a footballer anyway. And it seemed like working in the city and becoming a banker was the closest I can get to kind of that fast life. But also, that incredible income. But for whatever reason, I wasn't able to quite get into the city, it coincided with, I guess, the financial crisis. So, in a way, they weren't recruiting as they once were. But also, written on my end, the lack of confidence and the lack of resilience. You know, I gave up quite quickly, to be honest. So, I graduated from uni. And then, I did work in a bank. I worked in the bank or building society called Nationwide ... So, I had to like kind of reflect and think about okay, you know, what am I good at? What do I like? And I always worked with young people in some capacity. I've worked with young people for an incredibly long time. So, it's okay. I want to work with young people in some capacity. And like I said, I did a degree in history. I got grade A level in history. So, I said, okay, let me marry the two. Let me become a teacher because I love to work with young people, but I love to use my skills of history ... I wanted to make sure that my students didn't have the same kind of experience I had growing up with not like encountering black history. So, in order to make sure that they learn about the Black History that I want them to learn about, I had to learn more about it because I wasn't taught that in school. So, then, you know, you kind of go on a journey where reading, reading, consuming things, and then I think it was in the aftermath of George Floyd's murder. I was approached to co-write a textbook. So, that's where kind of the author thing came from. A couple of years ago, I was nominated for like a National Diversity Award. And that presented opportunities as a public speaker. And then, as you can see, like my memory, I'm quite observant, I pick up stuff. So, from when I was young people always told me, and I'll always pick this

Figure 66. Joshua T. Garry.

stuff up. And I remember that, okay, this is a form of history. And history is not all about, what happened to kings and queens, it has a place. Of course, it does. But, history is about what happens to us. And then so, my kind of journey is, doing kind of those two. So, as you can imagine, a textbook which kind of lends itself to that. It was on the Notting hill; on the migration story of Caribbean (inaudible) I'm currently doing a master's at the University of Oxford. What am I doing? My thesis is exploring decolonization that's what it's exploring. And so, in order for me to explore decolonization, once again, there's a historical hell left. I've got to do my racism, got to compile my argument, etc, etc. And yes, that's kind of how we've found it here.[256]

Joshua Tamunopreye Garry (Josh Preye Garry) is also the 2022 National Diversity Award winner and a graduate student at the University of Oxford. He began teaching in 2014 and taught in several London schools. As Head of History, Josh led the creation of a curriculum that highlighted previously excluded communities in the UK, such as African immigrants. He co-authored the textbook for Pearson's first-ever Black British GCSE. As a public speaker, he has spoken at world-renowned companies such as Goldman Sachs, Kantar and the Migration Museum. Joshua is also an MSc Student at the University of Oxford, which focuses on approaches to decolonising the English curriculum. He regularly completes CPD in the History and local communities and creates learning and teaching resources for teachers.[257] As part of the national recognition for his outstanding work, according to the National Diversity Awards website, which states:

2022 Shortlisted Nominee - Positive Role Model Award: Race, Religion & Faith. Growing up, Josh Preye Garry struggled to see how and where he fitted in. Despite having no substantial support network, Josh worked hard and his passion for teaching and educating was born. Currently heading up the History Department at Platanos College, Josh is on a crusade to drive forward the conversation around Black History, and why it is integral to British History. In addition to leading on an A-level module on African American Civil Rights, Josh has played a key role in developing a Key Stage 3 curriculum that reflects the backgrounds of his student body, contributed to a new GCSE, and co-authored a GCSE course that explores Black British History. Proud recipient of a fellowship from the Historical Association, Josh is a shining example and a display of hope to a generation of young people who will follow in his footsteps.[258]

Joshua is a good example of the upwardly mobile, young Ijaw multitalented professional of London, who has a keen sense of his Ijaw culture and is ready to investigate and learn more about his own people. He has since been able to harmonise both his Ijaw identity and his British/Nigerian legal identities, while growing up in London, largely due to the upbringing given to him by his parents. As a young professional, he is already positively impacting the London Education sector by actively taking part in educational work that uplifts and broadens the UK educational curriculum to include more ethnic minority history. A GSCE's Examiner and Education Consultant, currently Joshua lives in the London suburbs with his family.

Ms Patience Agbabi: Poet and Lecturer

Patience Agbabi was born to Ijaw parents in 1965 in East London. Her father Mr Clement Agbabi is a retired person, a lawyer by training, who hails from Ekumugbene of Oporomo Ijaw Clan of present day Burutu Local Government Area.[259] Agbabi FRSL, is a sought-after poet and performer. She has spent almost 30 years celebrating the written and spoken word in the UK, Europe, Scandinavia, Africa, Asia and the USA. Active on the literature and arts scene, she was on the Council of Management for Arvon from 2009 to 2016. Her work often gives voice to the voiceless, bridging the gap between page and stage, high art and popular culture, poetry and prose; paying equal attention to formal structure and the dynamic of performance.

She read English Language and Literature at Pembroke College, Oxford and has an MA with distinction in Creative Writing, the Arts and Education from the University of Sussex. She holds honorary doctorates from the University of Worcester (2018) and the University of Kent (2019), is an Associate Member of the English Faculty at the University of Oxford until 2025 and was made an Honorary Fellow of Pembroke College, Oxford in 2024.

Figure 67. Patience Agbabi.

She has lectured in Creative Writing at Greenwich, Cardiff and Kent Universities and has delivered readings, lectures and seminars at over 50 universities in the UK and abroad. Since 2008, she has been a Fellow in Creative Writing at Oxford Brookes University. Additionally, she has 25 years' experience delivering workshops in secondary schools at all levels. Recently that work has focused on Sixth Form, on specific *Canterbury Tales* or her poem *Eat Me,* a set text for A' Level English Literature on the Edexcel Exam Board.

In 2004 she was nominated one of the UK's 'Next Generation Poets'. Her work has appeared in a broad range of anthologies, on TV and radio, The London Underground and human skin. She has published four poetry collections, *R.A.W.* (Gecko Press, 1995), *Transformatrix* (Canongate, 2000), *Bloodshot Monochrome* (Canongate, 2008) and *Telling Tales* (Canongate 2014).

Agbabi's work is inspired by the full spectrum of the arts. She has worked on numerous high-profile multimedia projects including *Metamorphosis: Titian 2012* at the National Gallery, which led to delivering workshops in the gallery with the general public; and a three-month project with Year 8 pupils on the painting *Diana and Actaeon.* She has participated in a broad range of residencies from Eton College to Flamin' Eight, a tattoo and piercing studio in North London; from The Historic Dockyard at Chatham to Harewood House, a stately home outside Leeds. There she wrote her poem 'The Doll's House', shortlisted for the Forward Prize for Best Single Poem 2014.

She was Canterbury Laureate from 2009 to 2010 and received a Grant for the Arts and an Authors Foundation Grant to write a contemporary version of *The Canterbury Tales.* This fourth collection, *Telling Tales* was shortlisted for the 2014 Ted Hughes Award for New Work in Poetry and Wales Book of the Year 2015. She has toured this book extensively in the USA including the universities of Harvard, Yale, George Washington University and The University of California, Irvine.

Her poem 'The Refugee's Tale' appeared in *The Refugee Tales* (Comma Press, 2016) and she has participated in The Refugee Tales annual walks ever since to raise awareness around asylum seekers' issues. In 2017, Agbabi became a fellow of the Royal Society of Literature. And in 2018 she was Poet-in-Residence at Brontë Parsonage Museum, Haworth. Agbabi's debut middle-grade novel *The Infinite* (Canongate, 2020), launched *The Leap Cycle,* a time-travel adventure series featuring a British Nigerian neurodivergent hero. This was shortlisted for the Arthur C. Clarke Award and won Wales Book of the Year: Children & Young People category in 2021. It was followed by *The Time-Thief* (2021) and *The Circle Breakers* (2023). The fourth and final book of the series, *The Past Master,* appeared in February 2024.

Figure 68. Rowland Ekperi.

Patience is an example of a young Ijaw person who took a radical pathway into the creative literary arts and has made a success of herself despite conservative views of the type of professions people should specialize in. Currently Ms Patience Agbabi lives in Kent, with her family in the suburbs of London.

Mr Rowland Ekperi: Housing Chief Executive, Community Leader

Rowland Ekperi hails from Odoni community of Oyiakiri-Ebeni Clan of Ijaw people. He was born in February 1955 in Ghana to Ijaw parents. Rowland's early education involved attending Academy Primary School Sapele, Metropolitan College Lagos and University. On relocating to London in pursuit of further education, Rowland attended Southwest College London, Henley Business School, University of Brunel, London. Mr Rowland Ekperi came to the United Kingdom in the 1980s. The stated reason for coming to the United Kingdom, was a deep desire for further studies, mainly self-sponsored. Once in the UK, Rowland discovered a greater purpose for his existence, and in his own words:

> So, God has put me here for a purpose. One, bring Britain and Ijaw areas very close. Britain has some link with Ijaw land. And unfortunately, our Ijaw leaders have not been able to exploit that fully and now I have the privilege through late Dappa Biriye who took me to places. I was in this country but, I didn't know what was happening in the UK. Dappa Biriye, old politician now took me places, unlocked doors. I now realise how important Ijaw land is. I would try

to mobilise as many Ijaw persons as possible so that, Ijaw here would be a bridge between Britain and Ijaw land. And that was the reason why some of us have tried to stay here, trying as much as possible. Where there are issues in Ijaw land, we carry placards. In fact, my children they love that. They are all grown up, successful people but, they like to go demonstrate with cousins and me. I came here as a student, to do what I had to do and I believe in trying to build the relationship between Nigeria and Britain, we are trying to promote the two countries, culture, economics, empowerment environment, preach peace in all the globe. We've contributed much.[260]

Ekperi has worked in the banking sector, academics/education and housing sector. Currently, he is the Chief Executive Officer of Mace Housing, a medium sized Housing Association that provides social housing to various social categories and vulnerable people of London. It is within the area of academics and housing, that Rowland has contributed immensely not only to the London economy, but the wider UK society. He has worked extensively in academic research groups to create and implement policies for the National Health Service (NHS) and the Housing Sector. He is also an active, well sought after public speaker and Housing Sector specialist shaping Housing policies for the UK. On his work with the Housing Sector as head of the Mace Housing Group, this is what he has to say in our interview with him;

I am the Chief Executive. Again, my interest there is the word, 'cooperative'. We don't call them tenants, we call them members and the ethos, and the beliefs are based on the common good. I got in there because the organisation was in tatters, you know. I went there to change the culture of the organisation. You know, people believe that everything is free. Nothing is free in life. You have to contribute, and you don't expect people to contribute all the time. You don't treat people anyhow, because they are homeless. Because they have low paid jobs, you treat them like trash? No, I wasn't going to take that nonsense. I also wouldn't accept that some housing groups are meant for some special people … Mrs Thatcher open up a lot of things in this country. So, some of us have become, because we were prepared. That's why some persons who are clever said 'opportunities always favour the prepared mind'. So, that was how in that period I found myself in Mace Housing Corporate Group and we started to dismantle the very backwardness … If you want to define people's character, people's value, you want to build their aspirations, a home is very important. I can tell you, Mace has well over 500 units at the moment, and we really take care of people with low income. We also take care of people that are unemployed etc. ... The most important thing that drives us, one thing that we have done that most housing associations are now copying again, is our advancement of British society and it is also having some sort of impact for the amount of money that Britain pays out to people who are unemployed in terms of their housing costs, now they call it, Universal Credit, right … So, I started with Mace to set what is called a product called SEAP. SEAP was designed by me and my colleagues in Mace to make sure to provide repairs, maintenance,

administration professional skills, training, intensive training. Then, I also look
at the rental income management, which is, we designed the course contents,
we sought approval from qualifications awarding bodies, we secured them and
our drive to make sure those people in Mace that are employed and don't have
skills, they come into those programmes to learn. Then, from there we can
employ them directly, or we can find employment in housing associations for
them. My dear brother, that was a big move in the housing association sector ...
So, these are some of the contributions, we are still making. From time to time,
I go out travelling, the National House Federation called me to come and
deliver papers. We go over there deliver papers, introducing what is happening
in practice at the private level, try to marry financial management processes and
procedures for the private sector, bring down the experience in public sector
organisations, for them to be more efficient in the allocation of scarce
resources, monitor and see what is happening. That has been some of my major
roles in the social housing movement, occasionally contributing articles to
some professional journals as well.[261]

Regarding his immense contribution to the Ijaw Community in London and
the UK as a whole, Ekperi can be said to be a silent philanthropist. He has
served in various capacities as a member of the Ijaw People's Association of
Great Britain and Ireland, including being the President from 2004 to 2008. He
was instrumental in upgrading its sole property and turning it around into an
income generating asset, enabling the association to fund its welfare activities
without overburdening its members. He also worked within the IPA to bring
the Ijaw people and the UK government, to a better understanding of the
relationship between oil and gas exploitation, environmental degradation, and
marginalisation of the people of the Niger Delta, with the series of conferences
and gatherings under the heading of Boro Day UK. In this regards he did
extensive work with the UK Parliamentary Groups on bringing to the attention
of the UK government, the injustices meted out to Ijaw people of the Niger
Delta Nigeria:

> And then we made sure the British government understands the Niger Delta
> region provides the oil, palm kernel, rubber, and those things we promoted. And
> British people, policymakers understand that. So, there's always that link to
> power brokers in Britain. That is the more reason why I'm begging and
> pleading with all of you, we need to have links here in Britain. In so doing, we
> are helping to promote the economic advancement of Britain. We're helping to
> protect British markets in Nigeria, and equally, we expect our people to exploit
> our positions here to do that ... And I think policymakers that are around some
> of us, know exactly where we stand on that. In the past, before anything about
> oil pollutions, they will run around IPA. If I'm not here, they call Benaebi, then
> Edema who became a powerful commissioner under Governor Obong Victor
> Attah. The network, the networking. Then also this Ogoni guy, Atama also. So,
> one contributed so much to building the Niger Delta and that is the more reason

why this group is still very important to me. It's very important to me, if we can unite, a lot of achievement can be made. Britain has enjoyed the presence of all of us here. They are looking for people like all of us, whether we can play active role in Nigeria to help protect their people's interests and I tell them it's possible, but it is not going to be business as usual. There must be mutual understanding, mutual benefits, and enlightened self-interest. Yes, I agree. You have something we want; we buy from you. We have something you want; you buy from us, but on par. We also have to promote the African free trade platform. We were instrumental. Where people talk about WTO and all that nonsense. You are an economist, you know, the WTO terms of trade, Africa and Europa and whatever, is heavily skewed against Africa. So how do we change that, IPA was at the forefront during my time. Thank goodness I had, you can call him a godfather, up till now he calls me his godson. He is not an Ijaw person…I liaise with him, he was able to set up the African Free trade zone, which AU, African Union has now have tried to promote and thank goodness an Ijaw son, Dr Eradiri is heading that in Addis Ababa. So, these are the things we've done for Ijaw People, Ijaw community, Niger Delta community, the entire Nigeria and probably Britain as well.[262]

What informed him of this work with the British Establishment, was his understanding that the Ijaw people and the UK have had a long history of trade relations and interaction from the 19th Century till date, and as a good citizen of both Nigeria and the UK, it is his duty to make sure that the Ijaw people and the UK, both benefit from a mutually beneficial partnership.[263] Currently, Ekperi is a Trustee of the IPA as a part of his continued service to the Ijaw community of London. Mr Rowland lives in London with his family, and travels regularly to Nigeria and other parts of the world.

Mr John Eperebofori Opuogulaya: Chartered Accountant

Mr John Eperebofori Opuogulaya was born in Lambeth London in 1977 to Ijaw parents that hailed from Wakirike Ijaw of present day Rivers State, Nigeria. They came to the United Kingdom to study and after completing their studies, while John was still a small child, returned to Nigeria. After completing his primary and secondary education in Nigeria, John returned to the United Kingdom in 2003. He attended the University of Westminster, where he studied BSc in Accounting and Business management and then went on to do professional studies in ACCA, achieving full accreditation ACCA in 2009. Furthermore, John proceeded to do an MBA Business Administration at Brunel University, London. He has also done various professional trainings. John has worked in various organisations including charity, and public accounting organisations and now currently works in the aerospace industry, where he has developed different specialist skills over the years. John's personal experience of career progression in UK society is typical of many

Figure 69. John E. Opuogulaya.

young Ijaws who are determined to get ahead, despite the odds;

> After my degree in accounting and business management, one of the barriers I
> faced at a time was that of cultural difference. So the accent, my accent was
> quite different at the time. And most of my experience of my schooling, both
> primary and secondary was in Nigeria. So, it was quite a difficult time for me
> to break into the [accounting] professional at the time. So, what I did was, I had
> to volunteer for an accounting firm. I went to them, and I said, I want to work
> for you for free. I want to volunteer, and they said, "Okay, come on board, what
> can you do?" I said, Well, whatever you give to me, I am going to do. So, I
> started then as a normal desk man, a desk boy, gradually started learning,
> shadowing various accounting staff at the time. And that really helped me break
> into the industry, the accounting industry at that time. And after that, once I
> built myself when I got the experience or this experience required, I then
> moved to various industries.[264]

John also got actively involved in the London Ijaw community by
volunteering his time in several Ijaw community associations. In one of his
interviews, he states how he did this:

> I belong to Ijaw communities. I am the President of Wakirike Community UK,
> and also the chairman of the Ijaw National Congress, Europe. And also, we
> have the Rivers State community but that is partly, it basically covers the state,
> not just the Ijaw clans. I will say, I have given the number one thing I have
> really contributed to the Ijaw community, is my time and using the experience
> I have got over the years, the professional experience. I have brought it into the
> community, developing the community. So, the Wakirike community, I

Figure 70. Ms Amanda Epe.

remember I joined the Wakrike community in 2008. And then it was about, you know, struggling with the [membership] numbers and all that. And when I joined, I now was able to influence and invite people within my age group to join, because the Wakirike community was formed in 1953, and most members were elders, and the elders were a bit scared that the community might be extinct because the youngsters were not joining or showing interest. So, when I joined, I started invited my peers to join. And I was made the secretary at the time and whilst I was secretary, I used that, to help develop the organisation, reach out to our members. Put in place, setting welfare packages, that will help our elders, you know, reach out to them, and help them in various areas like members that require mobile wheelchairs, making contributions to help in those areas. Now, also is it in 2010? I joined the Ijaw National Congress, Europe, and then I was made the financial secretary. And one of the initiatives, one of the things we did was to help our people back home with I think, in 2012, there was a major flood back home that affected a lot of people. And what we did, we come together contributed not just money, but medical facilities, clothing, and all that, and shipped them to Nigeria. And we as members travelled to Nigeria, went to various communities that were affected and distributed these medical equipment. So basically, my contribution here, even now as President is basically bringing the Ijaws together, bringing the Wakirike people together, you know, for us to bring our various experience, knowledge and qualifications together, to help build ourselves here, and use that opportunity to help our people back home. So that is what I have done over the years, the brief things I have done over the years to help our people here, and contribute to our community here and back home.[265]

Currently John Eperebofori Opuogulaya lives in London with his family. He is a strong member of the Ijaw community of London.

Ms Amanda Epe: Educator and Author

Amanda Epe is a woman of Ijaw descent, whose father hails from Agbere in present day Sagbama Local Government Area of Bayelsa State. Amanda has been an active young lady, very much interested and focused on her Ijaw heritage and quite visible in the Ijaw community circuit in London. Through the years she has worked in the airline industry, education and personal professional development.

Known in the wider London and UK society, Amanda is also a multi-award winning author, poet, writing coach and creative producer. According to the National Literacy Trust;

> Amanda Epe is a multi-award-winning author, poet, and writing coach. Her memoir *A Fly Girl Travel Tales* is listed in The Mirror's best travel books to read in 2020. She has performed poetry locally, at London Poetry café and live digitally. She offers creative writing workshops for all ages in schools up to sixth form as well as adult sessions, championing creating stories. Amanda has over two decades delivering creative education with SEN, BAME, girls groups, and mainstream students in schools and community settings. She has delivered talks/presentations in schools on human rights equality for International Women's Day, End Violence Against Women Day, and Black History Month. The sessions and talks help to promote self-esteem, confidence, equality, and mental well-being as well as to develop literacy. She has testimonies from her Black, Asian minority, and refugee students that have become authors. She has an enhanced DBS certificate and BA, MA Education Studies.[266]

Some of Amanda's achievements have been in the Writing and Book Author field. She is the author of the following books; 'A Fly Girl' listed in Forbes, Lonely Planet and the Mirror as top ten best travel books. She is also a film maker of heritage films on women pioneers and aviation WW2 Service Men and Women. Working on inclusion stories in education for African and Caribbean children and empowerment of girls and women. Her literary and creative works have been recognised by Pride of Brent Award. She is a BEM honours recipient and received the RAF BLAC Awards for Best Writer. Currently, Amanda Epe lives in London.

Mr Macdonald Imaitoghi Joseph Mopho: Lawyer

Macdonald Imaitoghi Joseph Mopho was born in 1964 and hails from Emelesua of Abua/Odual Ijaw clan, in present day Abua/Odual Local Government Area of Rivers State, Nigeria. He is a Lawyer. Regarding his personal educational advancement in the UK, he also states in his interview;

Figure 71. Mr MacDonald I. J. Mopho.

I got employed with the Embassy of Nigeria, Abidjan and worked there from December 1988 - January 1991, before coming to England in February 1991 for further studies. I went to the University of Essex, Colchester where I did a BA Conversion Certificate in Philosophical Studies (Justice, Ethics, Philosophy and Human Rights Law). Then, I went to the University of Bristol where I studied Law and Philosophy before enrolling for the Diploma in Advanced Legal Practice at De Montfort University, Leicester, and subsequently completing my Master of Laws, LL.M., degree, in 2000, following my Diploma in 1999.[267]

After Bristol University Macdonald explains how his professional life took off;

When I finished my course at Bristol University, I had opportunity to volunteer with the Citizens Advice Bureau for advice work training and I did. They trained me. They sent me to trainings on public law, housing law, social security law, employment law, county court representation and several other relevant courses to enhance my ability to give quality and standard professional legal advice to members of the public and to be able to train others. I completed my training of about 18 months, before I secured a full time paid employment in the Citizens Advice Bureaux, first as an Advice Worker in Camden and then in Bromley where I was Deputy Manager and Advice Session Supervisor. After that I got employed in the commercial and private sector such as Capita Group plc, where I was a Legal Services Commission Manager and Supervising Legal Adviser of several solicitors and barristers who were employed as legal advisers to deliver the Specialist Quality Mark advice on Employment Rights, Housing Law, Debt and Social Welfare Benefits. While I was with the Citizens Advice Bureaux in 2001, the Secretary of State for Transport advertised that they wanted some lay persons to join expert medical advisors, to advise the Secretary of State for Transport on Alcohol, Drugs, Substance Misuse and Driving. With my background as a Citizens' Advice Bureaux Adviser and Social Policy Coordinator, I felt I was a suitable candidate so, I applied. And I was invited for interview and subsequently appointed by the Secretary of State for Transport in October 2001. I sit in the Panel for seven years: 2001- 2008. I was also appointed as an Independent Member and chairman, Standards Committee, London borough of Newham Council. Then as a Lay Member, Independent Advisory Group, General Practice Extraction Service, Health and Social Care Information Centre for England and I sat in that capacity from May 2012 - June 2015. We were a 9 Member Panel and we made policy recommendations on data extraction for clinical and indirect clinical use. The House of Commons MPs for the Health Select Committee commended our Panel in 2015 for excellent work on data governance and recommendations. As we speak, I'm currently sitting as a Lay Faculty Examiner in Communication Skills with Patients at the Royal College of Obstetricians and Gynaecologists Part 3 Final Revision Course for doctors who want to qualify as Obstetricians and Gynaecologists. I have been doing this since 2018. Outside that I work as a Legal Adviser/Consultant as well as a Commercial and Civil Disputes Mediator. I speak on human rights issues at conferences and write Christian and law books, respectively.[268]

Macdonald has authored International Human Rights Law books that are reference books for International Human Rights Law scholars, researchers for the MPhil/PhD students and legal practitioners with interest in human rights. Professionally, he is a Member, (MCIArb), and The Chartered Institute of Arbitrators in 2006, and was admitted as a Pioneer Fellow of the Civil Mediation Council for England and Wales in April 2021. More professional development came in the form of enrolling in the Certificate Course in Public Financial Management with the International Monetary Fund (IMF), Harvard University Certificate Course in Religion, Conflict and Peace; and a Professional Certificate in Leadership and Communication. All this specialised knowledge is being put to use in the service of the Ijaw people and UK in general. Mopho also finds time volunteering his time and energy in service to his people and community as a member of the NDPiD, dedicated to finding solutions to the various problems and issues affecting the Niger Delta Region, and the community in London. He currently lives in the London suburbs.

Anthony Harcourt Otokito: Retired Civil Servant and Community Leader

Mr Anthony Harcourt Otokito, hails from the town of Otuokpoti of the Ogbia Ijaw clan, in present day Ogbia Local Government Area of Bayelsa State. In pursuit of the legendary golden-fleece, Anthony has been living in London since 1976 and is a citizen of the UK and Nigeria. Otokito studied at Nottingham Trent University and did other professional courses. He is a Certified Chartered Accountant. He has spent over 24 years in the UK Public sector, specialising in public sector VAT/taxes and funding of Capital Investment Programmes. He has numerous years of working closely with HM Revenue & Customs (HMRC) on Taxation & VAT matters, where he has been lead officer on these matters on behalf of the authorities. He eventually retired as Group Finance Manager. Having spent many years giving his best the UK public sector, Anthony Otokito is also in the private sector where he is Executive Director of London-based Finance Consultancy firm, KitCrest Consulting, which specialises in Taxes/VAT and advising on funding streams for capital programmes/projects.[269]

Otokito is a familiar name within the Ijaw community of London, where he is known for his community welfare activities. He is a member and one time President of the London Tari Club (LONTAR), a welfare association made up of mostly Ijaw persons. He was also the President of Ogbia-UK Community (UK and Ireland) and he is Director Diaspora & International Affairs for INDG (Ijawnation Development Group) - an organisation dedicated to promoting the interest of all Ijaws both in the Niger Delta Region of Nigeria and in the Diaspora. Recently, he was appointed INC-Europe Admin on the INCW (Ijaw National Congress-Worldwide) Platform, keeping up his active service to his people. He has made remarkable contributions to advancing the general welfare of Ijaw people, diligently working towards the development of the Ijaw people and promoting our rich cultural heritage in the UK. Otokito's commitment to the advancement of the Ijaw people, is demonstrated through his unwavering dedication and tireless efforts in creating awareness and fostering unity among the Ijaw community residing in the UK. His passion for preserving our cultural heritage and strengthening the bond of kinship is undeniable. His leadership qualities and wealth of knowledge have been instrumental in mentoring and empowering fellow Ijaw individuals, ensuring that our heritage continues. Many young Ijaws, have tapped into his fountain of knowledge in his endeavours. Otokito has consistently worked towards the best interests of Ijaw development. His unwavering dedication to enhancing the socio-economic prospects of our people, has impacted the Ijaw community. Through his visionary initiatives and collaborations, he has facilitated

Figure 72. Mr Anthony Otokito.

numerous opportunities for Ijaw professionals and entrepreneurs, fostering growth and prosperity within the UK community. Furthermore, through his active membership and participation in the welfare associations, Otokito's efforts in promoting Ijaw cultural heritage in the UK have been instrumental in preserving Ijaw traditions and raising global awareness of our rich cultural tapestry. Through cultural events, exhibitions, and educational initiatives, he has showcased the beauty and uniqueness of the Ijaw identity, ensuring that the Ijaw heritage remains vibrant and celebrated within London. Otokito lives in London with his family.

Archbishop Doye Teido Agama: Religious Leader

Archbishop Doye Teido Agama was born in Shirley, Southampton, England in 1956. Archbishop Doyé Agama was fostered as a baby within a white English family. Archbishop Doye Agama's father was His Royal Highness, Chief Frederick Abiye Agama, the Ogbotom Edede of the Epie-Atissa Clan of Ijaw in Bayelsa State, Nigeria. His maternal grandfather, Chief Nelson Kemeninabokide Porbeni, was the Etonkepua of Kabowei Kingdom, and the Ododomedo of Asideni in Delta State of Nigeria. Bishop's mother, HRH Chief

Beatrice Agama (nee Porbeni) arrived in England with his father in 1953, where they both came for higher education studies. Agama as a boy ,went to Nigeria with his natural family in the early 1960's and returned to the UK in the early 1990s as a part of further education and to explore the religious side of life. He has remained in the UK ever since, occasionally travelling to Nigeria on various assignments. Agama's professional life spans both the UK and Nigeria. According to the website https://www.apostolicpastors.info /bishop-doye-agama:

He is a former Telecommunications Consultant to the oil Industry, Central and Local Government and the Emergency Services. He first started work as a teaching assistant in 1973, and has also been involved at various times in Community Development and Regeneration work since 1975. Archbishop Doyé has participated in Bid Management, Technical and Operational Studies, Requirements Assessment and Gap Analysis Reports, Best Value Reviews, Strategy Reviews, Risk Assessments, Business Process Re-engineering and Business Case Development. His involvements have often covered the full program/project life cycle. The technologies Doyé has specialised in, have included a variety of computer networks, as well as landline and mobile telephony, HF, VHF, UHF, microwave point-to-point, satellite systems, sonar and radar. Doye has held certificates in Microsoft and Cisco Networking Technologies etc. He was also a consultant in the transition to Airwave for one of the largest UK Police Forces. Organisations he has worked for in the past include: The Post Office, Thames Valley Police, the Department of Work and Pensions, Community Service Volunteers, the College of Venereal Disease Prevention, Wigan MBC, Liverpool City Council, Praxis-HIS Consulting Limited, Mason Communications, Durham City Council, Telford and Wrekin Council, British Nuclear Fuels, CAMCO, WASCO-OILTOOLS, First Aluminium, MAERSK Lines, Single Buoy Moorings, Air Liquide, SEACOR Global Santa Fé and Nowcam etc. He has worked at local and regional levels for some of the biggest charities in the United Kingdom, including NACRO and Community Service Volunteers. Coming to clergy ministry in mid-life, he was first ordained in 1994 and became a Pentecostal Bishop, ten years later. He has frequently been called upon by Churches, Charities, Central and Local Government, the Emergency Services and other organisations in the United Kingdom for advice (and training) on community relations. He also aims to bring Christian (and other religious leaders) together with civic and business Leaders, for community benefit. He is a former member of the Council of Manchester Cathedral and Director and Trustee of the Ecumenical Council for Corporate Responsibility, ECCR (2009 till 2011). He served four years as a member of the Valuations Tribunal (2008-2012). He also served for several years as a Forcewide Chaplain to Greater Manchester Police Force, and is a former Member of GMP Independent Advisory Group, North Manchester Division. In early life, he had also previously worked as a Documentary Film Maker, Actor and Jazz Musician, and has also run innovative alternative education for "NEETs" those otherwise not in employment, education or

**Figure 73.
Archbishop D. T.
Agama.**

training. He has attended various Middle Level and Senior Management courses over the past 30 years. He is a current member of Chatham House (The Royal Institute of International Affairs), and is Alumni of the Experienced Strategic Leaders Programme of the Windsor Leadership Trust held at Windsor Castle (Spring 2011). Archbishop Doyé is Alumni of the Cranfield University School of Management and a member of the Cranfield Management Association. He is a Fellow of the Institute of Consulting and holds their highest Certification, the CMC. He is currently an Associate Member of the UK Restorative Justice Council and a Member of the Centre for Crime and Justice Studies. In addition, he holds the BA Theology (Church Admin & Dev) 1994, and MA (Pastoral Counselling) 1996. He has been honoured with doctoral degrees (Honoraris Causa) from Italy and the United States of America. He has been a member of the IEEE (the Institute of Electrical and Electronic Engineers, USA), the British Computer Society, British Institute of Public Sector Management etc. He is also a member of several Christian and cultural charities ... He has been married to Rev (Mrs) Helen Agama for over 30 years. Together they have 5 children and several grandchildren; and have helped start community outreaches for thousands of younger people across Greater Manchester and the UK. They are also Co-Pastors at Way of Life, in Moston, North Manchester. His hobbies include walking, visiting historic buildings and reading good books.[270]

Archbishop Doye Teido Agama has worked extensively with the IPA in London, during the year 2000 decade through the Boro Day conferences, highlighting the injustices against the people of the Niger Delta and jointly making presentations to the UK Parliament, regarding the issues of resource exploitation, environmental pollution and climate change adaptation/resilience. This is captured in one of his interviews;

> Okay, I would say, as I've hinted that my effort has been towards the broader minority ethnic community, because I see these problems as being common to most of us and that if we approach it collectively, then probably it will be more effective. As one of the known or recognised minority ethnic leaders in the UK, I was asked at various times to attend high level meetings, to make contributions to discussions at city level at a national level. To interact with parliamentarians, visit No 10 Downing Street, as the case might be. But these were not headline efforts. As a servant, you need to go by the master's instruction. So, for me, it is as much a miracle if I pray for you, you have a headache and we pray and it goes. Equally, if I find myself with opportunity to discuss certain issues with key people who can really make a difference, then that is a miraculous opportunity. Also, I don't take it lightly. So, I think I've made some contributions along the way. We've also attended meetings with the Diaspora. In the United States, for example, the joint College of African American Bishops attended the conference over several years, to interact with them and discuss issues of how people can work together because I believe, if certain problems are to be tackled, the churches have to be a part of it and until we have ministers who have the knowledge and the language to express the knowledge of some of these things, then we are incomplete. And so, we've tried to be part of that.[271]

Some of Archbishop's publications include the following;

✦ Agama, DT *Ancient Prayers For Today,* 2011 Chakram Ltd, Manchester, England

✦ Agama, DT *A Word For Your Now,* 2012 Chakam Publishing, Manchester, England (a booklet of 70 small pages)

✦ Agama, Doyé (2015). *An apostolic handbook. Volume one,* Guidance on faith and order in the Apostolic Pastoral Congress. Peterborough, GB: FastPrint.

✦ Agama, DT *An apostolic handbook. Volume two*

✦ Agama, DT *An apostolic handbook. Volume three,* Ancient prayer secrets of the first apostles and the early church, 2015 Fastprint Publishing, Peterborough, England (a re-publication of Ancient Prayers For Today - see above)

✦ Agama, DT *Africa, Christianity and the Bible - Our Global Destiny,* 2016 Fastprint Publishing, Peterborough, England

✦ Agama, DT *Strategic Leadership in the Charity Sector - a selection of perspectives,* 2016 Fastprint Publishing, Peterborough, England

Dr Boma Douglas: Engineer

Dr Boma Douglas was born in 1959, and hails from Abonnema in Kalabari Ijaw of present day Akuku Toru Local Government Area Rivers State, Nigeria. Dr Boma did most of his early education and university education up to degree level in Nigeria. His coming to settle in the UK coincided with his looking to do a Masters Degree while on vacation in the UK in 1988, by which time he was an already qualified Structural Civil Engineer. In his own words;

> And we actually came to the UK, you know, for honeymoon. And it so happened that within the period, I also wanted to investigate the universities who were offering engineering, you know, at postgraduate level. And I was opportune to have so many opportunities; you know, at my disposal, because when we arrived, I was already a fully qualified civil engineer, you know, civil and structural engineer. So, I wanted the Masters. I wanted to go in to do a master's degree. So, I made the inquiry and almost three possibilities came up, one is Strathclyde, one in Southbank and, you know, and then one in London. So, the main reason for coming to England was actually a honeymoon.[272]

After further studies doing his Masters and then Doctorate degree, he took the decision along with his wife Mrs June Douglas, a qualified lawyer, to take advantage of the permanent residency permit given to him and since then, has been a full British citizen. This was done with regards to his young family at the time with the convenience of educating them in the UK and not disrupting it by returning to Nigeria. Since then, Dr Douglas has contributed his wealth of knowledge in building the local London economy and the wider economy of UK. In the interview for this book, he elaborates further;

> I came into this country as a civil engineer. I mean, back in Nigeria, you know, I was working for a construction firm as a project engineer, working on roads, building design and supervision of rigid pavement and multi storey construction and all that, as a project manager. When I came into this country, and I went in and did my master's degree in environmental engineering, because you see, I was like, everyone was going into structures, hydraulics within the civil engineering sector and I thought I should go into something more contemporary. And that was why I went into environmental engineering because that sort of keys in into things about climate change, renewable energy and the building services. So, I did my master's degree, and got all that out of the way and went in, worked for the National Health Service as energy manager. You know, looking at multi storey buildings, multi-site situation within the NHS where you have the PCTs, and so on. So, I was looking after the energy consumption on most of the buildings and, you know, working with the other teams; mechanical and electrical teams, and making sure that the energy content is well looked after. So, I did that for some years. And eventually I went in, I was given an employment by WS Atkins, who, is one of

Figure 74. Dr Boma Douglas.

the biggest energy companies within the United Kingdom. They were based in Oxford ... so I was hot desking, I could be in London, I could be in Birmingham, you know. So, I was doing energy audits all around the country. I go to commercial sites, go to Metropolitan Police sites, magistrate courts, all the prestigious you know, sites, but you will be cleared to go into such places anyway. So, I was going into such bases, conducting the audits and then you will now write a report, do the calculations and all that. They write a report, make recommendations as to what they need, to change within either the plants or equipment or fabric, you know, those sorts of things. And then you write a report, so that they will now give feedback to either government, or depending on who you are reporting to, the owners of the schools. It could be sometimes the schools are owned by church, church council or you know, sites are owned by government, that sort of thing. So, you make recommendation as to what they need to change. So, I did that for quite a number of years. And at some point, you know, I now became a chartered engineer, when I was with WS Atkins as a chartered engineer. And now that is with the EI, the Energy

Institute. So, I now went on the membership panel, what they call the membership partner, that is the body that accredits all chartered engineers, listening to those who are seeking to be chartered. So, we sit as the peer review group of people who will look at the qualifications of engineers, look at their skills, qualifications, say they have a doctorate or master's, we look at all that. And then, we make recommendation to the panel ... The Peer Review Panel and I was on panel as well. So, that is where we make the decision. And if we say yes, the person becomes a chartered engineer, and you start to practice in this country as a chartered engineer. And after a while, I became the chair of the London and home counties branch of Energy Institute, which is about maybe 4000 engineers and professors, you know, that I became the Chair of the branch, I think, about three years whereby all the engineers who have within the London home counties will meet up. You have a database of them, you communicate with them, you will organise conferences and all that sort of thing, the key person in charge of them. So, I had done that for three years. And then I was nominated to be on the board of the energy Institutes. And the Energy Institute is not just for UK Energy institute, it is all over the world. And there is about 11 Man Committee, which is the board of the EI, I think I happen to be the first Black on that panel. And so, you know, I was a member of the board. The board membership is like you a member of the trustees of the Energy Institute. So, the board looks after the human resources or the ethics of the whole organisation. So, I was there, you know, for another three years. So, within that particular year, if you go into Companies House and check, you will see that I was there. Those are information that is there for life, so those know, interesting thing that as an Ijaw man to be in such sort of position, it is something I kind of thank God for, because it is not an easy thing. But even after all that, I still remain on the membership panel, whereby every couple of months, you send in emails of applications, which are to be considered ... I still do those things like energy audits, you know, for clients, but I do that in my time. So that is, you know, that is my story" (Dr Boma Douglas)[273]

Mr Boma Douglas, a past Chair of the Energy Institute (EI), London and Home Counties Branch, and a member of the Governing Council. He is a Chartered Energy Engineer. He is an Assessor and Interviewer on the Membership Panel of the EI. Dr Douglas has a PhD and an MSc in Environmental Engineering. He is also a Civil and Structural Engineer with vast experience as a Projects Engineer on multi story structures, rigid and flexible pavement construction. And as we can see from the interview, he has worked with various government agencies and large corporate consultancies in the UK including WS Atkins. He is an expert in Energy Efficiency and Low carbon technologies.

Apart from his professional career as an Engineer Consultant impacting positively the UK economy, Douglas has also played prominent roles within the Nigerian and Ijaw community in London. He is a Trustee of several charitable and community organisations in the UK. He has been a chairman of the Central Association of Nigerians in the UK (CANUK) an executive member and trustee of the Kalabari Central Association of the UK, and also an active member and trustee of the IPA. In these capacities, he has contributed immensely to the welfare of the UK Nigerian community and the Ijaw community in London. Furthermore, Dr Douglas had been on the Governing Board of Turney School in Dulwich and Archbishop Sumner School in Kennington. He is also the President of the Engineering Forum of Nigerians in the UK (EFN) and a Patron of Patron of Nollywood Entertainment Ltd UK ZAFFA and the Voice of Hope Foundation. Dr Douglas is a British and Nigerian Citizen, an outstanding Ijaw person with vast experience in community support work. He lives in London with his family.

Barbara Tombra Odisi: College Lecturer

Ms Barbara Tombra Odisi was born in the late 1960s and hails from Ogobiri town of Mein Ijaw in present day Sagbama Local Government Area of Bayelsa State Nigeria. She did her early schooling in Warri and Lagos and got her first University degree from Rivers State University (RSU), Port Harcourt. She worked as a Graduate Assistant Lecturer at the Niger Delta University (NDU) before relocating to the United Kingdom to undertake a Masters degree in 2003. She has since attained an MBA in Finance, MSc in Accounting and Finance and a Post Graduate Certificate in Education (PGCE). As soon as Barbara arrived the UK, she got herself busy contributing her expertise to the local economy. As she studied, she worked in retail for 12 years and lectured in Business for 8 years. Currently, she is a Lecturer with Coventry College.

Barbara's story is a good example of the spirit of personal advancement of the Ijaw person, the eagerness to acquire knowledge, education and advance in UK society against all odds and without shying away from her people. As soon as she arrived the UK, she came to London and identified with her people, immediately joining the IPA and becoming an active member. From 2003/4 till date, Barbara has been a steadfast member of the IPA, contributing to the welfare of its members and the Ijaw community in London. She has been two times assistant secretary and general secretary of the IPA She has been a part of the significant events organised through the years that the IPA has organised in London, be it the Boro Day or other events that help to bring unity to the Ijaw people of London and UK. In the past, Ms Odisi used to live part-time in London and commute up to Leicester. Presently, she lives in Leicester and comes to London from time to time, especially to attend IPA meetings and see her fellow Ijaw people. Tombra Odisi is married with 2 sons and lives in Leicester.

Figure 75. Barbara Tombra Odisi.

Dr Amabetare Biu

Amabetare Biu is just one of several persons of Izon (Ijaw) descent who have specialised in medicine and are currently working in the healthcare sector in London and the wider United Kingdom. His roots are in Patani Town, Kabowei Kingdom of present day Delta State Nigeria. He is truly an International figure, contributing to healthcare delivery in the UK and Nigeria simultaneously.

Dr Tare Biu as he is known to his friends and associates, had an extensive education and career in Nigeria before coming to the United Kingdom for further studies. His intention was not to migrate but, to study further in the Medical Health sector. Before arriving in the UK, Dr Biu in his younger days attended the prestigious Federal Government College Warri between 1967 and 1973 and proceeded to the University Of Benin Medical School in 1973. He graduated MBBS with distinction in Child Health in 1979 and won the Glaxo prize for best student in Paediatrics. After his Youth Service, he worked with the Nigerian Airforce Medical Service, Onikan and Ikeja Barracks in Lagos. He was granted in service training to do his Residency at the University of Benin Teaching Hospital as a supernumerary, where he obtained the FWACP in the Faculty of Paediatrics.

He proceeded to the UK in 1989 for subspecialty training in Paediatric Gastroenterology. He trained in leading Children Hospitals in London and Bristol obtaining the DCH, MRCP, MRCPCH and FRCPCH in 2004. It was in London, because of his exceptional brilliance that Prof Walker Smith of the then Queen Elizabeth Hospital for Children head hunted him to be a part of his

Figure 76. Dr Amabetare Biu.

team in 1991. Since 1991, Dr Amabetare Biu has opted to stay in the UK and further develop his expertise and contribute to developing the London and wider UK health sector, specialising in Paediatrics health. His young family at the time, was also a factor that made him to stay in the UK and eventually take up British citizenship. After working extensively in London, Dr Biu moved to other Health services outside London, notably Bristol, England.

As a part of his international global outlook, outreach and philanthropy, Dr Biu contributes to the development of healthcare in Africa. He was appointed the Royal College of Paediatrics and Child Health Strategic Regional Adviser for West Africa in 2012. He has contributed to improving healthcare delivery in the Niger Delta, Nigeria and was part of the team that set up the Niger Delta University Teaching Hospital in Okolobiri, Bayelsa State Nigeria. He is also a Fellow of the West African College of Physicians and a regular resource person, at the Child Neurology Society of Nigeria Annual Conferences. One of his goals is to see the success of the Bayelsa Medical University of Bayelsa State Nigeria, which he helped establish, so that it attains International recognition in healthcare training and provision. But, his focus still remains the United Kingdom, because of its vast opportunities for professional development and cutting edge research. Dr Amabetare Biu continues to contribute his full expertise to the UK Healthcare sector from his base in Bristol. He is an Emeritus Consultant Paediatrician with the North Bristol NHS in Bristol, UK and until recently, honorary Senior Clinical Lecturer, University of Bristol Medical School. He is a Member of the Royal College of Physicians of Ireland, Fellow Royal College of Paediatrics and Child Health (UK), Fellow

Royal Society of Medicine. He holds a Diploma in Child Health from the Royal College of Physicians, London. He was also elected Fellow of the Royal Society of Medicine. He is a Neurodevelopment Paediatrician with expertise in Child Protection, Forensic Paediatrics and International Paediatrics. Biu presently, works as the Consultant Neurodisability Paediatrician assessing children with behaviour difficulties for ADHD and Autism in Wiltshire Community Children's Services.

Despite moving to Bristol, Dr Biu continued to contribute to the welfare of the Ijaw community in London and UK in general. He attends regular community events and was very active in the 2000s, in community improvement affairs. On this note, he continues to contribute to healthcare development in his place of origin as well as internationally. He has several publications in internal journals to his name and has given numerous international guest lectures on Public Health. Biu currently lives in Bristol, England with his family.

Review of Ijaw Professionals Impact in London and the UK

The Ijaw community in London is several thousand strong and has to a large degree, successfully socially integrated into the wider London and British society, whilst maintaining key elements of their traditional Ijaw culture. We could not interview all the Ijaw people, who are successful residents of London, especially the younger professional generation who are working and have contributed excellently to London life via their professional work in the following sectors;

Architecture
Banking and Finance
Catering
Education & Teaching Profession
Enterprise and Entrepreneurship
Housing Sector (Social Housing)
Industrial Food Manufacturing
IT and Computing
Law
Local Authority & Civil Service
Medicine
Maintenance & Cleaning
Nursing and Midwifery
Police
Politics
Professional Football

Rail Transport (technical and drivers, national rail and underground services)
Social Services
The Creative Arts
The NHS, Healthcare
The NHS, Social Care
Transport services (minicab)
University Teaching
Security

REFERENCES

227. Personal family testimony records of Edna Knight 04/09/2023
228. Ancestry.co.uk accessed October 2023.
229. Personal family testimony records of Edna Knight 04/09/2023
230. Edna Knight Interview 04/09/2023
231. Edna Knight interview 04/09/2023
232. Ancestry.co.uk accessed in October 2023
233.Testimony of Ombrai Oguoko, son of late Morris B Oguoko, oral interview 21/08/2023
234. Ancestry.co.uk accessed in October 2023
235. Ancestry.co.uk accessed in October 2023
236. Testimony of Laraine Okorodudu, daughter of the late Laurence Okorodudu, oral interview 12/09/2023
237. Testimony of Laraine Okorodudu, daughter of the late Laurence Okorodudu, oral interview 12/09/2023
238. Interview with Rev Francis B Akpanari 22/08/2023
239. Interview with Rev Francis B Akpanari 22/08/2023
240. Oral Interview (Date) Ekineh states; "You see, Nkrumah joined the communist movement. Supported. Nasser over sways. And they said when he got independence, many people in the colonial office were so happy (inaudible). I was at WASU West Africa Student Union, Nigeria when he came there to study law in 1946. In 1947, they asked him if he could be the secretary of the political party, He saluted and he said yes. And he went …"
241. Interview of Aliyi Ekineh via his daughter Sokari Ekineh accessed on 14/09/2023
242. Bishop Ebenezer Tamunoteghe Dimieari was an earlier Nigerian Ijaw Bishop to have been ordained by the Anglican Church (Church of England). He was consecrated on 29 June 1949, by Geoffrey Fisher, Archbishop of Canterbury, at St Paul's Cathedral (London, UK), to serve as assistant bishop to Cecil Patterson, Bishop on the Niger. He served mostly in Nigeria.
243. Family testimony. Oral History Interview of John Ogetti Kpiaye on 27/10/2023, 14:00hrs
244. IPA Archives, earlier in 1945 the Ijaw People's Union was founded in Liverpool, and therefore the foundation of the IPA in 1948 seem to have been a continuation of this, since many of the founders had once lived in Liverpool. Records sources from Ancestry.co.uk show that all these persons were in London by 1947.
245. Interview with John Ogetti Kpiaye 27/10/2023

246. https://en.wikipedia.org/wiki/John_Kpiaye, https://lintonkwesijohnson.com/lkj-records-artists/john-kpiaye/ accessed in October 2023

247. https://lintonkwesijohnson.com/lkj-records-artists/john-kpiaye/, https://en.wikipedia.org/wiki/John_Kpiaye, accessed in October 2023

248. https://en.wikipedia.org/wiki/John_Kpiaye, https://lintonkwesijohnson.com/lkj-records-artists/john-kpiaye/, https://www.discogs.com/artist/390500-John-Kpiaye accessed in October 2023

249. Larkin, Colin (1998) "John Kpiaye" in *The Virgin Encyclopedia of Reggae,* Virgin Books, ISBN 0-7535-0242-9, pp. 160-161, https://lintonkwesijohnson.com/lkj-records-artists/john-kpiaye/ accessed on February 2024.

250. Interview with John Ogetti Kpiaye 27/10/2023

251. Interview with John Ogetti Kpiaye 27/10/2023

252. Ancestry.co.uk accessed on 12/03/2024 London Electoral Register, Tower Hamlets, Stepney records Mr Vincent Akenkide, Mrs Irene Akenkide and Mr Young Kpiaye living at Brushfied Street in 1950. Mr Young Kpiaye was the foundation President of the IPA, while Vincent Akenkide was a member. Both were close friends along with other Ijaw men. IPA archives.

253. Interview with Edith Akenkide 20/10/2023

254. Interview with Edna Knight 04/09/2023

255. Interview with Datoru Ben Paul Worika 13/10/2023

256. Interview with Joshua Tamunopreye Garry 29/08/2023

257. https://joshuapreyegarry.com/#:~:text=Josh%20Preye%20Garry%20is%20the,a%20number%20of%20London%20schools. Accessed on 11/04/2024

258. https://www.nationaldiversityawards.co.uk/2022-nda-shortlist/josh-preye-garry/ Accessed on 11/04/2024

259. Interview of Patience Agbabi 05/04/2024

260. Interview with Rowland Ekperi 12/11/2023

261. Interview with Rowland Ekperi 12/11/2023

262. Interview with Rowland Ekperi 12/11/2023

263. Interview with Rowland Ekperi 12/11/2023

264. Interview with John Eperebofori Opuogulaya 23/08/2023

265. Interview with John Eperebofori Opuogulaya 23/08/2023

266. https://literacytrust.org.uk/storytellers-and-authors/find-uk-storytellers-authors/amanda-epe/ accessed on 13/04/2024

267. Interview with Macdonald Mopho 03/02/2024

268. Interview with Macdonald Mopho 03/02/2024

269. http://www.londontariclub.com/profile.php

270. https://www.apostolicpastors.info/bishop-doye-agama, accessed on 14/04/2024

271. Interview with Archbishop Agama on 16/08/2023

272. Dr Boma Douglas Interview 30/08/2023

273. Dr Boma Douglas Interview 30/08/2023

CONCLUSION

The story of the Ijaw (Izon) people of London, is indeed a fascinating one. We began the journey by looking at the Ijaw people in their original homeland, the Niger Delta of present day Nigeria, with a brief summary of the history and culture of the Ijaw people in the Niger Delta. We then touched on the earliest contacts that the Ijaws had with Europeans, firstly with the Portuguese trading mercantile visitors and then with the earliest English or British merchants who visited the West African coast. This allowed us to explore the historical understanding that, there were a number of reasons why Ijaw people found their way to the United Kingdom, arriving under various circumstances and timeframes.

Having found their way to the British Isles, the Ijaw people who chose to leave the shores of their original homeland in the Niger Delta, tried to make a success of their stay in Britain (London, the focus of the heritage story). Some were exiled against their will, but took advantage of the educational system to educate their children in the ways of the emerging British Empire. Later on, others arrived, worked, raised families and went back. While others stayed permanently and passed away in the UK and were even buried in the UK. Not everyone had the intention of becoming full British citizens, although the timeframe for some of the arrivals, falls within the period when they were automatic British citizens, by virtue of colonial status. Others arrived later and added to the younger generations born to the earliest arrivals, now become and constitute UK citizens or UK nationals, reconciling their identities as Ijaw, Nigerian and British persons. This is a phenomenon common to many immigrant communities in the UK. We outlined how some of the younger generation of 2nd generation Ijaws, especially of mixed Ijaw and English heritage, have managed their mixed heritage and cultural ethnic identities, trying to fit into both worlds and seemingly making a success out of it, despite the negative circumstance some of them faced at the time.

We looked at some of the interviewees and other persons with their outstanding professional contribution to the London economy and Ijaw community welfare and this brings into focus the reality that, these people decided to make a success of themselves in London regardless of the place and time they found themselves. They demonstrated the Ijaw spirit of truth, excellence and success.

We have outlined over 200 years of documentary evidence of Ijaw people coming to and living in London and the UK, while undocumented inference may take this back 500 years, with the arrival of West Africans in Liverpool. The Ijaw people's interaction with Britain or more correctly, the British mercantile class, has been mixed, with hostile, antagonistic reception and behaviours as demonstrated by the exiling of Kings, alternating with mutually beneficial relationships, exemplified by the international trade in palm oil. The fact that the Ijaw people of London, maintain a healthy relationship with the host nation of the UK and their homeland of Ijawland in the Niger Delta Region of Nigeria, is a testament of the harmonious relationship the Ijaws have tried to display, with all the people they encounter while sojourning in the UK. This sojourn has for many, turned from temporary residency into permanent citizenship status.

As a part of coping with the demands of London living, the Ijaw community associations will continue to function and thrive, providing the much needed welfare support that can only be received from within the community. Will these community associations eventually cease to function in time? Some of the interviewees expressed their opinion that they would like to see these organisations continue to exist and provide more and better support to the Ijaw community of London. The challenge then is, how the older generation hand over the baton to the younger 'more British' generation, and how they see the relevance of these organisation in their own lives. But, there appears to be optimism that the younger generations will hold on to their Ijaw cultural roots.

We are convinced therefore that, what we have documented and compiled, contributes to the historical heritage of the Ijaw community of London, and is a part of the wider Ijaw heritage of living in the United Kingdom from the 1800's to the present time. Furthermore, this heritage is a part of an even bigger heritage of immigrant communities in London. People speak about the Black Community in the UK and the arrival of the Windrush generation and very often, they omit or miss out the African populations that arrived either earlier or at the same time as the Windrush, also for the same reasons. These African persons came from former colonies or trading partners at the time and especially those who arrived during the first and second world wars, had a sense of fighting for the mother country, contributing to the liberation of Britain from the threat of Nazi Germany.

So, that is why we visited the Black Archive Centre in Brixton South London and took a picture of the Plaque dedicated to the African and Caribbean men and women of the armed forces, who lost their lives in the First and Second world wars, while some came to settle in London to work and better themselves. The East London Docks, the area once known as 'Black Harlem' provided an early home for both Ijaw merchant seamen and students, and this saw the birth of the first Ijaw organisation in London, the Ijaw People's Association of Great Britain and Ireland in 1948. From this early nexus, subsequent generations of Ijaws started moving to different areas of London to earn a living and make their home.

In summary and conclusion, Ijaw people living in London, did not happen by accident. It is the result of at least 200 years of interaction between the Niger Delta (Nigeria) and Britain, a relationship that is still going on today. And as one of the interviewees observed; as President of the Ijaw People's Association, he saw himself trying to improve the relationship between the Ijaws of Nigeria and the UK government because of the UK interests that are still being derived from the Niger Delta, turning the relationship around for the benefit of both; and how to position the Ijaws of London to provide that professional role of cultivating a mutually beneficial partnership between the Ijaws of the Niger Delta (Nigeria) and the UK government in the economic, scientific and cultural exchange that takes place between both nations.

INDEX

Printed in Great Britain
by Amazon